The Nickelo...

ALSO BY CHRIS MORGAN

The Comic Galaxy of Mystery Science Theater 3000:
Twelve Classic Episodes and the Movies They
Lampoon (McFarland, 2015)

The Nickelodeon '90s

*Cartoons, Game Shows and a
Whole Bunch of Slime*

Chris Morgan

McFarland & Company, Inc., Publishers
Jefferson, North Carolina

ISBN (print) 978-1-4766-8564-9
ISBN (ebook) 978-1-4766-4346-5

Library of Congress and British Library
Cataloguing data are available

Library of Congress Control Number 2021023905

Front cover image © 2021 Shutterstock

Printed in the United States of America

*McFarland & Company, Inc., Publishers
Box 611, Jefferson, North Carolina 28640
www.mcfarlandpub.com*

Hey Sandy

Table of Contents

Preface

What is this book?

It's *The Nickelodeon '90s: Cartoons, Game Shows and a Whole Bunch of Slime*. It lives up to that title.

So this book is about '90s Nickelodeon?

Yes, what I have done is write essays about every show that aired original episodes on Nickelodeon in the decade of the 1990s. Some of those shows began in the '80s and some of them ended in the 2000s, but they all aired episodes in the '90s. These are shows that were airing new episodes in the '90s, mind you. It does not include shows that had their rights bought by Nick so that they could show reruns.

What are these essays like?

I don't want to spoil too much, and I wrote a more proper introduction to this book as well, but I will try to satisfy your curiosity, imagined book reader. They are a mix of personal reflection and media criticism. I delve into the history of the shows, provide my personal critiques, and hopefully make them interesting reads. Personally, I like to think of it as something akin to a fun encyclopedia of '90s Nickelodeon, or talking to a cool, knowledgeable friend about the shows you loved back in the day and still love now. Yes, I just called myself cool and knowledgeable. No, I don't feel great about it, but I'm trying to sell a book here. I also included as a little subheading on every chapter some "lesson" one could learn from the subject of that chapter.

Who are you, anyway?

Fair question! My name is Chris Morgan. I have been writing about pop culture personally and professionally for more than a decade at this point. You may have seen my work on websites such as Uproxx, Paste Magazine, IGN, and many, many more. Like, an almost distressing number of websites at this point. This is also not my first book for McFarland. I am the author of *The Comic Galaxy of Mystery Science Theater 3000: 12 Classic Episodes and the Movies They Lampoon* (2015). I have been dedicating a generous portion of my life to entertainment since I was a child, and I have been writing about it for about the entirety of my adult life. Basically, it was inevitable I would write this book.

Are you going to talk trash about my favorite show?

There's only one way to find out, and that's to keep reading.

Introduction:
The Gak Generation

Someday you will die, but the '90s never will

In my early twenties, in a fit of anti-nostalgia, I threw out a bunch of my old stuff, especially school stuff like yearbooks. Right now, I bet you are super pumped that the book you bought about Nickelodeon is beginning with a banal and solipsistic personal anecdote. I'm just illustrating the point that our relationship with the past, and with our past, can be complicated. I honestly don't miss any of those old yearbooks—what would I have done with them?—but I have no qualms with the thorny concept of nostalgia like I did then. I also mentioned it because I don't want you to feel like this is going to be a book of rose-colored-glasses love for shows from the past. This is going to be fun, but it isn't going to be about me talking about how I loved a show when I was seven and therefore it is beautiful and pure and will never hurt me like the cruel, uncaring world we were born into. In fact, I don't intend to talk much about myself at all, except when necessary, because I'm not as interesting a subject as Nickelodeon. We're all here because, in some way, shape, or form, Nickelodeon was a big part of our life, and we maintain some connection to it. Maybe it's as pop culture devotees. Maybe it's nostalgic. In the end, we're all here because we're all interested in the quintessential network of our childhood.

Back in 1977, when cable was a primitive beast, Warner Cable debuted 10 channels on QUBE, one of the earliest cable television systems. One of those channels was simply called C-3. All it did all day, from seven in the morning until nine at night, was run a TV show called *Pinwheel*. It was an educational program in the vein of *Sesame Street* or *The Electric Company*. People and puppets interacted and taught kids about sharing. There was a character named Ebenezer T. Squint, which was basically an Oscar the Grouch rip-off, right down to being green. After a couple years of this, Warner figured a rebrand, and an expansion, was in order.

On April 1, 1979, Nickelodeon was born. It was the first-ever TV network aimed at children and entirely for children. There weren't ads at first, and Warner envisioned Nickelodeon as a loss leader. They wanted to be in

3

the market of being a TV channel for children. It made total sense. Adults have busy lives. Children, especially in the summer, could plop themselves down in front of a TV for hours. They had a friend, and their parents had a babysitter. You hook those kids in as viewers, and someday when you debut ads you have a built-in audience. Then they grow up and they are watching other Warner networks because they've developed an affinity for TV. You entertain kids, teach them some lessons, and in the end someday they grow up and spend their disposable income on the products they see ads for on television. I say this without cynicism, as somebody who was raised by television in some respects and regrets not a second of it.

Nickelodeon was chosen as a name over options like The Rainbow Network. The initial logo, along with the name, harkened back to the old-timey nickelodeon theaters. It's actually the only real connection anybody has to nickelodeons these days, given that we've all agreed to forget about Peter Bogdanovich's 1976 movie *Nickelodeon* starring Burt Reynolds and Tatum O'Neal. They dubbed it "The Young People's Satellite Network," which is a hilariously wordy and clunky tagline for a children's network.

The network's first bit of indelible history came in 1981 when they began airing episodes of a Canadian sketch show for kids they had ported over. You may know it as *You Can't Do That on Television*. In addition to introducing us to Alanis Morissette years before she was writing tunes partially inspired by Dave Coulier, *You Can't Do That on Television* brought green slime into the children's zeitgeist. When performers would say, "I don't know," they'd get slimed. The slime proved so popular it became a fixture of Nickelodeon, especially on the *Double Dare* family of shows. The crew on that program nicknamed the slime "gak," in reference to the street name for heroin. And from that bit of adult irreverence and drug slang, I got the name of this introduction.

Despite the hunger for slime (not literally, in most cases) the channel struggled for years. Reportedly, they lost $10 million in 1984, which is also the year that *Pinwheel* aired its last episode. Funnily enough, that show, while pretty much forgotten, is the most prolific show in Nickelodeon history in terms of sheer hours of television. Nickelodeon began to accept corporate underwriting. Looking to revamp the network, Fred Seibert and Alan Goodman, the men who were responsible for branding MTV in the '80s, were brought in to give Nickelodeon a makeover. Needless to say, it worked. Gone were the fusty, backward-looking bits of iconography. The duo introduced orange as the dominant color of Nickelodeon and created the "splat" logo that is emblazoned in our minds to this day. Suddenly, Nick was taking off. It was fending off threats from the Disney Channel and the Cartoon Network. In 1986, Nickelodeon—along with MTV, VH1, and some other networks—was sold to Viacom for $685 million. This was around the time the Nickelodeon we know and love was beginning to really take its footing.

More original programs were introduced, some of which will be featured in this book. The Kids' Choice Awards debuted in 1988. Nickelodeon opened its own production studio in Orlando, Florida, in 1990. This is where the journey of this book begins. To many, the '90s are synonymous with Nickelodeon and Nickelodeon is synonymous with the '90s. When I think of the '90s, I think of Nickelodeon, MTV, eating personal pan pizza from Pizza Hut because I had read some books, and learning the comedy rule of threes. Children of the '90s grew up on Nickelodeon, and it made an outsized impact on our lives, and created deep grooves in our brains full of cartoons, game shows, and bad child actors.

This book is for us. It's for those of us who have '90s Nickelodeon on our minds all the times. For those of us who have the first two seasons of *The Adventures of Pete & Pete* on DVD and are annoyed the third never came out. People who have the *Clarissa Explains It All* theme song burned in their brains. Our childhoods were defined by Nick, and we have carried it with us. This book is also for people who want to go a little deeper into these shows. There's nothing wrong with a vague, familiar sense of positivity because you hear the name of a show from your youth. If you like to stop at "Oh yeah, I remember *Angry Beavers*. What a fun show!" I don't blame you. However, I care too much about pop culture to leave it there, and I bet many of you are right there with me. I have made a living (or part of a living) writing about movies and TV. I wrote a book about *Mystery Science Theater 3000* (which is still available to buy … just saying). I love TV, and I love to write about it. I want to have discussions about the stuff I'm interested in, and Nickelodeon from the '90s is a big piece of (all) that.

That is why I wrote *The Nickelodeon '90s*. This book has a chapter dedicated to every show that aired original episodes in the '90s. That includes shows that started in the '80s and shows that started in 1999 and ran long into the 2000s. Some of these shows are cultural touchstones. Some of them have been mostly forgotten. I loved some of them then and still like them. Others don't hold as fond a place in my mind as they once did. On a few occasions, I was basically delving into a show for the first time, which was interesting. Maybe I dislike a show that you love, or maybe the opposite is true. That's all quite all right. This is a chance for all of us to take arguably the deepest dive into '90s Nickelodeon done so far.

There are some people who threw away Nickelodeon, metaphorically speaking, much like I threw away all those old yearbooks. This is for the rest of us. There are dozens of shows and hundreds of episodes that are burnt into our brains. Our relationship to these memories has changed over the years. Some of them aren't even distant memories. You can watch classic

Nick shows on DVD or streaming platforms. Few things in pop culture ever truly die. In a way, Rocko and Ferguson Darling and Alex Mack will outlive us all. When we're old, will we be sitting there remembering a random joke from an episode of *Doug*? That's not a question this book can answer. I also can't answer the question "Couldn't the producers of *My Brother & Me* find one child actor who wasn't total garbage?" All I can do is take you on a journey through a topic we're all interested in, and which many of us care about in one way or another. It may be intellectual. It may be emotional. No matter what, we're the Gak Generation. And not in the heroin way.

Aaahh!!! Real Monsters

Learn to embrace your nightmares,
even when they smell terrible like Krumm

The concept of humanizing monsters is something you are surely familiar with at this point. It's at the crux of *Monsters Inc.*, one of Pixar's more popular films, and also its sequel *Monsters University*, which is a movie that certainly exists. If you are of the generation that grew up on '90s Nickelodeon, though, and if you are reading this book you probably are, then you had already been indoctrinated into the world of monsters who are just trying to make their way in a world that is as scary to them as it is to us. That's because you watched *Aaahh!!! Real Monsters*, a show that practically begs you not to write about it with its aggravating title. Three As, two Hs, and three exclamation points. Keep that in mind for all future endeavors.

When this show, I really want to try and avoid typing *Aaahh!!! Real Monsters* as much as possible, comes to mind, the first word that springs forth is "grotesque." To be fair, that's also true of *Monsters Inc.*, but that's because the way humans are rendered in Pixar movies is by-and-large terrifying. The baby in *Inside Out* is a trip into the uncanny valley more distressing than anything this side of a David Cronenberg film. Of course, that is not Pixar's intent. Klasky-Csupo, the studio behind *Rugrats* who made this as a follow-up cartoon for Nickelodeon, definitely wanted there to be gross, revolting elements in this show. It was a selling point. Maybe it's akin to something like *Garbage Pail Kids*, with the idea in mind being that young boys like gross stuff so therefore they will like watching a bunch of weird monsters with messed-up visages. They may have been right.

Like the Pixar movies I keep referencing, even though the '90s kids in attendance right now don't need the comparison point, *Aaahh!!! Real Monsters* (I've mastered typing this out) does not posit a world where monsters terrify us out of malevolence or psychopathy. It's not a calling, but what is effectively a job. Aimed at an audience of children, *Aaahh!!! Real Monsters* makes it more relatable by focusing on three monster children who are in school to learn how to scare humans. Much how in school you learned, say, the multiplication table or how to read *Hardy Boys* books that have had all the problematic stuff edited out, these monsters are learning to frighten.

They get assignments. They have homework. The premise seems to be "Hey kids, you know how you hate school? Well monsters have to go to school too and they also don't like it!"

This allowed Klasky-Csupo to make a show about monsters that, somehow, was also relatable to kids in some way. Granted, beyond that one comparison, there is not a lot to relate to in the show. None of us are monsters who have to learn how to scare people. Besides, we all know the best way to scare somebody is to hide in a table on Ellen DeGeneres' talk show. Or pop a paper bag behind their head, provided you don't have access to Ellen's set. We also don't use toenails as currency.

That speaks to the high-level of grossness on *ARM*, an initialism I just decided to adopt. Our three main characters are Ickis, Oblina, and Krumm. Ickis is not terribly grotesque, and that's sort of the point. He's the focal point of the show most of the time, and he's sort of the everyman. Ickis has a hard time scaring people beyond the fact he's reluctant to do it. He looks like a bunny to a lot of people. Ickis can grow large to scare people, but he does it sparingly. Most of the time, he's just a little bunny-looking dude with an unimposing voice.

On the other hand, Oblina is like if a worm and an evil candy cane had a baby and she pulls her organs out from her mouth to scare people and gives them nightmares. She's messed up. Krumm carries his eyes around in his hands. When he needs his hands, he puts them in his mouth. There are many other monsters, including The Gromble, the headmaster of their school. Zimbo (voiced by Tim Curry!) sort of is like a bee with one leg and a humanoid face. Plus, the show is animated in that *Rugrats* style synonymous with Klasky-Csupo. There is an uneasy quality to that as is. In the realm of grotesque monsters, it just adds fuel to the fire.

This gives *Aaahh!!! Real Monsters* a real polarizing quality. Even if the monsters have the edges sanded down and are the protagonists of the show, one could imagine a kid, or adult, still being grossed out by the gang. It's akin to something like how I love *Futurama*, but any episode that has a heavy presence of the mutants never sits well with me. The monsters of *ARM* aren't on that level, but the show can be gross or revolting, with some degree of intent, and that's not for everybody.

It was also, for all its cleverness, not terribly good. There were definitely worse shows on Nickelodeon in the '90s, including in the animated realm. If you enjoy world building and different sorts of creatures and life forms, which is to say if you grew up to love stuff like *Game of Thrones*, this may have been up your alley. If you wanted quality jokes and storytelling, though, *Aaahh!!! Real Monsters* was probably never your favorite. That was true for me. I have no particularly fond memories of the show. There is no classic moment that we all, as a collective generation, think of. There are

52 episodes of *Aaahh!!! Real Monsters*, and since it was one of the cartoons on Nick that had two stories per episode that's a lot of stories. How many of them do you remember off the top of your head? I talk to people about Nickelodeon in the '90s fairly often, and this is not a show that ever really comes up. It's not in memes. It feels forgotten.

Aaahh!!! Real Monsters got good reviews. The critics at the time tended to like it, if not love it, effectively calling it a sweeter *Ren & Stimpy*. Comparison wise that makes sense, given the latter's extreme dedication to the gross. *ARM* wasn't like that. It was a soft gross, which is in and of itself kind of a gross phrase. The show was also evidently popular enough to merit a video game in 1995 for Sega Genesis and Super Nintendo. I may or may not have played it, but I definitely dig the visual style of the game.

Revisiting *Aaahh!!! Real Monsters* for this book raised my opinion of it. Not that I think the show is any better than it was then. If anything, it feels more facile in its storytelling, and it still lacks many jokes that pop. Oblina pulling her organs out is still weird and gross. That being said, it feels like this show is underrated, if only for its ambition. They did build a world and craft a bunch of distinct character designs. That's sort of what animation is for, but not everybody swings for the fences. *Aaahh!!! Real Monsters* is a fresh show, which is somewhat ironic given that the characters hang out in a sewer and one of Krumm's powers is that his armpits smell terrible.

After fittingly debut two days before Halloween in 1994, it feels like *Aaahh!!! Real Monsters* never really grabbed onto kids like other Nick shows. Maybe I'm just not the right person for it, and maybe the kinds of people I associate weren't either. One can imagine the *Nightmare Before Christmas* types getting an Ickis tattoo next to their Jack Skellington one. Television need not be homogenous. If somebody out there was dreaming of Tim Curry voicing a monster named Zimbo, they got it. For others, we learned not to be afraid of monsters, because now we were too busy shrugging them off.

The Adventures of
Pete & Pete

*Your family and friends will always
be there for you. Also, no fog, no fun*

I will just be upfront with you before I get started. *The Adventures of
Pete & Pete* is my favorite Nickelodeon show. It was my favorite as a kid
and it is by far my favorite as an adult. I have the first two seasons on DVD.
I bought the second season the day it came out. There are no other Nick
shows I have on DVD. When the third season didn't come out it really
bummed me out, because it features two of my favorite episodes. I have
written about it extensively already in my professional life. One of the first
big features I wrote for a particular website was about the music of *Pete
& Pete* and it's as long as any chapter in this book, if not longer. Iggy Pop
was interviewed for the piece. It's still one of my favorite things I've ever
written. This show is so good. Part of me just wants to free associate about
everything I love about this show. One of my former internet aliases was
"Captain Scrummy." However, I am a professional. I will handle this professionally. Let me tell you the tale of two brothers named Pete, a tattoo named
Petunia, the strongest man in the world, and the plate in a suburban mom's
head and why it was so wonderful as a kid, and still is.

In the late '80s, Will McRobb and Chris Viscardi were working in the
promo department for Nickelodeon. The network was looking for content, and McRobb and Viscardi decided to work together to try and come
up with some shorts that could be plugged into the lineup here and there.
McRobb's initial idea was indeed called *Pete & Pete*, but it was about a boy
and his dog, both named Pete. Eventually, that would become two brothers named Pete. Big Pete and Little Pete Wrigley were born in concept. The
two were joined by Katherine Dieckmann, who is vital to the story of this
show as well. She was coming off directing some R.E.M. videos, including
"Stand," which McRobb told her he was a fan of at their 10-year high school
reunion. They needed a director for their shorts, and they chose Dieckmann. She meshed well with their sensibilities and indie rock attitude. She's
also responsible for the fact the initial *Pete & Pete* theme from the shorts
was an R.E.M. cover of "March of the Wooden Soldiers."

Pete Wrigley and his brother Pete Wrigley. Little Pete (Danny Tamberelli) is on the left in his traditional plaid hat. Big Pete (Michael Maronna) is more willing to show off his trademark red hair (Nickelodeon).

Cast into the roles of the brothers Wrigley were Michael Maronna (Big Pete) and Danny Tamberelli (Little Pete), two redheads who could easily pass as brothers. When interviewed for my article back in the day, McRobb referred to the minute-long shorts as "singles," compared to the albums that were the full episodes when they started to air. The first *Pete & Pete* short aired in 1989 and in total 26 of them were made. You can see some of that *Pete & Pete* voice in there, but obviously this isn't a show. They aren't fleshed out. Like I said, they are a minute long. However, you can watch them now and definitely feel the show that *The Adventures of Pete & Pete* would become.

The success of the shorts led to five specials being commissioned. The first of these specials, "Valentine's Day Massacre," aired (fittingly) on February 9, 1991. All five specials are credited as being written by McRobb, with Dieckmann directing the first four of them. For the specials, they needed a new theme song, and thus a spinoff of Mark Mulcahy's band Miracle Legion was born, *Pete & Pete*'s own house band Polaris. McRobb has called Miracle Legion's "The Backyard," *Pete & Pete* in a song, so it was a fitting choice. Polaris created a new theme song, which would become the iconic Nick theme song, "Hey Sandy." Everything about it is written into my DNA, including the lyric that is incomprehensible. It's my favorite TV theme song ever. It's just straight-up a really good song. Music is indeed woven into the show's ethos. In the second special, "What We Did on Your Summer Vacation," we get appearances from both Kate Pierson and Michael Stipe. Those were both thanks to Dieckmann. Stipe plays Captain Scrummy, a low-grade ice cream man who peddles Sludgicle bars. He even says that Big Pete looks like a "bona fide Sludgicle man." Hey, Mr. Tastee, the usually ice cream man in Wellsville, has skipped town. Captain Scrummy was all they had left.

At this point, I probably need to get into what, exactly, this show is about. Other than, of course the adventures of the brothers Pete. It's a real slice-of-life show set in the fictional town of Wellsville, where it feels like it is always fall except when it is explicitly another season, usually summer or winter. The town always looks so beautiful in fall. We're so fortunate *The Adventures of Pete & Pete* was a single-cam show, and that they hired excellent directors. No Nick show looked better than *Pete & Pete*. While the Wrigley family live in suburbia, there world is just a smidge off around the edges. Little Pete has a tattoo of a pinup woman named Petunia. Joyce Wrigley, the matriarch of the family, has a plate in her head that can cause problems. For much of the show's run, Little Pete's best friend is Artie, the Strongest Man in the World. That may seem weird, but Artie is pure of heart. He's a superhero, and he's there to protect the kids of Wellsville, specifically Little Pete, who he calls "My Little Viking." Again, it doesn't play as weird, and it isn't weird when you watch it somehow. Artie, played perfectly by Toby Huss, wears thick-rimmed glasses, a blue-and-red striped shirt, and red long johns. He's apparently friends with Muriel Hemingway and a turtle named Clark. One time he stopped being a superhero and became an aluminum siding salesman.

Superheroes are needed in Wellsville, because the town is full of villains as well. Folks like Big Pete's nemesis "Endless" Mike Hellstrom, who has been stuck repeating the same grade in high school for years. There's Papercut. There's Pit Stain. The town is a strange one indeed. There's even a meter man who can see the future when he reads meters. Chris Elliott plays him. Not that everybody in town is bad. Big Pete's best friend is the third-most-important character on the show, Ellen Hickle. Their relationship is complicated, because Ellen is a girl, and his friend, but is not his girlfriend. On occasion, their potential feelings for each other are explored. In one of my all-time favorite episodes they do finally go on a date. However, Big Pete has gotten some terrible advice from "Endless" Mike, who gives him said advice (and his car) in exchange for Neapolitan ice cream. Ellen is upset that Big Pete put the moves on her too fast, but the day is saved by Little Pete. You see, this is all happening on one of Little Pete's favorite days, when Daylight Saving Time ends and you "fall back" and hour. Little Pete considers it time travel (get your riboflavin!), but by reliving the same hour you can fix your mistakes. Big Pete is able to resolve things with Ellen and they go back to being friends. It's a genuinely moving message delivers with better acting, directing, and writing than you get on most kids' shows.

Little Pete eventually gets a friend in Nona F. Mecklenberg, played by Michelle Trachtenberg. She always wears a cast because she enjoys the itchy feeling. Her dad is Iggy Pop. Well, not literally. He's just played by Iggy Pop doing suburban dad drag. I couldn't appreciate that as a child, but I do love it now. Bus driver Stu Benedict is a depressive with serious mental health issues who is heartbroken over the end of his relationship with bus driver Sally Knorp. One time he hit a perfect drive at the golf range after freezing up for days on end and it gives him a beautiful moment of catharsis more powerful than what half of TV shows have ever done. Also in that episode Big Pete works at the driving range in a bear costume to avoid embarrassment. Frank Gifford cameos as himself. This show rules. Although, it is not perfect. In the third season, as Big Pete aged out of the general age of Nickelodeon's audience, Little Pete became more of the focal point. He got a couple more friends, Kreb Scout Monica Perling and Wayne "The Pain" Pardue. I never loved either of them. Then again, I never loved Big Pete's friends Phil and Teddy either.

Like I said, there is a heavy streak of eccentricity running through *The Adventures of Pete & Pete*, but I think it's pretty much perfect. It rarely goes too far on the quirk. The absurdity lands, mostly because it tends to be so funny. The show is rich in detail that fleshes out the world. As a kid, I had never seen a show quite like *Pete & Pete*. You don't see characters like Artie every day. There is genuinely something special about this show. It is as fresh and original as anything I've seen in kids' programming, and it's got more going for it than a lot of shows for adults as well. There are few shows where I can just joyfully recount details like this. I mean, in the special where Mr. Tastee disappears the Wrigley family digs up not just a car at the beach, but specifically a 1978 Cutlass Supreme. That is just such a brilliant detail.

The Adventures of Pete & Pete is decidedly the funniest show from '90s Nickelodeon. The writing is extremely sharp. It doesn't feel like a kids' show other than the fact the main characters are kids. Even so, I honestly feel like it is as much for adults as children. It always feels reflective, if not necessarily nostalgic then wistful. If you are in a certain mood, *Pete & Pete* can hit you in a way that makes you feel melancholic. I am not one of those people who longs for his childhood. Being an adult is way better than being a kid. Even I can't help being moved by the mood set by *Pete & Pete* at its best moments. You could easily pitch *Pete & Pete* to somebody who hadn't seen it as a show for adults that just so happened to not be raunchy and had a wholesome quality to it. I bet they would believe it. Not that *Pete & Pete* is square. Far from it. You can just watch it at any age and appreciate it fully. That's incredibly impressive. There are a couple jokes that make me laugh out loud in every episode. You rarely get those groaning clunkers so common in programming for children. McRobb, Viscardi, and company never spoke down to their audience. They respected everybody who would be watching it.

The craftsmanship goes beyond the humor, though. There is a lot of nuance in the storytelling. While the world of Wellsville is absurd, even in that absurdity you can find moments that are relatable. Take, for example, the episode where Little Pete fakes being sick and then explores what happens in the world during the day when he's normally at school. Yes, he gets a marshmallow of Dwight Eisenhower stuck up his nose. Sure, LL Cool J plays a teacher at Little Pete's school who throws a luau because Little Pete isn't coming in that day. It also touches on so much of what you feel as a kid when you are home from school. Not every episode is that relatable, and that's not bad. In one of my favorite episodes, season three's "Pinned," Big Pete joins the school wrestling team only to see "Endless" Mike transfer schools and go through deranged ploys to get a chance to wrestle Pete. Oh, and he does it while dressed like a '90s pro wrestler. I love everything about it. That's silly, but it's still funny.

Mixed in with that brilliant silliness, though, is more earned emotion and gravitas than anything Nick has ever done. It can truly be a touching show. I don't intend to keep just telling you about episodes, but they reflect my points, and also they are never far from my brains. In "A Hard Day's Pete," Little Pete sees a mysterious band practicing one day. It's Polaris, though he doesn't know that. Never a fan of music before, he starts a band (math teacher Miss Fingerwood is on bass, naturally), so that he can remember that song—his favorite song—and play it so that he doesn't forget it. After playing so many other people's favorite songs to raise money to pay his dad's electrical bill, finally Little Pete remembers the song and his band plays it. It's a moment of triumph. Yes, the band is called The Blowholes.

Family, friendship, crushes, first jobs, they all get covered. Maybe Big Pete and Little Pete fight over a bowling ball with mystical powers. In the end, their relationship is more important. A pay phone in Wellsville has been ringing for 27 years and on the hottest day of the summer Little Pete finally decides to answer it because it's driving people mad. It turns out that it's a man who had a crush on Joyce all those years ago and was just waiting for her to answer. Now, if you apply real-world logic to that, it's insane and creepy. However, in the world of *Pete & Pete* where everything is heightened and can even border on magical realism, it's a moving testament to the endurance of human emotions. How many shows for kids can tackle big topics and bigger emotions without just hitting you over the head in as obvious a way as possible? *Pete & Pete* didn't have to resort to that.

The acting is almost uniformly good. Maronna and Tamberelli are both really good as the brothers Pete. Alison Fanelli, who didn't really act after *Pete & Pete*, is good as Ellen. Huss is so great hamming it up as Artie. Then you watch him on something like *Halt and Catch Fire* and you realize he can do drama as well. I also loved Damian Young's high-strung performance as Stu Benedict. The sentence "Passengers will refrain from KILLING MY SOUL!" will always stick with me. Hardy Rawls and Judy Grafe fit right in as well-meaning sitcom parents. Rick Gomez kills it as "Endless" Mike. So many actors, and non-actors, stop by in roles on *Pete & Pete* I couldn't have appreciated as a kid but I dig them now. In addition to Iggy Pop, Adam West eventually plays Little Pete's strict principal. Janeane Garafalo is in an episode. Steve Buscemi plays Ellen's dad Phil in multiple episodes. Bebe Neuwirth, who I love as Lilith on *Cheers* and *Frasier* plays a mail carrier. James Rebhorn and J.K. Simmons show up. Musicians like Juliana Hatfield, Debbie Harry, Marshall Crenshaw, Gordon Gano, and David Johansen all make appearances. Hell, Patty Hearst is in an episode. It's truly incredible to watch now as an adult.

Even more impressive than the casting, though, is the music. The soundtrack of *Pete & Pete* puts any other show for kids to shame. You have to start with Polaris, of course. In addition to "Hey Sandy," the song that becomes Little Pete's favorite "Summerbaby" is really good. I'm partial to "Waiting for October," and "She Is Staggering" has a great little hook to it that popped up a lot. When things got somber, you were going to hear the harmonica part of "Your Long White Fingers" by the Gothic Archies. Some people talk trash about shows or movies overly relying on music cues to set a mood, but it's part of storytelling. That harmonica part just feels sobering and bleak. When I hear The 6ths "Falling Out of Love with You," a sad and beautiful song about the end of a relationship, I immediately picture *Pete & Pete*. Specifically, Ellen using semaphore for some reason. Of course, they never really used the lyrics from that song, just the killer guitar part in all its jangly glory. This all comes from the dedication from the likes of McRobb, Viscardi, and Dieckmann. They never undersold any part of the show. It is not a perfect show, but there are no weak points to it.

After those five specials, they made three seasons and 34 episodes of *The Adventures of Pete & Pete*. Needless to say, that wasn't nearly enough. They couldn't churn out episodes like a game show, though. This show looked good. It was shot well. You needed to hire talent. You had to shoot on location, in this case primarily in South Orange, New Jersey. While we are never told where Wellsville is, in my mind it has always been in New Jersey because of this fact. The show just feels like the Northeast, be it winter, summer, or fall. They aired the final episode on April 1, 1996, an episode called "Last Laugh" fittingly about a prank. However, that was not the last episode in the show's production, as the final episode aired out of intended order. The last true episode of *Pete & Pete* is "Saturday," which feels fitting to me because it's an ensemble episode that shows what everybody in town is doing on their Saturday.

While "Saturday" is a good episode, I am truly irked that *Pete & Pete* had to suffer from Nickelodeon's disdain for series finales, the better to air a show in random order for endless reruns. If any Nick show deserved a series finale, it's this one. And yet, it couldn't even get its final season shown in order. Do I hate Nickelodeon now having thought about this? Maybe. I'm definitely not going to be sending Stick Stickly a Christmas card this year. Reruns did indeed air for a few years, and like I said the first two seasons came out on DVD, which I quickly snatched up. I even listened to the audio commentary. That's how I roll. When TeenNick, a Nick offshoot, started doing a '90s block, of course *The Adventures of Pete & Pete* was a part of it. The fan base for that show remains fervent. There have been multiple reunion events over the years. People have Petunia tattoos. Maronna and Tamberelli, the brothers Pete, even started to do a podcast together called *The Adventures of Danny & Mike*. The theme song? "The Backyard" by Miracle Legion, of course. People who love *Pete & Pete* seem to love it intensely. I get that. It sticks out among '90s Nick shows for many reasons. We just didn't see other shows like this. It was unique. It was special.

I will go back to my article once more to wrap things up. When discussing the show in the big picture, McRobb called it the "ultimate first record" show, referencing the fact that first records tend to be special because the artist has had their whole life leading up to it. "It's a celebration of all the little things about being a kid that you forget about as you get older, but as a kid are larger than life. Really celebrating all the little things of childhood. It was almost trying to get kids to be nostalgic for their own childhood while they were having their own childhoods," he said. Viscardi, meanwhile, declared, "I would say the thing that we always talked about when we were making the show was we wanted every single episode to be funny, sad, strange, and beautiful." I certainly think they succeeded at that and then some. No Nick show is funnier. No Nick show is sadder. No Nick show is more beautiful. Yes, I did skip strange. There's a show with a cat and a dog that are conjoined siblings and a show with a sponge that lives in a pineapple. Those shows are stranger, but also in a way that is kind of affected. *Pete & Pete*'s strangeness feels more earned and substantive. Accuse me of bias if you must, but I am wearing my critic's hat when I say that. It says "CRITIC" in rhinestones, and I have to live up to that declaration.

I feel like I somewhat managed to avoid just gushing about *The Adventures of Pete & Pete* and just listing my favorite jokes and episodes like a written version of that Chris Farley sketch. You know, the one where he's a Chippendales dancer. I didn't even make too many dumb jokes and pop culture references in this chapter. I was too busy articulating all of what makes *Pete & Pete* the pinnacle of Nickelodeon in the '90s. It deserves all the praise I gave it. You know what else it deserves? The third season to be released on DVD. I know DVDs aren't popular anymore. Just give us the third season. If my book can somehow make that happen, I will consider it a success.

All That

The idea of a *Saturday Night Live*–style show for kids just makes sense. They say your favorite *SNL* cast is the one from when you are 13, but what about kids who aren't 13 yet? The kids that can't stay up late on a Saturday night and shouldn't be made privy to a series of clumsily-constructed fellatio double entendres? A sketch show for kids that aired at a reasonable hour was a great idea. If you can get kids actually starring in it, that's also beneficial. While I am somewhat squeamish conceptually about the idea of professional child actors, putting a bunch of tweens and teenagers together so they have friends to hang out with is better than being the precocious kid on some sitcom where your costars are a bunch of embittered TV actors. Being able to hang out with (hopefully) friends and make comedy sketches? That doesn't sound too shabby. Thus, in 1994, *All That* was born, and it became one of the seminal '90s Nickelodeon shows.

Like most things in life, *All That* began at Millard Fillmore High School. What does the mostly forgotten 13th President of the United States have to do with a sketch show from the '90s? It was the setting for the sitcom *Head of the Class*. The show ran for five seasons on ABC and focused on a group of honors students at the high school. Sort of an inverse version of the Sweathogs. They were joined by their history teacher Charlie Moore, played by Howard Hesseman, who is best known as Dr. Johnny Fever from *WKRP in Cincinnati*, a show hurt but the fact a bunch of music had to be scrubbed from it for reruns. The same thing happened to *Daria*. Life can be cruel. Hesseman left after the first four seasons, and was replaced by Scottish comedian Billy Connolly, who played Billy MacGregor.

One of the kids in the group was Dennis Blunden, who was a computer genius and a wisecracker. He was sort of the rapscallion of the bunch, coercing some of his other gifted students into his schemes. For some reason, I want to compare him to Dan Fielding from *Night Court*, but without the womanizing. Another of the students was Eric Mardian. He was the outsider of the group, but given the focal point of the show (gifted students) he stood out because he was a tough guy who rode a motorcycle and didn't really care about academics. Dennis was played by Dan Schneider. Eric was played by Brian Robbins. This is where the *All That* journey begins.

Schneider and Robbins were friends and they both had an affinity for writing. Filled with the audacity of youth, they wrote an episode and then pitched it to the producers of *Head of the Class* and, to their surprise, the producers bought it. Skill, hubris, and cronyism all paid off for Schneider and Robbins, and their path post-acting was starting to unveil itself.

While cast members on *Head of the Class*, Schneider and Robbins were asked to co-host the 1988 *Kids Choice Awards* alongside Tony Danza and Debbie Gibson, a pairing that screams 1988. This is what got the duo on Nickelodeon's radar. Robbins also got involved with his friend, the producer Michael Tollin, in their own production company. They were mostly making documentaries when Robbins was asked by the brass at Nickelodeon if he was interested in making a TV show. He pitched the concept of *All That*, which is literally just *SNL* for kids, and brought along Tollin to help him produce and run the show and brought Schneider on as the head writer. With that trio in place, and with the go ahead from Nick, they went about finding their cast, even before they had written the pilot. Which, you know, makes total sense, because it would be insane to write a sketch show without a cast in place.

A nationwide talent search yielded an original cast of seven: Angelique Bates, Lori Beth Denberg, Katrina Johnson, Kel Mitchell, Alisa Reyes, Josh Server, and Kenan Thompson. While some of those names, and faces, have stuck with me, I have to admit I had no real memory of Bates or Johnson before going back to the show for this book. To be fair, Bates was only on the first two seasons, making her the first of the original seven to go. Only Server lasted the full six seasons of the initial run of *All That*. It was a sketch show, after all. Cast members come and go. Over the initial six-season run, which ended in 2000, I would say there were three notable cast members added in Amanda Bynes (who basically replaced Bates in the cast), Danny Tamberelli, and Nick Cannon. Bynes was one of the breakout stars of *All That*, but I will discuss her more in *The Amanda Show* chapter. Cannon is remembered for his career post–*All That* more than his work on the show, and Tamberelli was already known to *All That*'s audience when he joined the show, as he had starred in *The Adventures of Pete & Pete*. I guess that kind of makes him like when Christopher Guest and Billy Crystal joined the *SNL* cast? If you read the *Pete & Pete* chapter, I'm sure you can guess that I was hyped for Tamberelli joining the show. It probably is also worth noting that *All That* always had a rather diverse cast, which hasn't always been the case for even *Saturday Night Live*.

You know how sketch shows work, right? There is no overarching storyline, though there are recurring sketches. Pretty much every episode began with the cast all hanging around as "themselves," usually causing stress for their "stage manager" Kevin. Kevin was played by Kevin Kopelow, who was a writer on the show and eventually co-head writer with his writing partner Heith Seifert. He was a solid counterpoint in terms of energy to the kids, though his role was that of a two-dimensional adult authority figure, mostly there to be made fun of and mistreated. After that, we'd see a handful of sketches. Unlike *SNL*, *All That* was only a half-hour long, which curtailed the total sketch number. Then, things would end with a musical guest. The vast majority of the acts on the show were from the realm of hip hop and R&B, which wasn't my thing then and isn't now. Although, when they stepped out of the hip-hop realm it was usually for boy bands or, like, Sugar Ray, which also wasn't for me then or now. I suppose it was too much to ask for Pavement to stop by the studio down in Orlando, or in Hollywood after the show moved production to the West Coast. Basically, I could have turned most episodes of *All That* off a few minutes early. I wouldn't, of course, because I had to watch the next show on Nick. And the next show. And so on and so forth until Nickelodeon turned into Nick at Nite and then eventually I would fall asleep.

In terms of quality, *All That* was a sketch show. It was hit and miss. I don't know if there has ever been a single sketch show that had an episode that just killed it for every sketch. Even *The State* would usually have a middling sketch or two in an episode. *All That* worked for me as a kid, and it surprisingly held up decently well as an adult. There are bad sketches. Some of them are lazy and barely fleshed out. Some of them just fall flat in performance. Admittedly, some of them probably worked on me as a child but now the jokes are so obvious that I can't enjoy them any longer. Take, for example the librarian sketches. Denberg would portray a librarian who was always yelling, "Quiet, this is a library!" She's make a ton of noise herself, but if anybody else made a peep, the yelling would commence. The loud librarian is about the most facile joke possible, but given how fully Denberg committed, it could have worked once. Making it a recurring sketch was probably a mistake.

Also, I hated the "Ear Boy" sketches, mostly because it was Cronenbergian body horror. I didn't need to see Pizza Face, Egg Head, and Four Eyes. I did enjoy the Ross Perot jokes, though, more for the audacity of parodying Perot on a show for kids. I enjoyed Detective Dan, and Server was perhaps my favorite of the original cast members. I also liked Denberg, who hosted "Vital Information," the show's version of *SNL*'s "Weekend Update." It was a little bit more about deadpan one-liners, but maybe it's not surprising that a guy who became a professional writer enjoyed the sketch that was all about joke writing.

That being said, you can't talk *All That* without talking Kenan and Kel, who ended up with their own show. They clearly were favorites of the folks on the show, and I can see why. Kenan had plenty of recurring characters, such as Pierre Escargot, but if we're talking *All That* and breakout sketches, then this is the time to talk "Good Burger." Mitchell will forever be a part of the filament of pop culture for his role as Ed, the clueless cashier at Good Burger. The vocal intonations of the character, and his catchphrase "Welcome to Good Burger, home of the Good Burger, can I take your order?" are burnt into my brain.

Ed, along with Thompson and Mitchell, were so popular that it led to a *Good Burger* movie. It was written by Schneider, Kopelow, and Seifert and directed by Robbins. The movie features a young Linda Cardellini and an old Abe Vigoda. There's more acting from Carmen Electra than traditionally recommended. At the beginning of the movie a baby is thrown through a basketball hoop and it never stops being insane to see that. It's not a good movie, but it has some genuinely solid moments, and enough bad-in-a-fun-way moments, that it's worth watching once. Or just watch the music video for the "We're All Dudes" song by Kel (as Ed) and ska legends Less Than Jake. Hey, *Good Burger* made money. In the end, that's the goal for studios.

All That is lucky that technology has lent itself to carving up old pop culture for our own benefit. You can throw a good sketch on YouTube from back in the day and set aside the bad ones. If you want to watch "Ask Ashley" you can, and you don't have to sit through a whole episode. That's how

Kenan Thompson as his *All That* character Pierre Escargot. Yes, he usually wore a raincoat in the bathtub (Nickelodeon).

a lot of people watch new episodes of *Saturday Night Live*, let alone old episodes of *All That*.

   All That as I knew it ended in 2000 after the sixth season. It came back for four seasons in the 2000s, but I did not watch. As of this writing, a new, fresh reboot has started airing on Nick. Mitchell and Thompson are executive producers, and Kel also occasionally acts on the show. As for Kenan, well, he took to sketch comedy quite well. Thompson has been a cast member on *Saturday Night Live*—which is like *All That* but for adults—since 2003. He is the longest-serving cast member in the history of a show that has been around since 1975. Frankly, that's incredible. Other cast members have gone on to various levels of success in the business. It's not uncommon for child actors, even child stars, to have their careers end in early adulthood, by choice or otherwise. I don't know what every *All That* cast member is up to. I do know Danny Tamberelli has played in bands and, from firsthand experience, I can tell you that Denberg and her friends are quite good at *Simpsons* trivia.

   What about the men who created the show? Tollin has had an incredible producing career, including producing *The Last Dance*, the Michael Jordan/Chicago Bulls documentary that was seemingly watched by every sports fan. He also directed *Summer Catch*, *Radio*, and a *30 for 30* documentary on the fall of the USFL, for which Donald Trump was largely responsible. The man clearly loves sports. Robbins has done a lot of directing as well outside of *Good Burger*. Granted, that includes directing bombs like *Norbit*—which may have cost Eddie Murphy an Oscar—and *A Thousand Words*. He probably cares zero percent, as Robbins is currently serving as the President of Nickelodeon. And yet, if I were to ever meet him, I'd mostly want to talk about his role as Steve Williams in *C.H.U.D. II: Bud the Chud*.

   Then, there's Schneider, who basically became the main creative force behind Nickelodeon television. This is not hyperbole. Schneider created the following Nickelodeon shows: *The Amanda Show*, *Drake & Josh*, *Zoey 101*, *iCarly*, *Victorious*, *Sam & Cat*, *Henry Danger*, *The Adventures of Kid Danger*, and *Game Shakers*. Now, I haven't seen any of these shows outside of *The Amanda Show* and a YouTube clip of a *Victorious* episode that was a parody of '70s *Match Game*. For the generation just younger than mine that grew up on Nick, Schneider was maybe the biggest influence in their cultural life. He had a role in our generation's as well. The *New York Times* literally called him the "Norman Lear of children's television." Then, in 2018, Nickelodeon cut ties with Schneider. There were reports of problematic behavior, including anger issues and potential sexual impropriety. It was the end of an era, and the downfall of a legacy. The lack of ethics that made Dennis Blunden a fun character on *Head of the Class* isn't as fun in real life. The fall of Schneider is a stark reminder, not that we needed one, that are childhoods aren't sacred and can't always remain untainted. Who would have thought that the worse thing I associated with *All That* would no longer be the "Ear Boy" sketches? Time makes fools of us all.

The Amanda Show

There's this thing in life called diminishing returns

Amanda Bynes was discovered by a Nickelodeon producer through a comedy camp at the Laugh Factory in Los Angeles. She joined the cast of *All That* in 1996, the first new cast member the show added after the original seven were hired. Bynes was 10 years old at the time. That means she had been at a comedy camp and done standup by that age. This is, to me, pretty messed up. And so begins the journey that led to Amanda Bynes becoming a TV and movie star for a fleeting moment.

Clearly, the people at Nickelodeon were big fans of Bynes, who had been acting since she was seven. I will certainly acquiesce that she was more talented than a lot of kids. Even professional child actors who are preteens are bad. They don't have timing. They don't have skill. They can barely recite their lines. Many of them had jobs on Nickelodeon. Bynes was precocious, but she wasn't playing precocious, because that's more for TV shows and movies aimed at adults. They are the ones who chuckle mildly at a kid acting wise beyond their years. Or, if you're me, two seconds of Chlöe Grace Moretz in *(500) Days of Summer* makes your eyes bleed. Bynes was just a kid on a show for kids, and because she wasn't terrible at doing sketch comedy those kids were able to find her funny. I'm not going to say she was good, because I am an adult and have watched professional comedy acting for many years with my adult brain, but she knew what she was doing, and Nickelodeon thought they had a star on their hands.

Bynes started appearing as a panelist on *Figure it Out*, and then, in 1999, was given her own sketch show, simply entitled *The Amanda Show*. This was big for Bynes, as well as the creator of the show, the now-disgraced Dan Schneider. It was his first of many creations for Schneider. This is also maybe the only spinoff sketch show I can think of. Many sketch show actors go on to their own shows or movie careers. Chevy Chase literally left *Saturday Night Live* after one season in the '70s. Goldie Hawn appeared on *Rowan and Martin's Laugh-In*. Eventually they would star in *Foul Play* together. Usually actors are moving beyond the realm of sketch comedy. Bynes was only 13, though, so maybe they didn't want to overreach. Regardless, 13 year olds normally don't get to star in shows, let alone shows with their names in the title. Having said that, it's something that shouldn't be normal. It's quite weird. I am not a fan of the fact *The Amanda Show* existed.

Exist it did, though. To be fair, there were other cast members on the show, including future Nick stars Drake Bell and Josh Peck. I only know this through osmosis. You see, I did not watch an episode of *The Amanda Show* when it aired. Bynes is a couple months older than I am. By the time she was starring on her own sketch show, I had moved on from watching Nickelodeon by and large. I was watching *Saturday Night Live*. I was a teenager. Childish things had been put away. Besides, they weren't really showing *Pete & Pete* or *Rocko's Modern Life* by 1999. There were also a couple adults in the cast, including John Kassir, best known as the voice of the Crypt Keeper on *Tales from the Crypt*. He would have called this "The A-maim-da Bones Show." Danny Bonaduce appeared in two episodes.

I don't have a ton to say about *The Amanda Show*, and only in part because it wasn't present in my childhood. It was basically a worse version of *All That* with a focal point performer as opposed to a true ensemble. There were *Judge Judy* parodies and a now wistfully dated parody of Blockbuster video with the first-draft name of Blockblister. The show ran until 2002, finishing off with three seasons and 40 episodes under its belt, not including six best of episodes.

In 2002, Bynes, still a teenager, got her first movie role in *Big Fat Liar*, where she costarred with fellow teen sensation Frankie Muniz. The movie was co-written by Schneider and Brian Robbins, who was one of the creators of *All That*. That same year she began starring in a sitcom called *What I Like About You*, where she played Holly, the spunky younger sister of the strait-laced and responsible Val, played by Jennie Garth. While I never watched this show on WB, it aired for four seasons and 86 episodes, which in television terms is an unqualified success. Seems like your classic mismatch comedy, from what I gather. Was it co-created by Schneider? You'd better believe it! This time, he teamed up with Wil Calhoun, who had written on *Friends* previously.

Bynes moved from there to getting a chance to star in a couple of films, including *She's the Man*, a riff on William Shakespeare's *Twelfth Night* that by all accounts was well received. She also starred in *Sydney White*, where she played Sydney White. I remember it existing but only while writing this book did I find out that it is a riff on *Snow White*. Bynes also played Penny in the musical version of John Waters' *Hairspray*, the one with John Travolta stepping into the dress of Divine, and appeared in *Easy A* in 2010. That movie helped to turn Emma Stone into a star. Alas, while her star was rising, Bynes' star was crashing. I know stars don't crash, but just let me have my clumsy turn of phrase anyway.

In 2009, she was cast in the movie *Post Grad*, but dropped out of the production. The same thing happened in 2010 when she was cast in *Hall Pass*. Granted, I can't blame anybody for dropping out of *Hall Pass*. Everybody else who stayed in the movie should have followed suit. Unfortunately, Bynes' decision didn't seem to be a matter of realizing she was in a profoundly stupid movie. Later in 2010, Bynes declared she was retired from acting. Soon thereafter, she would rescind that retirement, but she has not acted since.

The problems in Bynes' personal life started to become the only times we heard about her. Bynes was charged with a DUI in 2012, and was charged with marijuana possession in 2013 when she reportedly threw a bong out her window. There were strange tweets. Calls for gynecological assassination rung throughout the internet. Her behavior was bizarre, and it grew increasingly concerning. Suddenly, she was being detained for allegedly starting a fire in a stranger's driveway and was hospitalized involuntarily due to concern about her mental health. This led to her parents filing for conservatorship over her affairs. Once she started tweeted about her erratic tweets being a result of a microchip her father had planted in her head, it had become abundantly clear that Bynes' mental health was in serious jeopardy.

Indeed, Bynes has said that she was diagnosed with bipolar disorder, which certainly is in line with her behavior. In 2018, after years in the wilderness, during which she studied fashion, Bynes popped back up in our lives. She said she was sober and apologized for some of the things she had tweeted. She talked of potentially returning to acting. That hasn't happened, and Bynes' social media activity hasn't exactly stopped being distressing. There is no magical cure for bipolar, and I refuse to make any presumptions of how she feels and what she is doing to manage her disease. I do know that it is a mental illness that often starts manifesting itself in your early twenties, which lines up with certain things that happened in Bynes' career. In a weird way, I'm glad she got to have such a robust career in her childhood. Otherwise, she may have not gotten to have any sort of career at all. That feels like it would have been truly tragic.

Of course, the actuality is quite tragic as well. Things are terrible! A lot of child stars have issues in adulthood as is. There is no way to know what Bynes' life or career would have been like were she not struggling with her mental health. All of our childhoods pass us by, which is a good thing. Being an adult is better than being a child, in a vacuum. Still, we all lose a little something when we make the transition from one stage of life to the next. Bynes sadly lost a lot. It is incredibly strange to sit here in the present and watch *The Amanda Show*, knowing what the future held for her. If

I could sit through a dozen Blockblister sketches in exchange for Bynes' mental health to be in a better place, it would be a trade I'd happily make. I can't. Reality is what it is. This chapter ends on a bummer note. Even the Crypt Keeper wouldn't make a joke right now.

The Angry Beavers

*Getting along with siblings
(and network executives) can be hard*

Eventually, Nickelodeon cartoons stopped being remarkable. This is not a mark of quality, mind you. I mean that it stopped being notable that Nick was making new animated shows. The first three Nicktoons debuted the same day in 1991, and that was significant. The next couple of shows were also noteworthy. By the time *The Angry Beavers* debuted in 1997, on the other hand, we had been enjoying over half a decade of Nicktoons. We had seen hundreds of new episodes, and even more reruns. Reruns play a part in the story of *The Angry Beavers*, at least, if you dig into the lore. Oh, there is *Angry Beavers* lore, and it's more interesting than you would imagine. Especially if you watched *Angry Beavers* as it aired.

The show focuses on two beaver brothers, Norbert aka Norb and Dagwood aka Dag. They move out of their parents' house and live together in the forests of the Pacific Northwest. Dag is high strung and dumb. Norb is a bit chiller and more mild mannered, the relative brains of the duo. They bicker, argue, and fight. Sometimes their relationship is tumultuous. The Beaver brothers (their last name is Beaver) have a sibling rivalry but also fit into the classic tropes of television comedy. You could call them an odd couple, if you were feeling so bold. Their personalities are distinctly different, creating a juxtaposition of attitudes and approaches to problems. It's Storytelling 101 in terms of developing a comedy show. Not that I'm knocking Nickelodeon or show creator Mitch Schauer. The odd couple pairings in sitcoms have existed for decades for a reason. It works, and as far as I know it had never been done with talking beavers before.

Dag was voiced by Richard Steven Horvitz, a successful voiceover actor. Norb's voice was provided by Nick Bakay, best remembered for voicing Salem the cat in the *Sabrina, the Teenage Witch* show starring Nick alum Melissa Joan Hart. I had a brief preoccupation with Salem from *Sabrina*, because when Salem was being portrayed by a puppet it looked so incredibly fake in an amazing way. I would watch GIFs of that horrendous puppet doing things like reading a book, stirring a cauldron, or dressed like a costume pimp and declaring, "Money, bay-bay!" In short, Salem rules. Norb was much more dexterous than Salem, what with being animated, but he lacked any kitsch factor unfortunately. *Angry Beavers* also lacked any notable characters outside of its main pairing. I spent hours on end seemingly every day as a kid watching Nickelodeon and so much of what I saw is etched in my memory. There are lines of dialogue and tertiary characters I haven't seen in over 20 years that I still remember. I have to be honest and say that before returning to the show for this book I didn't remember a single *Angry Beavers* character other than Dagwood and Norbert.

There's a shrew named Truckee who loved his truck, a lizard named Bing, a love interest for Norbert named Treeflower who is a beaver that's a champion snowboarder, a vegetarian bear that loves funk and sounds like Barry White, and so on. There's also a stump named Stump that shows up at various events and "interacts" with Dag and Norb even though Stump never actually does anything. It reminds me of Jerri Blank's father Guy on *Strangers with Candy*. There's a bit of an absurdist streak running through *Angry Beavers*, but that's not uncommon for cartoons. I wouldn't call *Angry Beavers* "out there," but that's not a bad thing. Some shows veer too much in that direction and become intolerable miasmas of "random" elements. As an adult, there are a few tertiary characters that are way more interesting to me. The show has something of an antagonist known only as "Scientist #1" which I imagine is a riff on those nameless characters you find in movies, namely old sci-fi movies. I specifically mention those because Dag and Norb enjoy B movies, particularly those made by Oxnard Montalvo. There's even an episode where the Beaver brothers have to help Montalvo defeat the monsters from his movies in real life. Also making appearances are Dr. Cowtiki, an actor who plays a scientist in Montalvo's movies, and actress Toluca Lake (voiced by Adrienne Barbeau), who is something of a B movie scream queen who also worked with Montalvo. A B movie actress named Toluca Lake is so far up my alley that I have no choice but to doff my cap to *Angry Beavers* for that one. If only those characters had shown up more.

Unfortunately, not everything on *Angry Beavers* is as fun as Toluca Lake. Revisiting the show, I didn't get a ton of laughs. A lot of jokes are corny, or barely jokes. The show relies too much on "transgressive for children" material. You know, fart jokes and underpants jokes. Stuff that you may find to be edgy as a kid, but as an adult don't really register. It just feels like lazy comedy, lowest common denominator stuff. The pacing is also strange sometimes for a cartoon show. Usually they are jam packed with action and incident. Watching my first episode of *Angry Beavers* in 20 years I was struck by the amount of time between jokes, or moments of outright silence. It feels a little clumsy at times, which is weird when you can control every single element of the timing. As a kid, *Angry Beavers* was far from my favorite Nick show, but I did enjoy it. My opinion isn't any stronger on it as an adult. It feels like Schauer and company were maybe in over their heads.

Or maybe there was just too much nonsense to deal with, to hear the folks who worked on the show tell it.

As the stories go, Schauer often ran afoul of Nickelodeon's management, particularly when it came to standards and practices. This is surprising, given the envelopes pushed by *Rocko's Modern Life* and *Ren & Stimpy*. However, when different people are at the top of the pyramid, everything can change below them. In 1996, Herb Scannell had taken over as president of Nickelodeon. According to Micah Wright, who was a writer for *Angry Beavers*, the words "shut up" were bleeped in an episode of the show because Scannell didn't like when kids said "shut up," and he figured it TV characters didn't say it then kids wouldn't either. Which, you know, is definitely not true and also a weird thing to concern yourself with. To think that the network that birthed *Ren & Stimpy* was now clutching their pearls over a beaver saying something so harmless marks quite a sea change. Indeed, you can see the proof in the pudding of the "shut up" incident. They literally bleeped it, only drawing more attention to it, and then later replaced it with "hush up" using ADR. Eventually, shows that had an adult audience such as *SpongeBob SquarePants* and *Fairly OddParents* would be greenlit under Scannell, but Schauer's beefs with the network were never resolved.

They also went to the end of the show, when *Angry Beavers* was cancelled after four seasons and 62 episodes. The final story to air, "Shell or High Water," is about the brothers going to the beach and building sandcastles. Simple enough, though I can't help but notice the play on "Hell or high water" given the disputes about content between the network and the show. This was not the intended way for the fourth season to end, though. Seeing the writing on the wall, the *Angry Beavers* crew was going to throw caution to the wind, and this is where the lore of the never-aired series finale "Bye Bye Beavers" is born.

In "Bye Bye Beavers," Dagwood and Norbert were to find out they had been cancelled. Not in the modern use of the term, but in the literal TV sense. The episode begins with Norbert receiving a letter informing the brothers that their show has been cancelled and that they are just cartoon characters on a TV show. Most of the episode is Norb trying to calm Dag down and explain to him their reality. Which is to say, they aren't real. They also take shots at Nickelodeon for not supporting their show and preferring to just air reruns ad nauseam instead of creating new content. If you watched Nick as a kid, that's a criticism that has legs. To add to the meta nature, Horvitz and Bakay referred to each other as "Nick" and "Richard" on occasion, with a "Salem" also thrown in there for good measure. Whether or not that would have lasted to the episode airing we don't know.

That's because "Bye Bye Beavers" did not air. In fact, they didn't even finish production on it before the episode was nixed by the network. While

Nickelodeon had allegedly signed off on the idea, when they saw how it was all coming together they had second thoughts and pulled the plug. That makes sense, and not just because of the biting commentary which honestly they couldn't have thought would make it to air, right? Series finales weren't part of the routine for Nick back in the day. After all, finales are, well, final. It makes it harder to bring a show back, and it also makes things feel strange in reruns. Without a finale, you can just create an infinite feedback loop of episodes. There is no end point. There is just a wheel of reruns. "Bye Bye Beavers" was not just a series finale. It was a finale that pulled no punches and tore down the fourth wall. Imagine being a kid and seeing characters acknowledging that they are TV characters and telling you that the show you liked is over. It could be jarring.

Like most Nick shows, even the live-action ones, *Angry Beavers* didn't get a series finale. The only reason we know "Bye Bye Beavers" isn't just talk from embittered television professionals is that the audio of Bakay and Horvitz recording has been leaked online, as has some storyboards. Do I wish "Bye Bye Beavers" had aired? Of course. While I tend to not actually enjoy the fourth wall being broken down this much, for a petty series finale I can dig it. The idea of a cartoon beaver talking about how his animated show has been cancelled is kind of amazing in its way. We missed out on that, though. That makes *The Angry Beavers* a mediocre cartoon with a shrug of a final episode instead of a show that went down in history in a blaze of glory. You know what show actually did that? *Strangers with Candy*. I didn't realize these shows had so much in common. As a kid, *Angry Beavers* gave me a bit of entertainment. It also taught me two things. One, beavers have a second set of eyelids that are translucent so they can see while they swim underwater. Two, James Buchanan was our only bachelor president. I wish the crew on *Angry Beavers* had been able to end the show on their own terms, and also for the Dag and Norb to have been able to say "shut up" to each other. Before I bring this chapter to a close, I also have to wonder why the show was called *Angry Beavers*. The "Beavers" part makes sense, but they weren't particularly angry. Are they angry sometimes? Sure, but not to an unusual degree. In fact, Norb is quite chill. The title doesn't really make sense. They could have called it *The Beaver Brothers* or *Beave Us Alone* or something. It's too late now. It's too late for a lot of things. It's not too late to say "bye bye" to these beavers, though.

Animorphs

The most dangerous animal of all is not man,
but a man that can turn into, like, a tiger or something

When I was in elementary school, there was a book series with a supernatural bent that seemingly every kid I knew was devouring. That book series was *Goosebumps*. Also, *Animorphs* existed. I am joking to a degree, because I do remember *Animorphs*. They certainly were in the cultural zeitgeist for children. And yet, I can honestly say I do not recall a single conversation I had with any friends about *Animorphs*. The book series was written by Katherine Applegate and her husband Michael Grant under the name K.A. Applegate starting in 1996. They wrote 54 books in the series between then and 2001. Apparently they were published by Scholastic, which explains in part why I was aware of them. Like I assume most elementary school students in the '90s, I would receive a Scholastic book catalog a few times a year. I even bought some books from it. I definitely remember seeing the *Animorphs* books in there. Additionally, I was aware of the *Animorphs* series, which aired on Nickelodeon in the United States and which is the focal point of this chapter. I did not watch it then, though. It began airing in 1998, but *Animorphs* skewered older than some of Nickelodeon's programming, so I could have certainly watched it in the beginning. I didn't. I wasn't interested in it.

To be fair, I only had tangential interest in *Goosebumps*, the R.L. Stine series that skewed more horror than the sci-fi of *Animorphs*. I read some *Goosebumps* books out of cultural obligation, since my friends were reading them insatiably. They were always checked out of the library in my school. I ended up reading a few, and also came into possession of a book called *Gooflumps* which was a parody of *Goosebumps* I do not recall actually reading. Speaking of which, I also found a single *Animorphs* book in the closet of my childhood bedroom, along with a Book It pin and some Beanie Babies I was sure were going to be a gold mine on the resale market when I was a kid. Either I never read that *Animorphs* book, or I started reading it but never finished it because I wasn't into it. It made no mark on me. *Animorphs* has less of a cultural impact in my brain than the 1983 NBC show *Manimal*, which featured a man who could turn into animals. It lasted eight episodes. I have seen a couple of them. It was an eminently worthwhile experience and I apologize for nothing.

The *Animorphs* TV series was actually a Canadian production, and Canada actually has had an outsized impact on the history of Nickelodeon. As I mentioned in the introductory chapter, the first hit on Nick, *You Can't Say That on Television*, was a Canadian import. *Animorphs* was made in Canada, and aired on a couple different Canadian channels, but in the U.S. of A it was purely an American venture. Although, episodes aired in Canada weeks before they aired in the United States. In Canada, the show ran from September of 1998 until October of 1999. In the United States it ran from September of 1998 until April of 2000. If you were an *Animorphs* fan, I hope you didn't have any Canadian friends dropping spoilers on you over AOL Instant Messenger or ICQ.

Animorphs is an example of a brand of entertainment I just can't get into: A mildly interesting premise bogged down in a bunch of world building nonsense. It's the same problem I have with, say, *Lord of the Rings*. I've watched the trilogy. It has good actors in it. I just don't care about lands and lore. When it's cheesy or overly convoluted it's even worse. Some of this fantasy and sci-fi stuff just seems to be an excuse to come up with different words and jargon. I know J.R.R. Tolkien was interested in that. In fact, he was arguably more interested in inventing Elvish words than, you know, telling an interesting story or developing character, and that carried over to the movies.

Animorphs is a striking example of this. Researching the books, and the TV show, for this chapter made my eyes glaze over. If I were to tell you that the show is about five people who can turn into animals, that doesn't sound too bad, right? It could be good. Then let's throw in an alien who can also morph into animals. Hey, why not? All right, now let me delve further into the morass that is *Animorphs*. An alien from the Andalite race gives the kids, and an Andalite alien, the power to morph into any animal they touch to share its DNA. Oh, and they need to fight the Yeerks, slug-like aliens who take over human hosts by crawling in their ear canal. Did I mention that this plot to take over the human of Earth is called "The Sharing," and that humans who are taken over are called "Controllers" for reasons I cannot comprehend? Naturally, you can only morph for two hours, or otherwise your morph is permanent. And be sure to wear tight clothes, because only tight attire can go with you when you morph. You don't want to de-morph and be naked! Just look what happened to David in *An American Werewolf in London!* The next thing you know you're running around the zoo naked and John Landis is having to shoot around the fact you're uncircumcised even though your character is Jewish. You know, the usual stuff.

I haven't even gotten into the fact that the Animorphs are telepathic in animal form or the rest of the convoluted nonsense that makes up the rules of the *Animorphs* universe. I'm not against world building or fantastical elements. I enjoy many of the Marvel movies, including the *Guardians of the Galaxy* films that featured a living planet in one of the movies. They just don't get bogged down in it. The jargon doesn't overwhelm me. Also, and this is key, the stories are good, the characters are interesting, the films are show well, the acting is strong, and so on. *Animorphs* doesn't have all that going for it. It has the budget of a Canadian's children's show and, frankly, bad source material. I know there are people out there who will literally buy almost any science fiction or fantasy book. Give them a book taking place in a far-off land with drawings of maps in the book and it will give them the joy of like 10 hits of ecstasy. Those kind of kids probably enjoyed *Animorphs*. I was not one of those kids, and I'm not one of those adults.

I cannot pretend, for a second, to care about Jake, Cassie, Rachel, Tobias, Marco, and an alien named Aximili. By the way, that alien was played by Paulo Costanzo, who had a role in the *Josie and the Pussycats* movie, which means he will always be OK in my book. Shawn Ashmore, who played Jake, the de facto leader of the Animorphs, has had a decent career for himself as well. He even played Iceman in the *X-Men* movies, which also did fantastical world building with a decent amount of success.

The first season of *Animorphs* was 20 episodes long, while the second season only got six episodes. Despite that, the second season introduced a race of androids called the Chee. Well, if you don't know how to tell stories or write characters, you can always stuff more crazy stuff into your show. Or your books, as the show was heavily influenced by books from the series. *Animorphs* ended with a three-part episode that brought no closure to the story. Then again, could there really be any closure? J.R.R. Tolkien at least had Mt. Doom and Sauron for ending his books. What were the Animorphs going to do?

I'm not against a show about people who can turn into animal. Hey, it works for Beast Boy in *Teen Titans Go!* This show is just such a snooze, though. Watching it, you can sort of figure out what's going on, but what I could comprehend I didn't care about. I don't want to undersell how bad this show is, though I am viewing it entirely though entirely adult eyes. It's incredible how much padding was in the episodes I watched. Like, I watched one episode that literally began with 30 seconds of padding. There are so many weird pauses. The morphing looks weird as hell, though I had to admit that the special effects don't look too bad there. I can't say the same when it comes to the aliens, who look cheesy as hell with zero charm to the low quality. Watching *Animorphs*, I also started thinking about how convoluted the justifications for them touching animals to collect their DNA for morphing must have begun. It reminds me of *Knightboat* (the crime-solving boat!) from *The Simpsons*. *Knightboat* is a parody of cheesy action shows, and the Simpson family complains that there is always an inlet or a canal or a fjord for Knightboat to use to catch the bad guys. Was there ever an episode of *Animorphs* where a circus is traveling through down and the caravan gets derailed and animals get loose in town.

Animorphs is a forgotten Nick show, and I feel like it is with good reason. On the other hand, have you ever watched those *Goosebumps* movies with Jack Black as R.L. Stine? Honestly, they're pretty good and clever. All my friends must have been onto something for going with that book series over the one about humans turning into animals and a bunch of overcomplicated nonsense.

Are You Afraid of the Dark?

We're all afraid of something.
Also, always be sure to put your fires out

To answer the rhetorical question posited by the title of the show I am covering in this chapter, no, I'm not afraid of the dark. Even when *Are You Afraid of the Dark?* was airing in its initial run that wasn't true. I don't recall ever being afraid of the dark, though I don't know if anybody is truly afraid of the absence of light. They fear what the darkness could be obfuscating. It's kind of like how people who are "afraid of heights" are really often more afraid of falling from a great height, for obvious reasons. That reason being it might cause Jimmy Stewart to develop an unhealthy psychosexual obsession with somebody who looks just like you. *Are You Afraid of the Dark?* was yet another Canadian import by Nickelodeon. The show debuted in Canada in 1990, though it didn't really have a regular spot in the Nick lineup until 1992, when it became a staple of the SNICK lineup until 1996.

It has not come up yet, so in case you aren't familiar SNICK was Nickelodeon's Saturday lineup dedicated to shows that skewed a little older. For Nick, that mean it was for tweens and young teens. Kids who could be up later on a Saturday but didn't have a car and couldn't go out. For kids stuck between two worlds, they could stay up on Saturday and watch the shows Nickelodeon felt was more up their alley. These shows could be a little more "mature," in one way or another. For example, the original SNICK lineup featured *Clarissa Explains It All* and *Ren & Stimpy*, two Nick shows that skewed a smidge older, and two debuting shows in *Roundhouse* and *Are You Afraid of the Dark?* The latter, and the subject of this chapter, was a SNICK staple for its entire run. In fact, it often aired at the end of the night for SNICK, which was traditionally 9:30. The better to send you off to bed with potential nightmares. Also, it made sure that only the kids who were able to stay up that late on a Saturday night would be up for *Are You Afraid of the Dark?* Nick seemed really determined to protect their viewers from accidentally watching the network's one true horror program.

Some might consider *Are You Afraid of the Dark?* the channel's answer to *The Twilight Zone*, but that is inaccurate in multiple ways. First, *The Twilight Zone* was the brainchild of a single mind in Rod Serling. He didn't

36

write every episode, but in addition to serving as the narrator his personal politics and ethos was splashed all over the show. *Are You Afraid of the Dark?* isn't nearly as distinct. The premise of the show is that a group of kids who call themselves the Midnight Society gather in the woods around a fire and one of them tells a scary story. They are all horror hounds and ghost story fans, which bands them together even though oftentimes they don't seem to have much else in common. That's largely because they wanted to have a mixture of archetypes and kids, I'm sure. Even if it flew in the face of reality, if they had a bunch of different personality types and interests, kids were more likely to find somebody to relate to, and maybe that would make them more likely to watch.

The show also didn't have a ton of time to really dedicate to the Midnight Society. They were just there for the wraparounds, a couple minutes at the beginning and a couple minutes at the end. It was really just a bit of filler, though on occasion the events would spark the story being told. Sometimes that makes it feel like the storyteller is adjusting on the fly, or is an amazing improviser. Let's see what they can do playing a line game. How many double entendres can you pull out of thin air, Gary? Gary, of course, being the leader of the original Midnight Society. These parts of the episodes largely felt perfunctory, but they also make the show feel different from *The Twilight Zone*. Rod Serling wasn't a character. He was just an emcee taking us into the twisted world of another dimension.

Another difference is that not every *Twilight Zone* episode was a horror story. It may feel that way in our memories, because many of the most famous ones are. The gremlin on the wing of a plane that freaked out both William Shatner and John Lithgow. The freaky kid with mind powers who could wish you into the cornfield. Even the one where Burgess Meredith's glasses break is about the end of civilization. Also, there was that Tower of Terror ride at Disney World I really dug that they've apparently turned into a *Guardians of the Galaxy* ride. I've watched many a *Twilight Zone*, and while they are usually supernatural or have a twist involved, they aren't all horror. Some of them are even comedic in nature. There is a famous episode about a woman who fears the arrival of "Mr. Death," but when he does arrive, she actually feels a tremendous sense of relief and peace after she has crossed over. *Are You Afraid of the Dark?*, on the other hand, is pure horror, and more in the vein of monsters, vampires, ghosts, and other assorted bogeymen. The connection between the two shows come from the fact that they are anthology shows with a supernatural, often spooky, bent. Also, the Midnight Society gathered around a fire and Rod Serling chain smoked cigarettes. I did not pull this connection out of nowhere, by the way. Every story on *Are You Afraid of the Dark?* began with "Submitted for the approval of the Midnight Society...." This is a riff on Serling's "submitted for your approval," something he only said on the show in three episodes but has become an iconic part of Serling's legacy.

While I was not afraid of the dark in the era of SNICK, I was afraid to watch this show. I will admit it. The show debuted when I was five. That's only fair. Even now, as an adult, I'm not a fan of horror. I don't mind a monster movie—and I have an affinity for a good horror comedy—but I don't like slasher films or anything built around innocent people being imperiled with intent. Even if it's supernatural characters like ghosts or vampires on the attack. It's not a matter of fear, but a distaste for human sadness being caused by malevolence. Which is to say, if there was an *Are You Afraid of the Dark?* for adults, I wouldn't be watching it now. As a kid, it wasn't even that I was afraid of things I had seen on the show. The concept of it spooked me. I was afraid of what I *might* see, not what I had seen. That's a classic bit of mental gymnastics kids do. You build something up in your head way worse than what you would actually see if you just watched the movie or TV show in question. I certainly was doing that when it came to *Are You Afraid of the Dark?* Are there episodes that would have freaked me out as a kid? Certainly, because some wild and freaky stuff happens. However, it's not like it was a gore fest or was some sort of slasher show dedicated to hacking up babysitters or their dumb, horny boyfriends. What I'm saying is that this is not an alarming watch for an adult.

It's also not a good watch. There are only so many good Canadian actors, and only so many good child actors, and don't get me started on the small number of good Canadian child actors. Some of the stories aren't too shabby, to be honest. The concepts are clever and the twists solid. They are spooky without getting too intense for kids, at least based on my perception. The execution, though, can't help but be lacking. We're talking some fairly low budget affairs. I was mostly amused watching the adult actors—all Canadian day players—sinking their teeth into their roles. Many of the stories require special effects, or at the very least good costuming and makeup. The show is largely not up to the task. They may have had to make a vampire explode into dust in the sunlight for their story, but that doesn't mean it looked good.

I'm glad *Are You Afraid of the Dark?* existed for kids back in the day. It was probably a nice stepping stone into the world of horror. I have never been a horror hound, though. I was a little too young for *Are You Afraid of the Dark?* during its 1992–1996 run on SNICK. Oh, I was a SNICK watcher, but I was always turning it off at 9:30 before it started. I mean, there was a spooky attic in the opening credits! In fact, the opening credits go in heavy on the obvious spooky tropes. In my mind's eye there is a creaky rocking horse blowing back and forth in the wind, but even if there isn't, that captures the ethos of the credits perfectly. It wasn't for me as a kid, at least in my mind, and now it still isn't for me. After all, I still don't love horror, and I also don't love mediocre Canadian shows for tweens. *Are You Afraid of the Dark?* has been rebooted a couple times. Once was in 1999, and I did check into those episodes for the sake of this book. I watched the episode "The Tale of Vampire Town" because it is notable for having a dark ending. Usually everything was all right in the end on *Are You Afraid of the Dark?*, but this time that wasn't the case. This episode also involves two adults trying to murder a kid because they assume he's a vampire, which is some kid show logic in action.

That reboot lasted two seasons, and the second reboot is ongoing as of this writing, though they've completely revamped the cast after the first season. *Are You Afraid of the Dark?* was an attempt from Nick to both foster a horror audience and to keep some of the kids who felt like they were growing out of being a Nick kid. Sure, *Doug* was too tame for them, but maybe the "scary" show would keep them watching. Plus, if I know anything about horror fans, they often don't really care about quality. No fan base is more accepting for what even they consider to be mediocre output. At the end of every episode of *Are You Afraid of the Dark?* the Midnight Society would put out the fire with a bucket of water. With this chapter ending, please do not pour water on this book. It's not necessary, and it will make the book harder to read going forward. Then again, it might lead to more copies being bought. Submitted for the approval of the Midnight Society, considering pouring water on your book and then buying a new copy.

CatDog

We all need time to ourselves (if we can get it)

In the movie *The Fly*, the David Cronenberg one, not the one from 1958 co-starring Vincent Price, Jeff Goldblum plays a scientist whose DNA is accidently spliced with a fly. At first, it gives him superhuman strength, but he starts to fall apart. His humanity is increasingly lost as he becomes a revolting and grotesque amalgam of a fly and a human. Goldblum's teeth and fingernails start to fall out, and by the end of the movie he is no longer recognizably human. In his final act, he instructs Geena Davis to shoot him in the head, putting him out of his misery. Cronenberg has called it a metaphor for aging and death and watching your loved ones slowly succumb to disease. I say it's about Seth Brundle turning into a fly man, but my personal film criticism theory is that every movie is about what happens in the movie and nothing else. I have no interest in metaphor, and I have a BA in film studies so I am allowed to say stuff like that and get away with it. Anyway, let's talk about *CatDog*.

To be fair, *CatDog* lacks Cronenbergian body horror or man tampering in god's domain. Instead, it's about a hybrid cat and dog who are brothers and conjoined. Funnily, whoever listed its genre on Wikipedia calls it a "black comedy," presumably because they must see a grimness in a cat and dog having separate beings but being forever joined together. Cat is on one end and Dog is on the other. They each have a head and a brain and two hands they control but that's it. The two are best friends, but is it by choice? After all, their personalities aren't terribly the same. Does Peter Hannan, the creator of *CatDog* thereby believe in nature over nurture, given that my guess is Cat and Dog have had strikingly similar life experiences? Also, why does Rancid Rabbit have so many jobs?

CatDog effectively takes the *Odd Couple* dynamic to its logical conclusion. What if the odd couple literally could not get away from each other? What if Tom and Jerry, or Ren and Stimpy or whatever cat and dog duo you imagine, were both two separate entities but also in some ways a singular being? Despite the otherworldly nature of Cat and Dog, the show does give them the stereotypical personalities you would imagine. Cat is smart and fastidious. He's the serious one. He has a "cat's personality." Dog, naturally, is dumb and lovable and goofy. He gets easily distracted by balls and garbage trucks. He is a quintessential, stereotypical dog for all intents and purposes. Look, the idea of a conjoined cat and dog was already probably a lot for kids to wrap their heads around. Why push things any further?

The show contains an impressive collection of voiceover performers, including a reunion of two of the cast members of *Rocko's Modern Life*. Carlos Alazraqui, the voice of Rocko himself, plays a couple characters. Dog, meanwhile, is voiced by Tom Kenny, which is obvious the second you hear him speak. Kenny played Heffer on *Rocko*, but you probably know him better as Persky from *Just Shoot Me*. Or maybe the voice of SpongeBob SquarePants. Billy West, the voice of Stimpy and about a million cartoon characters, pops up in a few roles. Maria Bamford has a couple roles, which makes sense for a woman who does so many voices in her standup. Then, there is the voice of Cat, Jim Cummings. He's not as much of a Nick regular, but the dude has done so many voices over the years. You've heard him as Tigger and Winnie the Pooh. You've heard him as the Tasmanian Devil. The man has been everywhere. Or, mostly, he's been in a booth somewhere doing voices and then a bunch of animation happens, some of it likely in Korea.

Among the characters outside of CatDog that stand out the most, the two I primarily think of are Winslow Thelonious Oddfellow and Rancid Rabbit. Winslow is ostensibly a mouse, though he does not look the least bit like a mouse to me, who lives in a hole in the wall of CatDog's house. He has a wisecracker's accent and a wisecracker's personality and it seems like he's mostly there to comment on what Cat and Dog are doing for the audience. Rancid Rabbit is basically every authority figure on the show. Sometimes he's multiple authority figures in a single episode. This feels like a clear conscious choice, and for that I admire the absurdity. There are also three Greaser Dogs who are bullies, Cliff Feltbottom, Shriek DuBois, and Ignatius "Lube" Catfield-McDog. Other characters have names like Lola Caricola, Mervis Pantry, Dunglap Daniels, and Mr. Cornelius Sunshine. There's a character named Randolph Grant who is a hip, famous cat who is a riff on Cary Grant. You know, for kids. And if that wasn't enough of a current reference, there's another famous person in the show who is an actress named Tallulah Headbank, which is a reference on Tallulah Bankhead, an actress who was getting up there in years when she played Black Widow on the '60s version of *Batman*.

For a show whose two main characters are named Cat and Dog, *Cat-Dog* seemed to love coming up with unusual names for characters, and I'm all for it. I really dig a lot of those names. I'm also all for characters that are parodies of Cary Grant on children's shows in the '90s. All of that is my speed. The rest of *CatDog*? I can't say it wows me. Neither Cat nor Dog is terribly funny to me. The show's animation looks a little shoddy, especially background characters and settings. Storytelling is not terribly clever either. Also, let's face it: the premise is a little unusual. There is something disconcerting about seeing a being with two heads on separate sides of its body. Now, I'm not terribly disturbed by it, because the show is very cartoony. Cat and Dog don't seem distressed by their lot in life. Their conjoined status is not a constant burden to them. And yet, it's not exactly a bowl of whimsy.

CatDog debuted on April 4, 1998, a sneak preview right after the Kids' Choice Awards that year. If you were wondering, Alicia Silverstone won for Favorite Movie Actress for *Batman & Robin*, beating out such tough competition as … Uma Thurman in *Batman & Robin*. Kids of 1998, you had terrible taste. By that point, I was already phasing out of watching Nickelodeon, so I wasn't a *CatDog* watcher at the time. I was familiar with it, as at least one of my siblings watched it. The theme song definitely has been in my brain for 20 years at this point. The show just didn't have any hook to me, and I imagine the fact it was about some cat and dog hybrid surely played a part in that. In fact, it wasn't until I started working on this book that I knew they were considered conjoined twins and not simply one being with two heads. Knowing that, it feels weird to me they call the show *CatDog*. Don't treat them as if they are one. They are separate beings with separate lives! And possibly separate livers! I don't know a ton about their anatomy!

By the time *CatDog* ended its run I was far too old to consider watching it. Although, that end to its run is an unusual one. The first three seasons of *CatDog* were totally normal from a schedule perspective. Each season consisted of 20 episodes and they ran from 1998 through 2001. Then, the fourth season was made up of eight episodes, and those episodes aired from 2001 through 2005. After the third season ended in May of 2001 a made-for-TV movie that makes up three of those eight fourth-season episodes aired in November of the same year. It was called "CatDog and the Great Parent Mystery" and featured Cat and Dog on a search for their parents. It seemed like a fitting ending for the show, but then five more random episodes popped up over the next four years. They probably should have just left well enough alone.

After so many shows about mismatched pairs, it feels right that when '90s Nickelodeon became 2000s Nickelodeon a show like *CatDog* was bridging that gap. It's a strange show, but maybe not as strange as you would imagine all things considered. In the end, it's about another odd couple. They just happen to be fused together in one body. All I know is that I hope Cronenberg never decides to make a movie out of *CatDog*. I don't know what kind of things he might get up to with that initial premise. It might involve Rancid Rabbit putting guns up to both Cat and Dog's respective heads. Or maybe Tallulah Headbank turns out to be really turned on by car accidents. For a show with a premise both simple and visceral, there isn't a ton to say about *CatDog*. There's nothing really special to it. Save for that voice cast, of course.

Clarissa Explains It All

*Apparently it's totally cool for your friend
to enter your home through the window*

What makes somebody cool? *Happy Days* would have you believe it's wearing a leather jacket, hitting jukeboxes and keeping an office in a public restroom at a local diner. Perhaps it's more ephemeral than that. When you're young, you feel like cool is objective and measurable. Then you grow up and realize that it's entirely subjective and what's "cool" is really just what you're into. You stop defining what's "cool" by what's popular with your peers, or at least I hope you do. You're an adult now. However, if I can put myself back in that child's idea of coolness being empirical, I do believe I can say something that is accurate: Clarissa Darling was super cool.

I already heaped praise on *The Adventures of Pete & Pete* in this book, but in terms of live-action Nick shows of my childhood, *Clarissa Explains It All* was right behind it. They were the twin pillars of the '90s, both featuring characters I loved and a fresh style of comedy that grabbed my child's brain. As an adult, maybe *Clarissa Explains It All* doesn't pack the same punch, but it still certainly stands out for a multitude of reasons. That tracks, of course. If Clarissa did anything, it's stand out.

While the brothers Pete had each other to rely on to carry their show, Clarissa Darling wasn't so lucky. Well, Clarissa seems to enjoy the spotlight, so she probably didn't mind. Hell, she spent a ton of time talking to the audience directly. She was literally the star of her own show, but in her world, she also carried herself like the star of her show. Clarissa did her own thing all the time, which is something that appeals to a lot of kids, and even to some adults I would imagine. There's a freedom to her teenaged life that we probably all dream of from time to time. I don't want to own a baby alligator I keep in my bedroom, though.

Clarissa Explains It All was created by Mitchell Kreigman and hit Nickelodeon in 1991. It was the second-ever live-action original from Nick, and it debuted the same year as the first three Nicktoons. Indeed, 1991 was a huge year for Nickelodeon. Clarissa was notable for being the first female lead for a Nick show, although to be fair by that point they had basically only been creating ensemble shows and *Doug*. Still, it's worth noting that nevertheless in the grand scheme of things. Not that *Clarissa Explains It All*

Clarissa Darling (Melissa Joan Hart) in her impeccably decorated bedroom. Perhaps she is reading something that she will eventually explain (Nickelodeon).

was marketed specifically to girls, nor should it have been. There's something for everybody in *Clarissa Explains It All*, especially if you were the type of tween who was going to grow up to be the kind of kid with They Might Be Giants posters and an unrelenting creative streak.

When the show began, Clarissa was a 14-year-old ninth grader at Thomas Tupper Junior High School, which I appreciate because I too went to a seventh-through-nine grade junior high instead of going to a ninth-through-12th high school. I did see a contemporary *Los Angeles Times* story that called her 13, but the *Orlando Sentinel's* piece from the same time called her 14, and the paper of record in the city that Nick's studio was based in feels more trustworthy to me. She is our point-of-view character, our friend, our confidant. We go through her life with her as she experiences the normal teenager stuff, plus some not-so-normal stuff. Clarissa is basically supposed to be our friend, but one whose life is worth watching. As opposed to our actual friends' lives. Plus, for a typical Nick watcher, she was a little older. She was aspirational. We could imagine being like her someday, if only we could get our hands on a baby alligator.

To try and describe Clarissa, you could say she's Ferris Bueller without the dead-eyed sociopathy, Parker Lewis without the smarmy declaration that he "can't lose." She's cool, yes, to the extent that means anything.

Maybe in that I just mean she's confident, especially for a teenager. Clarissa is smart without being a know it all. She's funny with intent. Her interests are idiosyncratic without feeling like affected quirk on the part of the writers. She marches to the beat of her own drum, which is most easily understood in her clothes. I know many a child of the '90s, irrespective of gender, who consider her a style icon. Her clothes are colorful but they don't always match in the traditional sense. They still work, though. Clarissa can pull her outfits off in a way, like, that one dude on *The Big Bang Theory* can't with his deliberately clashing outfits. OK, I know his name is Howard and he's played by Simon Helberg. I know stuff about pop culture. I'm writing a book on Nickelodeon. It is what it is.

And yet, Clarissa isn't too perfect, what some may classify as a "Mary Sue" character. Clarissa makes mistakes. She doesn't always win. This isn't *Entourage*. Sure, she's not some anti-hero with intense flaws, but this is a show for children. It's supposed to be fun, light, and maybe teach you a lesson or two about being yourself or understanding your parents better. For that, Clarissa Darling is the perfect character. I might even say, in a voice barely audible for fear of admitting it to even myself, she's a better character than either of the Petes on my beloved *Pete & Pete*.

Clarissa has many sources of conflict, but the primary issue in her life is her younger brother Ferguson. Ferguson is basically what would have happened if *Family Ties* hadn't wanted to be sympathetic to Alex P. Keaton. The issues with Fergface go way beyond typical annoying little brother stuff. He's a Young Republican who worships at the loathsome feet of Ronald Reagan. All Ferguson wants to do is get rich, and he doesn't care how he does it. The kid knows a scheme, and he will do what it takes to get what he wants. He has some skills to his game too. In one episode, Ferguson manages to become a bit of a ladies' man against all odds. He gives his childhood blankie to the first girl he is dating and she finds it incredibly sweet (much to Clarissa's shock). Not happy with having one girl in his life, Ferguson builds a contraption to help him produce exact replicas of his blankie, right down to the drool stains. All in an attempt to garner the interest of as many girls as possible. Fortunately, his plan is found out and he loses them all, but Clarissa feels bad she accidentally played a part in this and takes Ferguson to his big school dance in the guise of a character she created for the occasion. Ferguson gets the loss, but it doesn't cut too deep, and Clarissa manages to both win and lose.

As for their parents, Marshall and Janet Darling are nice enough. Marshall is an architect and a quintessential goober of a TV dad. Sweet, well-meaning, but largely ineffectual. Maybe it's his flower child roots. Maybe it's the fact he always seems to be wearing a long-sleeve plaid short tucked into light blue jeans. I wouldn't believe he was a hippie of a bygone era if it wasn't spoken of in the show. Mrs. Darling has more of that Earth mother vibe left to her. She's an artsy type with an environmentalist streak and an interest in healthy eating. Perfect for a kids' show in the '90s, she likes to make tofu dishes. What a time to be alive when "tofu" could serve as a punchline. I could have used more seitan jokes, personally. The Darlings are ideally attuned for this show. They are nice and friendly and willing to give out advice or support when needed, but they seem genuinely oblivious enough to let their kids get away with some of their schemes behind their backs. Not negligent, but not strict. Exactly what a kid would want.

Finally, let's throw that ladder up against the house to introduce Sam Anders, Clarissa's best friend. While he is a boy, during the run of *Clarissa Explains It All* they very much just seem like friends and nothing more. Sam is upbeat and cheerful, the optimist to Clarissa's sarcastic realism. He lives with his dad, as his mom—who we meet a couple times—left to go become a professional roller derby athlete. I believe this show is what introduced me to the concept of roller derby, but they made it seem more like pro wrestling, which it kind of was in televised form. Shout out to my fellow *RollerJam* watchers. The most-notable thing about Sam is the fact you knew he was arriving when you would see a ladder appear in Clarissa's second-floor window. When the ladder would hit the house, Clarissa would often say "Hey Sam" before he even appeared. Yes, Sam entered his best friend's house via a ladder. The Darlings must have really trusted Sam. Also, I grew up in a safe suburb, and I feel like the Darlings live in one as well, but I can't imagine a family ever saying to themselves, "I see no problem with leaving a ladder on the side of our house beneath our teenage daughter's usually open window." Television is wild.

While Clarissa has other friends, such as Hillary and Olivia, only Sam really matters. Clarissa did some dating during the show's run, most notably dating Ferguson's former bully Clifford Spleenhurfer, a name I will never forget. There's no overarching storylines to *Clarissa Explains It All*, so each episode is pretty much a self-contained story build around some conflict or problem. Oftentimes Clarissa illuminates the issue by creating a video game based on what she's dealing with. Yes, Clarissa was a teenager who could create her own video games in the '90s, a true dream for so many. And yet, she didn't really seem interested in pursuing that as a career. Maybe she feared the crunch associated with the video game industry. Since Clarissa and company were actual human, as opposed to cartoons, that meant she got older as the show went on. That's probably why it moved to SNICK during its second season and stayed there. Eventually Clarissa is old enough to drive, old enough to be thinking about life after high school. She gets interested in journalism, and in the final season her role in the school newspaper becomes a bigger part of the show. It's natural development for the character, and that kind of dynamic storytelling is something I appreciate, especially from Nickelodeon. Too often the network seemed afraid of letting characters grow and change.

Clarissa also wasn't always an entirely sanitized show. One of Clarissa's friends smokes casually in at least one episode. Not in a "this is an anti-smoking episode" way. She smokes, Clarissa thinks it's gross, and that's that. Which reminds me, I didn't mention this in the *Pete & Pete* episode but multiple characters casually smoked on that show. Man, the '90s was forever ago. *Clarissa Explains It All* also wasn't afraid to mention "sex" or say "hell" on occasion either. It was a SNICK show, which perhaps gave it some leeway. I do not consider this a negative or a positive. I just feel like it's noteworthy. While I am using this paragraph to coagulate a series of stray thoughts, there is an episode where Clarissa creates a punk alter ego for herself named Jade, who catches the affection of a young James Van Der Beek. That episode is fun, but it was also written by Suzanne Collins. That would be the same Suzanne Collins who wrote the *Hunger Games* books. To me, Jade is her greatest creation.

Both *Pete & Pete* and *Clarissa Explains It All* are idiosyncratic shows, but in different ways. There's less wistfulness, emotion, and general absurdity in *Clarissa*. It's a bit more traditional, but still plenty good. Melissa Joan Hart became a star beginning with her turn as Clarissa. She's really good in the role and definitely has more screen presence than a lot of kids. I feel like she started to lose that a bit during *Sabrina, the Teenage Witch*, a much hammier, broader sitcom. Maybe she picked up some bad habits there, because her career just kind of hit an impasse. Not that she hasn't continued working. Hart is a key figure from my childhood, so she will always have that significance to me, but she definitely is no longer in the zeitgeist. She's not the only good performer on this show. Jason Zimbler, who played Ferguson, is also a strong performer. He manages to exude smarm quite well. However, Zimbler basically chose to give up on acting after *Clarissa* ended. Joe O'Connor and Elizabeth Hess, who play Marshall and Janet, are fine. You can see why their ceiling as adult actors was a Nick sitcom, but they are good for the roles.

There's a distinct '90s look to *Clarissa Explains It All* in terms of color choices and editing quirks, but that stuff feels fun now and was cool then. The production design on Clarissa's room was awesome to me as a kid and I still dig that level of detail. As a show, I would say *Clarissa Explains It All* is at an acceptable level for '90s sitcoms. It feels, quality wise, equal to a lot of good, but not great, comedies of the time. This one just happened to be for kids and gave them a character to possibly look up to. If not, they could still enjoy watching Clarissa as she navigated her life, best friend and personalized video games in tow. For kids who wanted to see a life a little more advanced than their own, but didn't necessarily want to watch married thirtysomethings, there was Clarissa Darling. Most episodes have one or two things that strike me in their cleverness or freshness. The joke writing can be broad in that sitcom way, but there are few groaners. The positives of *Clarissa Explains It All* are as much about feeling and environment as what people are saying and doing. You're kind of along for the Clarissa ride. It just happens to be a fun ride to be on. And that starts with the opening credits, of course. The *Clarissa Explains It All* theme song is such a perfect earworm. It pretty much just repeats "Na" rhythmically for a bit, but you'd better believe Rachel Sweet's song sticks with you after you hear it, especially when you watch a few episodes in a row.

Clarissa Explains It All aired from March of 1991 through October of 1994. In that time they squeezed in five seasons and 65 episodes, a respectable run. They shot a pilot for a spinoff in 1995 called *Clarissa* where she would have an internship at a New York City newspaper, continuing that trajectory for her, but it did not go forward. In 2015, Kriegman released a novel called *Things I Can't Explain*, which is about Clarissa in her late twenties. Now, if you do the math obviously that timeline doesn't work literally, but she's a fictional character so I can abide. I don't think I need to tell you I bought the novel and read it when it came out. In it, Clarissa is a struggling writer in New York (and kind of a jerk a lot of the time). Janet and Marshall are divorced. Ferguson is in prison for insider trading. Sam has disappeared. There is a flashback in the book to a time when Clarissa and Sam became a romantic item back in college. Yes, dear reader, I am here to inform you that there is a sex scene between Sam and Clarissa. Most sex scenes in books are bad. This one is particularly bad. Somehow, the guy who made his name creating a show for Nickelodeon couldn't write a good sex scene. Would I call *Things I Can't Explain* good? No. Would I call it absolutely vital reading for any *Clarissa Explains It All* fan? With all my heart.

Clarissa definitely stood out among the '90s TV landscape for kids. I enjoyed the show quite a bit as a kid, and I think I thought Clarissa was cool. I mean, she made video games after all. In truth, I probably didn't ponder that stuff much then. They say *Clarissa Explains It All* was notable because it appealed to both boys and girls. That certainly seems true, but it never occurred to me that it wouldn't be for me. Not that I'm trying to claim I was some sort of woke six year old. I definitely had my "this is for boys, this is for girls" ideas, but *Clarissa Explains It All* didn't fall into that. I was probably more concerned about "This show is for older kids" versus "This show is for babies" type stuff. Ultimately, it was a thing that was on TV that I was entertained by, and that was what I wanted as a child. Now, though, I get paid to write about pop culture and to make bold declarations and give strong opinions. I have to have takes on such matters. Clarissa probably shaped concepts of coolness for a lot of people. So did Sam, by proxy. Hopefully some kids learned to hate Republicans by associating them with Ferguson. As an adult, what I like about the character of Clarissa is the specifics that go into her personality. It is, in hindsight, admirably that she is a responsible person but still does her thing. She doesn't wear what is trendy. She's clearly smart, and does something "nerdy" like making video games, but that's never a defining thing about her personality. It's just another cool thing about her. You believe what Clarissa is into is cool as a kid because she seems to believe it's cool. There is no second guessing going on there.

Clarissa Explains It All is, at worst, my third-favorite Nickelodeon show from the '90s. There is a clear level of competency and quality in all its elements. It's an impressive showcase for Hart, but also for the character of Clarissa Darling. She has to carry the show. If you don't like her, you aren't going to buy in. If she isn't interesting, funny, or worth watching, you're turning away. They figured out how to make a character that could appeal to a ton of kids, and even to adults going back to watch the show many years later. I won't even make a joke about how she didn't explain it all. In fact, she explained very little. That doesn't feel like her style anyway. Clarissa was figuring out things for herself. She'd probably have wanted us to do the same for ourselves. That, as they say, is way cool.

Some Words on Nick Jr.

Screen time wasn't always considered evil

This is a book about Nickelodeon's original programming from the '90s. When I say that, I am talking about the hours of the day when the channel was considered "Nickelodeon," not the overarching channel. That's why every Nick show is getting a chapter. I don't want to leave the other aspects of Nickelodeon, and the experience of watching Nickelodeon, off the table though. Because of that, other aspects of Nickelodeon will get chapters. With that said, let's dig into the version of Nickelodeon for kids too young to go to school, Nick Jr.

As you may recall, Nickelodeon effectively began as educational programming for a fledging cable channel owner by Warner. *Pinwheel* basically became Nickelodeon over time. While the channel started to focus on entertainment, got ads, and left educational programming largely— but not entirely—behind, they never stopped thinking about its youngest viewers. The early-hour programming, called preschool programming, was rebranded as Nick Junior in January 1988, and then shortened to Nick Jr. by September of that year. What an important change that was. I'm being sarcastic, which is something that would be hard for a Nick Jr. viewer to understand. Brain development and all that.

The rebrand coincided with the premiere of *The World of David the Gnome*. Or, as it was known originally, *David, el Gnomo*. Yes, *David the Gnome* was originally a Spanish cartoon, and most of the programming in the early days of Nick Jr. was actually dubbed versions of foreign cartoons. Apparently Tom Bosley was the voice of the American version of David, who I will forever remember as the dad on *Happy Days*. If you are wondering, yes, I will be talking about Nick at Nite in a different chapter. I remember *David the Gnome*, but I don't think I necessarily enjoyed it. However, it aired when I was the proper age for Nick Jr., which gets to the heart of Nick Jr. conceptually.

It was for young kids, so all the programming was simplistic. When I was watching it in kindergarten, this wasn't a problem. I watched it and then would watch Nickelodeon after school. It was all entertainment to me. Then, I got older, and for many of us Nick Jr. was one of the first things we ever grew out of. We got too old for it. They were shows for "babies." We scorned Nick Jr.'s programming. Suddenly, we could see the seams. Even

though, compared to the adults in our lives, we were still profoundly ignorant and the TV we liked was largely trash, suddenly *David the Gnome* just
wouldn't cut it. And don't get seven-year-old me started on *Barney*. Oh, the
needless scorn I had for *Barney*!

In hindsight, I'm surprised how little original programming Nick
Jr. created in the '90s. So many of the shows, including *Muppet Babies*,
were imports. *Muppet Babies* was by far my favorite of the Nick Jr. shows.
I watched it every day before kindergarten while my mom took a nap
because she had three kids all five and younger and just needed 10 damn
minutes of peace. I have a distinct memory of accidentally falling asleep
and missing an episode of *Muppet Babies* and being so mad. I kid you not,
I still remember the dream I had during that unplanned nap. Garfield, the
Monday-hating cat, and I were running from Ronald McDonald. At one
point we all slid down a giant banister in a mansion. Apparently I had seen
a banister at some point in my life.

These imports are the Nick Jr. shows I grew, played, and learned on
("Grow, Learn, & Play" was a slogan for the channel in the '90s). By the
time they were really getting into originals I was too old for them. Their
existence frustrated me. If *Allegra's Window* or *Gullah Gullah Island* was on,
it meant something I wanted to watch wasn't on. I only knew so many channels as a kid. I just wanted the shows for me to be on TV. *Blue's Clues* wasn't
for me. It was clearly highly impactful on the younger generation, including
probably my younger siblings. I was too old to be yelling at my television,
though. I knew Steve couldn't hear me. That being said, I'm glad I saw some
Blue's Clues, because it allowed me to be amused when Steve Burns left the
world of TV programming and made an album called *Songs for Dustmites*
and appeared in the Flaming Lips' movie *Christmas on Mars*.

Nick Jr. was valuable in the '90s. It entertained us and occupied us
during the day when our parents needed a de facto babysitter. As I've said
before, I do not begrudge this or consider it an issue. Television did not
rot my brain and I enjoyed watching it immensely. It also gave you the life
experience of growing beyond something you once enjoyed. That happens
over and over as you grow up and mature. One day you are entertained by
Muppet Babies, and then you realize how slow paced it is and the jokes are
too obvious. One day you think *Family Guy* is funny and then you stop
being 13 and just saying inappropriate things stops cutting it as comedy.
While there are Nickelodeon shows from the '90s I still genuinely enjoy,
obviously none of them are from Nick Jr. In fact, I have never heard of any
nostalgia for Nick Jr. from any friends or acquaintances of mine. We truly
left all that behind. Even if the "Binyah Binyah Polliwog" song is forever
stuck in my head.

I do want to add one more thing. The only original Nick Jr. show from when I was of the proper age for Nick Jr. was *Eureeka's Castle*. It was a puppet show that took place in a castle that was also a music box. Eureeka was a sorcerer in training. There was also a dragon named Magellan, twin monsters named Bogge and Quagmire who lived in the castle's moat, and Batly, a bat who wore glasses and had trouble accepting when he was at fault. Case in point, whenever he crashed while flying he would insist that he "meant to do that." Poor Batly. He just couldn't let go of his ego. Also, why did a music box have a moat?

Anyway, there was an episode of *Eureeka's Castle* that was a riff on *The Monkey's Paw*. You know, being careful what you wish for and all that. Batly ended up invisible, but that doesn't matter. Bogge and Quagmire loved peanut butter and jelly sandwiches. They wished for a peanut butter and jelly sandwich. In a cruel twist, they became a peanut butter and jelly sandwich. A puppet of these two monsters in a peanut butter and jelly sandwich trotted out on the screen. I can say without hyperbole this was one of the most disturbing things I saw in my early childhood. It terrified me and the image haunted my brain for years. For all I know I never watched *Eureeka's Castle* again out of the fear I might accidentally see that. The only thing I can compare to for my child's brain was the episode of *Dinosaurs* where the patriarch of the Sinclair family is struck by lightning and is turned into a tree. To be fair, the puppet of that dinosaur-tree hybrid still looks weird as hell.

I did indeed learn something from that episode of *Eureeka's Castle*. I learned what I needed to fear. Eventually, I would grow and stop being afraid of that. Only then, could I play once more without the image of two monsters trapped in a peanut butter and jelly sandwich haunting me. Too bad I didn't take that accidental nap during that episode of television.

Cousin Skeeter

We can't choose our family

I have an ambivalence to puppets. Some people love them. I feel that's the bulk of the appeal of the Muppets. Much as I am a lover of pop culture, I must admit the Muppets have never done a ton for me. Rarely does anything Muppet-related ever rise above the level of "slightly entertaining." On the other hand, I love *Mystery Science Theater 3000*, including the puppets. However, the fun of Tom Servo and Crow T. Robot is not in the fact they are puppets, but in who they are as characters. I enjoy the concept of a man and his two robot friends making jokes about bad movies. Those robots just happen to be, practically speaking, puppets. All that said, when it comes to puppet-centric entertainment, I will take even something like *Muppets in Space* over *Cousin Skeeter*.

Nickelodeon didn't involve a ton of puppets in its '90s run, at least not on Nick proper. In the Nick Jr. chapter I will touch on a couple of puppet shows, and *Weinerville* had puppets as well, but no show really used a puppet like *Cousin Skeeter* did. It's the one *Muppets*-style blending of puppets and reality in storytelling that the channel did in the '90s. *Cousin Skeeter* is a sitcom where one of the main characters, and the titular character, is a puppet. He's also very much a Muppets-style puppet in the way he looks and moves. Indeed, Drew Massey, who has been a puppeteer for the Henson Company (and also for that weird puppet sitcom *Greg the Bunny*), was the primary puppeteer of Skeeter. He was helped by another Henson Company crew member Alice Dinnean, because that style of puppet can get complicated, especially when you are doing as much with it as *Cousin Skeeter* tried. In short, it can't help but feel that this show is indebted to Jim Henson and the Muppets in some small way. I would not say it lives up to that legacy, though.

Bobby Walker is just an ordinary boy living in New York City with his parents Andre and Vanessa. Then, one day, his cousin Skeeter from Georgia comes to live with him. Skeeter is different from Bobby. He's loud and brash and overly confident. Skeeter fashions himself a ladies' man and has an inordinate amount of celebrity friends. Sure, he's a little short, but he's a lot of personality in that package. His skills are litany. His tendency to rhyme for no reason a little tedious. What Skeeter isn't, though, is a puppet. Well, at least that is true in the world of the show. We as an audience see that Skeeter is a puppet. His face is felt. His fingers are smooth. He is unmistakably a puppet. However, within the show he is considered just as much a human as everybody else. Bobby doesn't see his cousin as a puppet. In Bobby's mind, he's living in *Perfect Strangers*, not that awful *Happytime Murders* movie.

This is the way it usually goes in the world of puppets interacting with humans. Kermit isn't a puppet. He's a talking frog, sure, and he plays a mean banjo, but he's not a puppet. This is just a choice for the audience's sake. To be fair, it's a hook. You tell me that your show is about yet-another odd couple and I shrug. You tell me one of them is a puppet and … well I personally shrug, but at least I'm curious. This also allows them to do a lot of physical comedy with Skeeter you couldn't do with a human. Although, if Skeeter is a human in the world of the show people are awfully blasé about some of the stuff that happens to him. I saw Skeeter crushed into a cube in a junkyard. If I saw that happen to a human, and they survived and walked around as a little box-shaped boy, I would be horrified beyond belief.

Beyond the inclusion of a puppet, there is nothing remarkable about *Cousin Skeeter*. The two get into misadventures, usually with Skeeter pulling the more timid Bobby into his schemes. Bobby also has a crush on his friend Nina, who is played by the actress Meagan Good. While her name is familiar to me when I looked at her filmography nothing jumped out at me as noteworthy. Bobby, by the way is played by Robert Ri'chard. Yes, there is an apostrophe in the middle of his last name. He's done some acting as an adult and followed up *Cousin Skeeter* by starring in the UPN sitcom *One on One*. Not a bad career for either of them. Skeeter, meanwhile, was voiced by Bill Bellamy doing a bit of a falsetto thing. Bellamy is an extremely '90s name, and I remember when *Cousin Skeeter* debuted the fact he was voicing Skeeter was part of the pull. In my memory, Skeeter's voice was annoying, and indeed when I revisited the show my first thought was, "Oh man I'm not going to be able to stand this for even a single full episode." However, it stopped bothering me after I adjusted to it.

What never stopped bothering me, though, is the quality of the writing. Oh, and also the fact this is a live-action show with a laugh track. It's really canned laughter, too. The laughter is more canned than shelf-stable peaches. Hearing those intermittent fakes laughs interjected into a show that clearly doesn't have an audience is jarring. And, of course, the fact the jokes that are being "laughed" at are so lousy doesn't help either. This show simply is not funny. I don't think I laughed at anything in *Cousin Skeeter* other than the opening credits. Those I laughed at because of how insane they are. Skeeter is basically dropped into a Puffy Daddy–style '90s music video. If I didn't know better, I would say that Skeeter is all about the Benjamins. Or the Pentiums. I feel like you are supposed to be amused by the opening credits, and I hope they are supposed to be found ridiculous. And yet, I still feel like I was laughing at them in a way that was not intended.

Skeeter says a lot, but none of it is really funny. It's all extremely broad, and there are a lot of sight gags. I don't recall any of them being all that amusing. The other humans are the straight people most of the time, but the occasion jokes they get barely register as jokes. There is some truly clunky dialogue in *Cousin Skeeter*. Literally, in one episode, Bobby said the line "The only think I know less about than lunchboxes is fixing lunchboxes." That's an insane line of dialogue. Is it a joke? Is that a think anybody would say ever? Also, why does Bobby know so little about lunchboxes? What is there to know? I don't go around saying things like "The only thing I know less about than shoelaces is fixing shoelaces." Although from now on I will, and then people will rightfully judge me as deranged.

That line is from an episode where Bobby gets a chain letter that says if he doesn't pass it on to other people he'll have bad luck. However, he's emailed this chain letter then prints it out to read it. It doesn't make sense, but they needed to do that to make the plot work, which is terrible writing. This is the level of freshness and ingenuity they were bringing to the TV landscape, though. They did the same chain letter plot that literally dozens of sitcoms before it had already done, and many had done better. A lot of the plots are pretty basic like that, but at least there was an episode where Skeeter wrestles called "Stone Cold Skeeter." Seeing a puppet in a wrestling ring is kind of funny, at least. Since I'm back on the topic of the puppet, though, while mostly Skeeter doesn't weird me out whenever you just see his legs/feet it is really disconcerting. I watched a scene where Skeeter is crawling under a bed that felt more like something from a David Lynch film than a Nickelodeon show. In Heaven everything is felt.

Cousin Skeeter ran for three seasons and 52 episodes, premiering in September of 1998 and ending in May of 2001. I recall watching it when it aired, and I think it is one of the last new shows I watched on Nickelodeon before I stopped watching it because I felt too old for the channel. The show wasn't good to me then, and time hasn't been kind to it. There are certainly worse shows than *Cousin Skeeter*, but it's just not good at all. Weirdly, this is in spite of the fact that Ri'chard and Good aren't bad child actors. They are both totally adequate. The show also has the hook of having a puppet character. Maybe those facts are what keep *Cousin Skeeter* from being too bad. I do have to admit that the puppet held interest to me that a human wouldn't. Of course, that could have just been curiosity. Perhaps after a few more episodes I would have grown accustomed to Skeeter being around and then it would have just been a dull, unfunny sitcom with a distracting and unearned laugh track.

You know what I wish? They had fleshed out the song used in the opening credits, a parody of the song "Steelo" by 702, into a full song and made a full-on music video for it starring Skeeter and that would have been that. There really wasn't much more to do with the character. Oh, and I also wish for world peace and all disease to be eradicated, since I'm wishing for impossible things. A puppet does not a successful TV make. Even when that puppet is friends with Dennis Rodman.

Don't Just Sit There

If you watch TV all day, you might have to watch Yahoo Serious

In the early days of cable, it seemed like a lot of the time networks were doing a little something called "killing time." Suddenly, networks had hours to fill in their schedule every day, but they had not generated much in the way of original programming yet. You could buy up reruns of shows from other networks, but it pays to have your own content. Also, if it can be cheap even better. A fledging network doesn't have the street cred or budget to go all in, at least they didn't in the '80s and early '90s. This led to many a cable network creating content that could really fill time on a relatively-low budget. These days, could you imagine a show like *Mystery Science Theater 3000* debuting on TV? For Comedy Central, then The Comedy Channel, it was a great idea to fill three hours a day with a show like that. It was easy to produce and had a cult following. There's a reason they used to air marathons on Thanksgiving. Joel Hodgson, the creator of *MST3K*, also created another of the first ever Comedy Channel shows, *The Higgins Boys and Gruber*. That show was just Steve and David Anthony Higgins along with Dave "Gruber" Allen sitting around a fake kitchen set talking and then throwing to clips The Comedy Channel owned the rights to. Think of the early days of MTV, when it was pretty much just VJs throwing to videos or just sitting on cheap sets talking. Nickelodeon wasn't all that different in its early days.

In the '80s, Nickelodeon was basically just games shows and programs like *Kids' Court*. They didn't really get intro scripted narrative programming until *Hey Dude*, which debuted in 1989. One year earlier than that, though, Nickelodeon figured they would go into a well that many a network has gone to in order to try and make some original content on the cheap. Namely, they created a talk show—mixed with a sketch show—they called *Don't Just Sit There*. It's the most '80s MTV thing that Nick has ever done. The only difference is that the show's equivalent of VJs were all kids. Yes, this was a talk show for kids hosted by kids with kids interviewing celebrities, including many an adult.

Really, I can't break down the premise of *Don't Just Sit There* anymore than that. Each episode would feature a few hosts on the set which was very much designed to look "wacky" but had a design that changed seemingly fairly frequently. I watched a few different episodes for this book and I swear the set was tweaked every time. The show took the Uncle Moe's Family Feedbag approach to decorating, and seemed to be trying to be as kooky as possible. I think I saw a zebra-print couch with a cow-print blanket draped over it. The walls were decked out with "fun" art here and there. Now, that doesn't stop the set from looking incredibly cheap, but when the set is so busy and stuffed with mise en scene they had the ability to hope you wouldn't notice. Also maybe they hoped you didn't notice how low-grade the entire look of the show was. I wouldn't be surprised if they taped episodes direct to a VHS that had already been used to record episodes of *Days of Our Lives* by somebody's mom.

The show would mix bad, unfunny sketches with awkward, but better than I expected, interviews. Again, these were kids doing the sketches and doing the interviewing. More to the point, these were kids on a show that was airing on a relatively-new cable network that began its run in 1988. These weren't modern, polished child performers. Even by the time *All That* rolled around things had changed. Episodes would also feature segments designed to give kids ideas of things they could do in their life. There would be food segments and scientific experiments and all matter of content designed to, well, get kids not to just sit there. While Nickelodeon needed people watching in order to generate ratings and revenue, it would have been gauche for a network aimed at kids to try and get them to sit in front of the TV all day. It was a bone thrown to those who might cast a jaundiced eye on Nickelodeon. Although, a lot of what they seemed to want you to do is get up, get out of the house, and go see a movie. As with any talk show, there was a lot of movie promotion on *Don't Just Sit There*.

Each episode featured a few different hosts shouldering the load. Matt Brown was a bit older than the others it seemed. The only one to have success outside the show is Will Friedle, who I watched interview "Weird Al" Yankovic around the release of *UHF* with maybe the worst turn-of-the-decade mullet I've seen. He played Eric Matthews, Cory's older brother, on *Boy Meets World*. Friedle has done a ton of voiceover work since then and his Wikipedia photo lets me know that, at least of 2019, he did not have a bad mullet anymore. One of the other hosts was B.J. Schaffer, who would very much like you to know he goes by Bernard now and that he is a police detective. I know this because I am assuming he wrote his own Wikipedia page. Schaffer now considers himself an author and released a short story collection called *Women and Other Monsters* in 2011. Cool guy. Other hosts including Wendy Douglas and Alie Smith. There was also a house band called Out of Order.

I can't pretend there is anything good about *Don't Just Sit There* other than it being a weird look into the past and a chance to see some interviews with folks you would never think about now. For example, I watched an episode where Matt enthusiastically interviewed Yahoo Serious prior to the release of his movie *Young Einstein*. Robert Englund showed up in another episode wearing a Freddy Krueger glove, but no makeup, and did bits about Freddy going to a dinner party. It's as bad as you would imagine.

Don't Just Sit There ran from 1988 until 1991, but its history is not as well chronicled as other Nickelodeon shows. That's partially because it was early in the network's history but also because it didn't lend itself to reruns. You can't promote *Young Einstein* twice, you know? This was clearly a show only a new network would put out. The sketches are essentially uniformly terrible. All of the kids are in over their heads both as performers and inter-viewers. A lot of talk show interviews are bad as is, especially if they are being done by Jimmy Fallon or James Corden. Imagine a kid trying to do that. It's extremely awkward to see a kid try and pull off a junket interview, even with somebody as game as Weird Al. Frankly, I don't know why some people in showbiz seem to operate under the assumption that kids would rather watch other kids on TV. I was happy to watch David Letterman's talk show as a kid, because I thought he was funny and he knew how to do inter-views. I would have rather seen adults doing something well than see kids doing something poorly. As an adult, that goes triple.

I did not watch *Don't Just Sit There* as a kid. I was way too young for it. It was gone before I ever had a chance. I did not know about it until researching this book, and it was trickier than any other show to find reli-able details about. Nick tried to recreate the MTV vibe for their audience who was not quite yet old enough for MTV themselves. I understand the impulse. I lament the execution.

Double Dare

Life is messy

What is the show that first defined Nickelodeon? You have a concept in your head of what Nickelodeon is. When you picture the network in your childhood, you have a specific image, right? Many things defined Nick in the '90s, and some shows stand out. Ultimately, though, to me *Double Dare* is the defining show of the early days of Nickelodeon. Without *Double Dare*, the channel that we knew in the '90s may never have come to fruition. Marc Summers may have never been born! Or something.

Double Dare precedes the '90s by several years, which is partially why it became such a defining show. The network was starting to get its legs under it in the middle of the '80s. It was developed the voice and image that we would come to know. The brightly-colored one that was fun for kids and involved a lot of mess and irreverence. Oh, and Gak, of course. The network decided they wanted to create a game show for children. They hadn't done that before. This book is full of game shows, but before any of them could come to fruition, *Double Dare* had to be born.

The initial idea for the game was a combination of trivia, truth or dare (the game, not the Madonna movie), and the board game Mouse Trap. Weirdly, jumping into a giant ice cream sundae wasn't part of that pitch. The show needed a place to film episodes, and they settled on the studio that belonged to the PBS affiliate in Philadelphia. Pittsburgh gave us Mr. Rogers, Philadelphia gave us a messy obstacle course. Sure, Philadelphians beat up a robot and booed Santa Claus, but they win this battle. Mr. Rogers has always been a snooze. That's a hot take, I know, but I stand by it. Few people on TV have ever been more boring than ol' Fred Rogers. Being a nice person doesn't make you good at being on television. Rogers would have made a bad host for *Double Dare*, but who would get that role?

Originally, there were two men in the running. One was Soupy Sales, who had been hosting shows for kids since the '50s. Of course, by 1986 that made him a little old for hosting a show like *Double Dare*. The other name? An upcoming young comedian named Dana Carvey. The producers at Nick were wise to recognize his talent, but of course they weren't the only ones. Before he could be given the gig Carvey got his audition for *Saturday Night Live*, and the rest is history. Frustrated they had lost out on Carvey, they auditioned over 1,000 people for the role. They winnowed that down to two potential hosts, and in the end the winner is somebody you know well: Marc Summers. I don't know the other potential how. Let's just say it was Michael Dukakis.

Summers is one of the definitive faces of '90s Nickelodeon. Hosting *Double Dare* is a big part of that, but he also ended up hosting *What Would You Do?*, which I get to later in the book. Summers was an extremely genial host. I wouldn't say he's terribly funny, but Summers had a warm, pleasant professionalism to him. He always seemed game, which was vital on a show like *Double Dare*. Summers could be the adult in the room, but he didn't come across like a stern taskmaster. He was your cool substitute teacher, but he was there every week. Eventually, Summers would make some waves when it as revealed he had obsessive compulsive disorder. This seemed like such a striking twist for a man who hosted a show like *Double Dare*. Hosting a show like *Unwrapped*? That seems more up his alley. However, it speaks to Summers' intense professionalism that nobody could imagine him having OCD while watching him hosting *Double Dare*. Summers would be joined by some other folks on the show. John Harvey, a Philadelphia radio DJ, would become the announcer, known as Harvey to kids of the '80s and '90s. I was a big Harvey fan. The stage assistants became sort of characters as well, specifically Robin Marrella.

The premise of *Double Dare* is as follows. Two teams of two kids are competing against each other. Early on, they both wore red, which seems like a mistake. Eventually, it became red and blue, the colors '90s kids are familiar with. I would have had them wearing bright yellow and bright orange, personally, for showing off messes better. The mess is integral to *Double Dare*. The show would begin with an opening physical challenge. In my memory, every episode would begin with the teams already in place and Summers would say, "On your mark, get set, go!" and then the challenge would begin, with Harvey filling us in. The team that won the first physical challenge would get control of the board.

Then, we get to the trivia. The team with control of the game would get the question, which was initially worth 10 bucks. They could answer it, or they could dare the other team to answer it for double the money, in this case $20. If that team got it right they got the money and control of the game. However, if they got it wrong the team that dared them got the money and kept control of the game. Ah, but the team that was dared could also drop a double dare on their opponents. Now, the question was worth 40 bucks! If that team didn't want to answer, they could take a physical challenge. If they won that, they got the money and control. Otherwise, both money and control went to the other team.

The trivia questions, asked by Summers, weren't too hard for me as a kid. A lot of them are easy, but on occasion they would hit you with a stumper. Maybe that was to try and drive kids toward taking a physical challenge. After all, as much as I enjoy trivia, a lot of kids were surely in it for the physical challenges. That was kinetic, and also crazy and messy. It's definitely more visual than question asking. Physical challenges involved having to perform a certain take in a certain amount of time. A lot of it involved filling a container to a line. Often that container would be on one of the kids' heads. Usually foodstuffs or various liquids would be tossed or shot at the container. Other times it would be about accomplishing a task a certain number of times. Memorably, one of the kids would be wearing big clown pants and their teammate would have to catapult pies into those pants. Even if you did a physical challenge right, you were probably going to get messy. Like Maria Kondo, *Double Dare*'s audience loved mess. It's chaotic and rare. Messes are scorned in day-to-day life, but on *Double Dare* you could make as much of a mess as you wanted. It was crazy to a kid, and it seemed like a lot of fun.

After all this we got to the real meat of the show. The team with the most money would go onto the obstacle course. The obstacle course consisted of eight different obstacles which would change from episode to episode. The order could change as well. You never knew what you were going to get. As a kid, I would look away from the TV and also mute it when the obstacles were being announced. Then, out of the corner of my eye I would try and gauge when the introduction was over. I wanted the surprise of finding out what was being included in the obstacle course as it was unfolding. Surely I was not the only one that did this. Of course, if the team didn't get through the entire obstacle course I would never find out the obstacles I didn't see, but that was fine with me. I knew them all by this point anyway.

You would complete each obstacle by finishing the task of it and getting an orange flag. As opposed to adult life, where all you get is red flags like an unwillingness to communicate through problems. Anyway, you would then hand that flag to your teammate who would complete the next task. For each obstacle there was a prize you could win, and the prizes would get increasingly nice. The final prize was basically always a trip, usually to a tropical resort with a deal with Nick or Space Camp. It is through *Double Dare* that I first heard of Space Camp. I never went there, but the librarian at my elementary school went there with his kid, so I got to see some first-hand footage of it once upon a time.

Some of these tasks would involve physical labor. The one I remember most of all is an oversized hamster wheel you would run in. You had to run in it until all six lights lit up, and then a boxing glove with the flag on it would drop down so it could be grabbed. "Big Bowl" featured you pushing a giant bowling ball to knock over giant pins, one of which had the flag under it. I remember obstacles that involved wading through a ball pit as well. Some of the physical labor challenges were also of the sloppy variety. The mess would be used to make the task trickier, though. "In One Ear" involved you crawling in one ear and out the other, but you had to crawl through a bunch of "earwax" to do so. "Sundae Slide" may have involved going down a messy slide and ending up in a giant sundae, but first you had to crawl up a slide covered in chocolate pudding. That's not easy. Vanilla pudding? A cakewalk, sure. But chocolate? Forget about it.

Then, there were the "find the flag" obstacles. On these occasions, you would have to find a hidden flag, and usually it was a messy situation. There was an awful lot of digging through big piles of food or slime. In "Soda Jerk" you stepped on pedals that made soda, and possibly the flag, fall down to you. Perhaps the indelible image of *Double Dare* is "Pick It," which was a giant nose (with big glasses). The nose was full of "snot," which was just Gak, and you had to lie down and dig through the nose until you found the flag. Is this gross? Sure, but also if you wanted to describe '90s Nickelodeon in one image it would probably be a kid in a messy-ass *Double Dare* getup with their arms shoved up that giant nose.

Watching the obstacle course was just so much fun as a kid. It was what the whole show was building to in many ways, which is not to say it couldn't hold my attention until then. I had my favorite obstacles, as we all do, and I was always glued to the screen to find out how the teams would do. Although, in truth, I was often watching a later version of *Double Dare* I will get to momentarily. The obstacle course remained the same, though, and it remained one of the pinnacles of game show achievement to me as a child. I wanted to run the *Double Dare* obstacle course so bad. It was entertaining to watch and made *Double Dare* stand out among children's programming. The show got so many strong reviews when it started to air, and I imagine the obstacle course was a big reason why. The thing was a stroke of genius, consisting of several smaller strokes of genius each and every week.

Because game shows are relatively easy to produce, the show got a 65-episode order for its first season, and they cranked those episodes out in only 23 days. I'd love to be a game show host. The show debuted on October 6, 1986, and aired weekdays at 5:30 p.m. It was immediately a huge hit. *Double Dare* literally tripled Nickelodeon's afternoon viewers and it became the top-rated original, daily show on cable. Sure, that was easier to do in 1986, but it is still incredibly impressive. It's not hyperbole to say that many of Nickelodeon's early viewers were drawn there by *Double Dare*. The show was the first breakout hit for the network. Summers became the face of Nick. *Double Dare* became its flagship program. It was a massive, messy success.

Bolstered by the network's first real taste of ratings glory, *Double Dare* was given a souped-up weekend version called *Super Sloppy Double Dare*. It was the same show but with more mess. Pity that cleanup crew, but when you sign up for a show like *Super Sloppy Double Dare*, you know what you're getting into. It is while making the *Super Sloppy* version of the show, which eventually became the sole version of *Double Dare*, that production moved from Philly down to Orlando and the newly-minted Nickelodeon Studios. In fact, it is an episode of *Super Sloppy Double Dare* that christened production down in Orlando. There was also a brief, 13-episode run of a show called *Family Double Dare* that aired on the fledgling FOX network in 1988. It didn't work there, but it would be brought over to Nick and became the new de facto version of the show.

Family Double Dare is the version of the show that I truly grew up on, since it debuted in 1990. The difference was that, instead of teams of two kids, teams consisted of two adults and two children. It became a family affair, which also meant having to change the nature of the trivia questions. Not that every adult on *Super Sloppy Double Dare* was a trivia whiz. They weren't all able to crush the obstacle course either. All of this was easier for most adults, obviously, but the show doesn't feel entirely different. It's just busier and more crowded. Hey, as a kid I dug it. In 1993, *Family Double Dare*'s run came to a close. First, though, they had to determine the champs. In the "Tournament of Champions," the two teams with the highest trivia scores from that season faced off, and then the two teams with the fastest obstacle course times that season squared off. Those winners then went head-to-head to be declared the final *Family Double Dare* champs. I know I watched it, but I don't recall who won. I just hope "Pick It" and the "Sundae Slide" were involved, as nature intended.

Not that *Double Dare* would die. After the turn of the millennium, we were given *Double Dare 2000*. The host was a guy named Jason Harris, who's not my real dad. Oops, I mean he's not Marc Summers. That version only lasted one season, maybe because they called the obstacle course the "slopstacle course" and it made everybody too depressed. And yet, *Double Dare* persisted. Yet another reboot happened in 2018. This time Summers came back, but he was joined as host by Liza Koshy, a Vine star and YouTube personality. Summers brought the iconography, while Koshy brought the youth and vigor. They made two seasons worth of episodes, but did not get a third. Evidently kids today aren't as enthused to watch people crawl through earwax and run in hamster wheels. Kids today are total chumps.

Hey, it's their loss. Nickelodeon may not be able to make *Double Dare* work any longer, but it basically built the network in the '80s. I don't think it would have become the network it did, the staple of the '90s it was, without *Double Dare*. In its initial run they made over 480 episodes. That's so many physical challenges, so much Gak, so much giant food. Now that I'm an adult, it doesn't appeal to me in the same way. I just don't find mess as much fun. It doesn't entertain me in and of itself. There has to be something clever to it or something absurd about it. You have to engage me more than just "Look at the mess we're making!" I'm a grown man. I could throw a whole pot of baked beans on my floor if I wanted to. It's just not that thrilling or exciting. Still, I imagine a lot of those obstacles would be fun, even now. When I watch reruns I no longer try and keep myself from seeing what obstacles are being included in the course, though. However, I do mute my TV and avert my eyes during the opening moments of *Chopped* to avoid spoilers.

Of course, I have nothing but honor to heap upon *Double Dare*. It helped define Nickelodeon. Without it, this book might not exist. Without it, my childhood may have been entirely different. Nick took a chance on creating a game show for kids. What it got was its first iconic game show. Oh, and its first iconic personality. Marc Summers will always be a TV legend in my eyes. He will always be synonymous with calm in the face of chaos and smiling through the insanity. I dare you to name a game show host from the '90s who has had a bigger impact on your life. And if you aren't up for the dare, you'd better be ready to fill a bucket with slime until it's over the line.

Doug

*Think big. Also, don't have kids if you
want to buy very expensive things*

The everyman is a common figure in culture. Not just on television or in movies, but even in literature. Before that dude filmed that horse to see if all four of its hooves were off the ground at once, there were everymen in stories. And, of course, everywomen and these days probably some everynonbinarypeople. Since those words don't seem to exist I figure I am allowed to make them compound words. It's what we call a neologism. Many characters are remarkable. Take, for example, Tony Stark. He's rich. He's brash. He lives a wild and crazy life. Also, he's Iron Man. When he puts on a suit he's a superhero. Tony Stark is special. He's uncommon. There may be certain elements of his personality that are relatable to many, but he's not living a life most of us can understand. In the world of Nickelodeon, there have certainly been unusual or uncommon characters. None of us are the strongest man in the world. None of us are talking beavers. Then, there is the biggest everyman in Nick history, which arguably makes him less of an everyman. I suppose he's really more of an everyboy, though. His name is Doug Funnie, and he was the main character of *Doug*.

Doug is the answer to a notable trivia question. It was the first Nicktoon to air. Nickelodeon debuted its first three original cartoons on August 11, 1991. *Rugrats* and *Ren & Stimpy* both aired that day. However, it's *Doug* that hit the airwaves first. By a matter of minutes, it opened the door. Those shows are a little more out there. *Rugrats* is about babies going on adventures in a world they don't understand and they can talk to each other. *Ren & Stimpy* is pure insanity and grotesquery. *Doug* is just about an 11-year-old kid with some friends and a crush on a girl whose last name is a condiment. That's not to say *Doug* is banal, of course. There's plenty of imagination running though it, especially in the character design.

Doug, the character, was created by Jim Jinkins many years before the show. He was an animator who liked to doodle, and creator Doug to be something of an alter ego. In fact, Doug's name was even chosen for its unremarkable nature. A friend convinced Jinkins to make a children's book built around Doug, called *Doug Got a New Pair of Shoes*. However, the book didn't sell. Instead, Doug made his debut in a 1988 ad for the Florida

Grapefruit Growers, and then he was also in an ad for the USA Network. After that, Jinkins got a chance to pitch his book as a show for Nick, in part because he had worked for the network back in the *Pinwheel* days. They liked the idea, and *Doug* got picked as one of the original Nicktoons. The first Nicktoon, as I noted.

Evidently Jinkins had created a massive and detailed pitch bible for the show, and it's clear. The world of *Doug* is rich. You know how people love *The Simpsons* in part because of the fact Springfield feels so complex and lived in? Over the years, we met so many denizens of Springfield and visited so many locations. There are restaurants, schools, and so many places that get revisited. From the get go, Bluffington, the city that *Doug* is set in, feels planned out. Jinkins deserves credit for the effort put into making the show a true world. I feel like I know Bluffington, and that goes a long way.

The show focuses on Doug Funnie, who like I have said is an everyman character. There is nothing terribly distinct about him, but he's not unlikeable. He even dresses kind of dull. His personality is reasonable, at least for a kid. If anything stands out, it's his imagination. Doug likes to draw, and he also writes in a diary seemingly every day. Or, rather, a journal. Doug Funnie has a lot in common with Walter Mitty, another everyman prone to flights of fancy. For example, Doug has a couple of alter egos. One is the superhero Quailman, and another is Smash Adams, a James Bond–style superspy. He also has a dog named Porkchop, who can skateboard, limbo, and has an igloo for a house. This ordinary boy has a pretty remarkable dog.

Doug's parents seem nice enough, but they were never notable characters. *Doug* really focused on the kids of the show. In fact, I feel like Doug's neighbors Mr. and Mrs. Dink make a bigger impact, and are maybe seen more, than Mr. and Mrs. Funnie. The Dinks, by the way, got their name from the acronym for "dual income, no kids." They are both successful, and thus Mr. Dink is always able to buy things that are "very expensive." They live the dream, save for the fact Mr. Dink seems like kind of a goober. I do not aspire to be like him, even if I desire his financial security. However, to get back to the Funnies, Doug has an older sister named Judy. She's very artsy and theatrical. We know this because she wears a beret and dark sunglasses all the time. Judy is the kind of person who likes to play the bongos and see art films, you know? That makes her quite different from her brother.

Doug's best friend is Skeeter Valentine, who is a happy-go-lucky kid who likes to skateboard and is maybe secretly a genius? He makes honking noises as his calling card. One time I perfectly imitated Skeeter's honk and then vowed to never do it again. Beebe Bluff is the daughter of the richest family in Bluffington. Yes, the city is named after their ancestors. Her money makes her feel a little out of touch with the other kids of the town.

Chalky Studebaker is an athlete. Connie Benge ... also exists? Roger Klotz wears a leather jacket and is a bully. He's even got stooges. However, he's not always the antagonist. Sometimes he has more of a frenemy relationship with Doug and the other kids at Doug's school. The assistant principal of Doug's school is the other antagonist, Lamar Bone. He's no-nonsense and he sounds like Don Knotts. In fact, he even kind of looks like Don Knotts. Mr. Bone also loves yodeling, an easy way of showing that he is out of touch and, presumably lame. Though he's not really a character, I do want to know that the principal of the school's last name is Buttsavich.

Last, but not least in Doug's mind, is Patti Mayonnaise. Doug has a giant crush on Patti. The kind of wholesome, all-consuming crush only a tween could have. Doug has a crush on Patti like you might have had a crush on a member of the Backstreet Boys. However, Doug sees Patti every day at school, where as you never were going to run into any of the Backstreet Boys. I think one of them was named Howie. Let's say Howie. Doug is head over heels for Patti, who seems nice enough but doesn't have much in the way of distinguishing characteristics. Her role seems to be "Doug's crush." Alas, Doug lacks the courage to say anything to Patti. In fact, he fears her ever finding out that he has a crush on her. Were he a little older, or a little less guileless and naïve, Doug's infatuation with Patti would seem creepy. Instead, it flies. Doug is harmless. It's not the kind of thing where as an adult I think to myself, "Man, this is actually kind of weird."

Needless to say, Jinkins came up with some incredibly distinct names for his characters. I didn't even get into Al and Moo Sleech or Skunky Beaumont. I bet Jinkins had a lot of fun coming up with these names. I don't blame him. Michael Schur, creator of shows such as *Parks and Recreation* and *The Good Place*, loves coming up with ridiculous names, even for characters whose names never get uttered. What would you expect from a man whose online alter ego is Ken Tremendous? The names aren't the only thing distinct about the denizens of Bluffington. They also look very distinct. Not just in terms of their hair and faces and attire. A lot of different colors were using in the design of the characters of *Doug*. Not your typical skin tones, either. Yes, Doug looks like a pretty traditional white guy, but Skeeter is blue. Patti looks like she has spent way too much time in a tanning booth. Chalky is green. Roger is yellow. Mr. Dink is purple. Bluffington is a true rainbow coalition. Those color choices were there from the days of the unpublished book. Jinkins "credits" the decision to some margaritas he had enjoyed. That's a fun story if true. Regardless, the color palate of *Doug* certainly helped it stand out.

When the show begins, Doug is new to Bluffington, having moved from a city called Bloatsburg. The first episode, which is one of the rare episodes that only tells one story, is called "Doug Bags a Neematoad."

Technically, it aired second, which is weird. In this episode he literally arrives to town, meets Skeeter, and is given a layout of Bluffington. It's all there in that episode. Doug meets Patti and immediately falls for her. Roger tricks him to going to a pond to try and catch a fictional creature called a Neematoad. He eats at Honker Burger, the hangout for all the teens. The episode perfectly lays out the show and its ethos.

Jinkins wanted every episode to have a moral, which feels a little heavy handed as an adult. I don't need to be taught the things kids needed to be taught, you know? The amount of times I have been taught to be myself by this point would be enough to cause me to want to disassociate from my own experiences, funnily enough. The plots aren't really that memorable. I just remember the beats from those stories. Doug gets a job in a mascot costume and doesn't want anybody to find out. That's been done a million times, and better than on *Doug*. And yet, I will forever remember the line "And why was he carrying those pants?" Doug and his friends start a band and Doug becomes egocentric about it. Do I remember the songs "Banging

Some of the *Doug* crew gather at the Honker Burger. Judy Funnie sips her beverage and casts a jaundiced eye on the proceedings. Mr. and Mrs. Dink join the kids for some reason. Mr. Dink can afford to eat like that because he doesn't have kids. Across from them, Doug, Porkchop, and Patti Mayonnaise share a milkshake. Roger Klotz looms over them. Meanwhile, Skeeter tosses a fry into the air, hoping to catch it in his mouth (Nickelodeon).

on a Trashcan" and "Think Big?" You bet! *Doug* actually has a lot of memorable songs. It also had a distinct theme song that was truly catchy. There was a lot of mouth music on *Doug*. It sounds weird, but it actually works.

Speaking of music, I can't talk about *Doug* without talking about The Beets, the most-popular rock band in the world of the show. Of course an everyman like Doug Funnie loves the world's version of The Beatles. Songs like "Killer Tofu" are currency these days for children of the '90s. I once wrote a fake oral history of The Beets for a website that ended up over 10,000 words. Honestly, it might be my favorite thing I've ever written. The Beets may be a parody, but they are part of what makes the world of *Doug* feel so alive.

Doug aired for four season and 53 episodes on Nickelodeon, with 104 individual stories being told. They were contracted to have another season of 13 episodes, but Nick declined the option. *Doug* hadn't generated the popularity of *Rugrats* or the cultural cache of *Ren & Stimpy*. It also apparently was too expensive for Nick's tastes. The show ended its run on Nickelodeon in 1994. In 1996, it would return as *Brand Spanking New! Doug* for Disney, often airing on Saturday morning on ABC. It lasted for three seasons and a movie in its new iteration, ending in June of 1999. Personally, I consider these episodes heretical. They don't count. They aren't *Doug*. They are a changeling masquerading as *Doug*. I even heard they showed the previously never seen Skunky Beaumont. The general consensus, even from people who worked on the show, was that the Disney episodes weren't as good. It would have been better if the show had just ended with the Nickelodeon episodes.

Doug matches its protagonist in terms of quality. It isn't remarkable. The show has some fun flights of fancy and a lot of the stories are relatable and down to earth. That's different from what a lot of animation does, especially for kids. Insane stuff happens on, say, *Rocko's Modern Life*. Nothing insane happens on *Doug*. One of the most-memorable episodes involves Doug trying to get up the nerve to eat liver and onions, which he hates, because Patti says she is serving it for dinner at her party. It was like a low-stakes sitcom, but animated and with kids as the protagonists. That's actually pretty cool, especially since with animation you can hire adults to do the voices and get better performances. That's especially true when you hire somebody like Billy West, a true voiceover legend. West voiced both Doug and Mr. Bone, which means he does quite the Don Knotts impression.

That being said, this subtle approach means there aren't a lot of laughs or impressive moments. It's pleasant. You rarely object to an episode of *Doug*, but you rarely love it. There aren't many big laughs. It aims for minor chuckles. The morals fall flat to me as an adult. Though Doug Funnie is an everyman, I never found him particularly lovable or relatable. Maybe kids don't want an everyman. Maybe they want sociopathic dogs and monsters who can pull their own guts out. *Doug* is remarkable for how unremarkable it is. Jinkins just told stories about a boy that was his alter ego he hoped would be nice and teach kids lessons like being honest. It's a solid little show. It's the first Nicktoon. It was just destined to be steamrolled by the flashier Nick shows that would follow. There's a reason Doug dreamed of being Quailman, after all. That's the kind of character people remember.

Fifteen

*You can reach great heights from humble
beginnings. Just ask Ryan Reynolds*

Canadians love teen soap operas. I have two pieces of evidence for this, and that's enough. To be fair, one of those is the eternal teen soap from the Great White North, the *Degrassi* series. Basically since 1980 there has been some version of a *Degrassi* show on TV. Each one is a teenage soap opera, which I presume I don't have to explain to you. Soap operas may have gotten their name from the fact the early ones were sponsored by soap companies, but they have become synonymous with serialized, melodramatic storytelling. Also, with incredibly cheap production values. Soap operas churn out the content. Now, take that concept, give it the budget of a Canadian TV show, and then throw a bunch of child actors into the mix. That's how you end up with the ludicrous teen soaps Canada has given us. That includes *Fifteen*, the subject of this chapter, though it was not nearly as prolific as your typical soap. They weren't cranking out episodes five days a week most weeks out of the year. You couldn't tell that by the production quality, though. However, before I get to *Fifteen*, let me return to *Degrassi*.

The version of *Degrassi* I am most familiar with is *Degrassi Junior High*, which aired from 1987 through 1989 in Canada. The show aired on CBC in Canada, a channel I am familiar with because I grew up in the Detroit area and therefore had access to it. It's the national channel of Canada, the BBC slathered in maple syrup. In the United States it would air on PBS. Lots of melodramatic stuff would happen. These kids couldn't seem to have a normal day. Eventually, basically the same cast would move on to *Degrassi High* from 1989 until 1991. Some notable characters include Joey Jeremiah, Snake, and Spike. Snake and Spike have real names, but I did not know them without looking them up. Joey Jeremiah was always wearing a dumb hat, which is how I remember him. The reason I have seen dozens of episodes of *Degrassi Junior High* is because my teacher would show episodes to us in my eighth grade Life Skills class. What's Life Skills class? Well once a week we would cook something in a kitchen, and we learned to sew and to balance a checkbook. However, once or twice a week we'd just watch TV. Sometimes it was *Degrassi*, other times it was *7th Heaven*. No, I don't think my teacher was religious. I think she was just very lazy and did not care.

Spike would have herself a teenage pregnancy, which begat a daughter named Emma, who led us to *Degrassi: The Next Generation*, which began in 2001 and aired for 14 seasons. If you know it, it's because a young Drake was one of the stars of this version of *Degrassi*. Truly, it is a Canadian rite of passage. Drake memorably was shot in the school shooting episode and ended up in a wheelchair. This ended his character Jimmy's promising basketball career. And yet Drake still shows up on the sidelines of Toronto Raptors games. Between the end of *Degrassi High* and *Degrassi: The Next Generation*, there was admittedly a bit of a gap in the Canadian teen soap world. Into that gap stepped *Fifteen*. Apparently the first intention for this show didn't really involve Canada at all, at least as far as I can tell. Originally creator John T. Binkley brought the idea to Disney where they did a largely improvised 13-episode pilot run. So I guess it was *Curb Your Enthusiasm* by way of *Degrassi*. I have not seen any of this show, it didn't work and they didn't move ahead with it, but I can't imagine asking teenagers to improvise a TV show. I've seen teenagers do improv. I would not build a TV show around it.

Binkley held onto his idea, though, and brought it to Nickelodeon and the Canadian channel YTV. This time the show went through, with production taking place in Canada at first. This meant the cast was filled with Canadian teenage actors, many of which were getting their first significant role. Up there, the show was called *Hillside*, named after the high school where the show was set, for the first two seasons. Down in the United States, it was always *Fifteen*, and it's the only teen soap that Nickelodeon has ever produced. Cast members would come and go, which is common for any soap opera, let alone one with kids. The fact the production location changed probably didn't help either. After one season shooting in Vancouver the show moved to Ottawa for its second season. That's a massive move. Then, the final two seasons were shot down at Nickelodeon Studios in Orlando, and even bigger move. This surprised me, given that I assumed the entire thing was a Canadian production from beginning to end. Then again, this would explain why the last two seasons looked a little better.

You know how a show like this goes. *Fifteen* features a bunch of kids dealing with the ups and down of being a teenager in as melodramatic of a way as possible. Granted, teens are often overwrought, but when you put that into a soap opera it gets even more over the top. They touch on all the typical serious issues. Parents getting divorced, teen drinking, sex, you name it. Everything is broad, right down to the bad boy Dylan who wears a leather jacket. He ends up playing in a band with another bad boy, Chris. Their drummer is a younger kid named Billy, who I will get to more later. The main couple at the center of the show is Ashley and Matt. Ashley is smart and successful and in a bunch of school clubs. She's a "good girl," and also quiet. By which I mean Laura Harris, the actress who played her, speaks so quietly she's barely audible at times. I don't know if it's a character thing or bad acting. Matt is the captain of the basketball team but also develops problems with drugs and alcohol. He's played by Todd Talbot, who went on to co-host *Love it or List It Vancouver*. Harris has also had a somewhat successful career as an adult, including roles in *24* and *Dead Like Me*.

All that said, I have to get back to Billy. He's the younger brother of Courtney, who was Ashley's best friend in the first three seasons. Billy looks up to Dylan and eventually becomes a bully because his parents split up. That is, until Dylan straightens him out. If *Fifteen* has any lasting legacy it's because of Billy, and specifically the actor who played Billy. You see, young Billy was played by Ryan Reynolds. Yes, *the* Ryan Reynolds. Van Wilder. Green Lantern. Deadpool. The guy who hung out with that other guy and that girl at a pizza place. Years before he became a movie star, Reynolds started his career on *Fifteen*. He's barely recognizable, and he's also a bad actor. Then. Now he's a total B-type performer.

To be fair, basically every kid on *Fifteen* is a bad actor. If this show was done in true soap fashion, they probably only got one or two takes, and that isn't going to cut it. The acting is bad. The dialogue is bad. *Degrassi* was never a good show, but it operates at a higher level of quality than *Fifteen*. I found myself laughing at how clumsy it is, and how stilted and awkward everything is. If you ask a kid who can't act to melodramatically emote over an over-the-top plot point, it's a recipe for hilarity. When you throw in a young Ryan Reynolds and it becomes even funnier. The opening credits are amazing too. They are so corny in that wonderful '90s way. When I saw one kid get introduced and then throw a basketball to another kid who was then introduced, I knew I was seeing some '90s glory in action. Additionally, apparently all but five of *Fifteen*'s 65 episodes were written by a guy named Ian Weir. That will give you consistency, but I have to imagine Weir was churning out scripts more concerned about quantity than quality.

Fifteen aired from 1991 through 1993, a time when I was much too young for a teen soap. It didn't last on in reruns on Nick at all, for obvious reasons. One, it wasn't any good, and two, it didn't fit with the direction Nickelodeon went. Sure, they did shows for older kids. That's what SNICK was for. None of them were dramatic teen soap operas, though. I was aware of *Fifteen* thanks to Reynolds' involvement, but if not for that we may not remember it. After all, how can this Canadian teen soap rise out of the shadow of the *Degrassi* monolith? It took a future movie star to make that happen. If you enjoy laughing at bad television, you can probably get some enjoyment from *Fifteen*. If you want to see how far Reynolds has come, you can check it out as well. Soap operas for adults starring adults are usually terrible. Even if *Fifteen* wasn't made at that production speed, it lives up to that reputation with its total lack of quality and slapdash production value. There's a reason my Life Skills teacher never showed us this show. She probably wasn't aware of it. Otherwise, I bet she would have. Anything to avoid having to actually teach.

Figure It Out

*The world can be chaos, but Lori Beth Denberg
is always here to try and maintain some sanity*

In the 1950s, the Supreme Court ruled that game shows weren't gambling, thereby legalizing them. Almost immediately, they became corrupt. *The $64,000* question used to stack questions against contestants they didn't want to win, though famously Joyce Brothers was able to overcome that and win anyway. The show *Dotto* had a match fixing scandal emerge in 1958 as well. Most notably, there was *Twenty-One*. Unsatisfied with how the show was going, producer Dan Enright decided the show should be rigged. A contestant named Herb Stempel, who had been fed answers, was strong armed into taking a dive for Charles Van Doren, a professor who became a fixture on television thanks to his fame from being on the game show. This served as the basis for Robert Redford's 1994 film *Quiz Show*, which is a better movie that *Forrest Gump*, *Shawshank Redemption*, and *Pulp Fiction*. It is not as good as *Ed Wood*, though.

In real life, the Supreme Court amended the Communications Act of 1934 to prohibit the fixing of game shows. The laws and regulations revolving around game shows became quite strict. They still are. At the time, a ton of game shows went off the air, and big money games shows took a while to return. Even now, you can see how serious game shows, even the fun ones, have to take things. When you watch game shows, you may see or hear a disclaimer that parts of the episode not affecting the outcome of the game have been edited. That's because nothing that involves the actual game play can be removed as per the rules governing game shows. There was a human toll on this as well. Van Doren resigned his professorship and lost his TV work. I say all this because *Figure It Out* was technically a game show on Nickelodeon, but how it could ever be considered a valid game show I do not know. While it may not have been fixed in a legal definition of the word, for all intents and purposes it was, all with the desire to give the kid contestants on the show a win. Even as a child I could see this, and it drove me nuts.

Figure It Out was a game show in the vein of *I've Got a Secret* or *What's My Line?*, a brand of game show I'm not a fan of. Each episode featured two games with three rounds per game. Every contestant had a secret talent.

Their talent was hidden on Billy the Answer Head, the name for the game board. The panel could see the prepositions and articles, but the other words were covered up, waiting to be unveiled. Like I just noted, there was a panel consisting of four panelists. They were almost uniformly Nickelodeon celebrities, with one of them tending to be an adult. The job of the panel was to try and figure out the hidden talent of the contestant.

There were three rounds that were each 60 seconds in length. A panelist would ask yes-or-no questions. If they got a yes, they kept asking questions. If they got a no, the next panelist would start asking questions. When they said a word that was on Billy the Answer Head, it would be revealed. After each round, if the contestant's talent hadn't been figured out, they won a prize. Oftentimes, they were props from defunct Nickelodeon shows like *Legends of the Hidden Temple*. To me, that would make for an amazing prize. If I could have the silver monkey out of their famed shrine today I would love it. After three rounds, the panelists got one final guess. If they still didn't solve it, then the contestant won the grand prize, which was almost always a trip, because this was Nickelodeon. Win or lose, the contestant would then show off their talent. There would also be clues given to the panel, sometimes pantomimed actions performed by the "Charade Brigade."

If this wasn't enough, there was also the "Secret Slime Action." This was an action that, when performed by a panelist, would get them slimed. We the audience would know what it is, but the panel wouldn't. It could be an action like scratching your head or saying a certain phrase. Sometimes, in a nod to *You Can't Say That on Television*, that phrase would be "I don't know." On occasion, it would be a choice that locked in getting slimed. For example, it could be "having red hair" or "having a twin," things that were already known traits and not anything the panelists could control in the moment. The panelists didn't have a chance. They would also slime people for "thinking" about something. This was either a bit or an example of telepathy in action that should have been way more disconcerting than it was. Clearly, the producers just really wanted to slime panelists. Sometimes they would barely be hit. On other occasions they would get absolutely drenched in slime, which is still funny. Then they would sit there all slimed up for the rest of the show. If this had just been for comedy, I would have been fine with it, but since somebody in the audience would win a prize if a panelist got slimed, it gets into a murky world akin to game fixing. We haven't even gotten as far into that topic as we are going to.

The host of *Figure It Out* was Summer Sanders. Sanders had an excellent swimming career, including winning multiple medals at the 1992 Summer Olympics in Barcelona. After that, she started dipping her toe into television, primarily doing swimming covering for NBC. The problem with being a swimming commentator is that people only care about swimming once every four years. Sanders would end up getting other sports-related jobs, including co-hosting *NBA Inside Stuff*, but she also was given a chance to host a game show with *Figure It Out*. Of all the Nick game show hosts of the '90s, Sanders is my least favorite. I'm not saying she was bad. She just was not a natural host. Which makes sense. She had never really done it before. Hosting a game show is different than sports commentary. The other Nick hosts were standups, comedians, and people who made a living adjacent to emcee work. Sanders had enthusiasm, but she didn't have the same presence as the best game show hosts. In a way, she presaged people like Snoop Dogg, Elizabeth Banks, and Alec Baldwin being game show hosts. People like Alex Trebek and Gene Rayburn would never get a chance in this modern era, which is a shame. Let people with natural hosting skills host game shows, please.

As for the panelists, much like *Match Game* in the '70s there were regulars among a rotating collection of celebrities and Nick personalities. The first chair traditionally went to an adult. That adult was usually Kevin Kopelow, the *All That* writer and producer who also played "Kevin" on that show. Along with Kopelow, there were two panelists that I distinctly remember, and they also came from the world of *All That*. They were Danny Tamberelli and Lori Beth Denberg. Tamberelli was mostly a goofball there to get laughs. He seemed less interested in guessing the talent than being funny. In this way, he is reminiscent of *Match Game*'s own famed funny redhead Patti Deutsch, one of my favorite panelists. Given that, it is fitting that Tamberelli was also one of my favorite panelists. Denberg seemed to take the game more seriously than anybody else. She also appeared in the most episodes of any panelist, asking questions in 115 episodes despite not appearing in the fourth and final season of the original run. Denberg could be funny, sure, usually in a deadpan way. However, she still took her role in the show seriously, seemingly thinking, "Hey, we're here to play this game, so let's play it." This makes her *Figure It Out*'s answer to Richard Dawson. I could sit here and compare *Figure It Out* and *Match Game* panelists all day. Clearly Amanda Bynes is Joyce Bulifant and Kopelow is Bill Daily.

I mentioned that Tamberelli didn't take things terribly seriously, and in truth—despite being the adult on the panel—that was often true of Kopelow as well. This brings me to a grudge I have been carrying since my childhood. I watched *Figure It Out*. I often laughed at the panelists. I was also often aggravated by it to no end. It was clear to me, even as a kid, that the deck was stacked toward the kids winning every time. The show wanted the contestant to win, and they did not bother hiding that fact. I can't say it was fixed, because they may have not told panelists to not care and not to try hard to figure out the hidden talent. Sometimes on *Match Game* the panelists clearly just think a bad answer that will never match is funny, and that also aggravates me endlessly. If you aren't going to take a game show seriously don't be on it! Even if it is a show for children! Anyway, like I said, I can't say for sure *Figure It Out* was fixed and panelists were actively taking a dive. I can say, though, so much clearly went toward the kids winning, and it goes beyond panelists obviously and overtly not caring about their own success.

For starters, so many of these "talents" the kids had weren't actually talents. This is not my retrospective feelings now as an adult. As a kid, I was annoyed by this in seemingly every episode. The kids would just do some random thing and it would be called a talent. Like, you could go to the producers of *Figure It Out* and tell them, "I can throw mustard packets into an accordion case" and the producers would say, "You're on the show!" That made the "talents" hard to guess. Then, to make things harder, they would word things in specific and clunky ways to make everything that much less intuitive. Early in the show's run, synonyms would count, so it didn't matter, but then they changed that. It seems obvious to me that the intent there was to make it easier for the kids to win.

So what we have with *Figure It Out* is a game show where kids showed off esoteric "talents" that weren't always talents and then panelists had to guess those talents despite them being worded awkwardly and with half the panelists not trying. No other game show on Nickelodeon made it this easy for the contestants. Compare *Figure It Out* to *Legends of the Hidden Temple* or *Nick Arcade*. Which show took the least amount of skill? Which show was easiest to win? By far it was *Figure It Out*. As a kid, I was mad at this. I wanted the game show to be fair. I wanted the panelists to try. I especially wanted the contestants to have actual talents. As an adult, when I watch game shows I am usually rooting for somebody. Maybe when you are watching *Chopped* there is some chef that drives you up a wall and you hope they lose. By and large, though, I am happy when a contestant wins on a game show. As a kid, if I felt a contestant's talent wasn't a real talent I would actively root against them. I wanted them to lose. I wanted justice in a cold and unfeeling universe. I also wanted Kevin Kopelow to get slimed, but that's a different desire altogether.

Unsurprisingly, I have calmed down a bit on this as an adult. It makes sense to me that they wanted the kids to win. Otherwise, what happens? A kid shows up and loses. They don't get the big prize and nobody walks away happy. The panelists had nothing to gain. Summer Sanders had nothing to gain. The kid winning and then showing off their talent was the happy ending *Figure It Out* wanted. I get that, but I also care about game shows. You can make a game show easy. I probably won't watch it, but I'll accept that. *Figure It Out* went a step further. It went through a ruse of a game show in many ways to try and trick the audience into thinking the game was more difficult than it actually was. *Figure It Out* was the game show equivalent of a sham trial. Their intents were noble, but the execution is a travesty for game show fans. There is a way to make a show like this with fun panelists cracking wise that also features a kid showing off a talent and getting a prize. It just doesn't have to be a game show, especially when you don't really seem interested in making a true game show.

The original run of *Figure It Out* ran four seasons from July 1997 through December 1999. The third season was dubbed "Family Style," and had nothing to do with the panelists sharing a big meal. It meant contestants could be siblings competing together or family members might show up on the Charade Brigade. Even Billy the Answer Head had a child. Then, the fourth season was "Wild Style," and all the talents involved animals. That means we got to watch dogs do things that weren't really talents. *Figure It Out* got rebooted in 2012 with some guy named Jeff Sutphen as the host. It lasted two seasons and ended in 2013.

Figure It Out had the potential to be the most fun of all the Nickelodeon game shows. After all, it had panelists who were professional comedians. The problem was the game they decided on wasn't any good. It was barely a game. Everything else about this show had clear flaws. Clearly, nobody brought the hammer down on *Figure It Out* for breaking the laws on game shows. That doesn't mean it wasn't annoying to me as a kid to see the show play out so transparently. The Charade Brigade weren't the only ones pulling off charades. The producers of *Figure It Out* were doing the exact same thing in their own way. Lori Beth Denberg deserved better.

Get the Picture

Don't be afraid to make changes

Television shows often tweak themselves, or go through out and out reboots. I'm talking when they are still airing, mind you, not when shows are brought back with a new cast as a "rebooted" version. Famously, *Newhart* was revised repeatedly over the first couple of seasons. Characters came and went. Eventually they found a format—and cast—that worked, and *Newhart* lasted eight seasons, including an iconic series finale. Remember the first season of *The Office*? Think of how they changed Michael Scott ever so slightly in the second season, and not just his hairdo. These tweaks and alterations don't always happen early in a show's run, and they don't always work. *Happy Days* rearranged their Titanic deckchairs for years. The less we say about Cousin Oliver on *The Brady Bunch*, the better. Nickelodeon wasn't immune to this either. As Big Pete got older, and aged out of the Nickelodeon demo, *The Adventures of Pete & Pete* started to focus more on Little Pete. This led to the introduction of more friends for him, like Monica and Wayne. Not coincidentally, my memories of the third season of *Pete & Pete*—my established favorite Nick show—are a bit less fond.

Game shows go through this process as well. *Match Game* in the '70s was really fun, but the '60s version was quite different, and not nearly as good. *Supermarket Sweep* was always adding and removing things, including David Ruprecht's iconic sweaters. Another game show that made quite a few changes between seasons is an early Nickelodeon game show by the name of *Get the Picture*. That's a little surprising, given that there were only two seasons, and also they both aired in 1991. Sounds like a short-lived show, right? Ah, but let's not forget the beauty of how easy it is for a network to crank out game show episodes. Yes, *Get the Picture* only aired between March and December of 1991, but they still produced 115 episodes. Hell, the second season is 75 episodes alone! They probably filmed them all in one month. Man, it would rule to be a game show host. Or even a game show writer.

Speaking of hosts, the man who was charged with hosting *Get the Picture* was Mike O'Malley. That's right, *Guts* host and Nickelodeon fixture Mike O'Malley was the host of *Get the Picture*. Since *Guts* figures more heavily into the history of Nick, I will save the O'Malley talk for that chapter. All I will say is that researching this book I found out O'Malley is only 54 years old, which is stunning. He's been around forever at this point. Do the math, and you can figure out that O'Malley was in his early twenties when he hosted *Get the Picture*. Specifically, he was 24. He definitely had a youthful energy, and the whole persona was already there. I can't champion his outfits, though. I like a bold fashion choice and bright colors, but the dude rocked some ugly ties throughout the dozens of episodes of *Get the Picture*. This was his first gig, though the same year he did play a cop in an episode of *Law and Order*. That role was a smidge smaller than this one.

Get the Picture, which had the clumsy tagline of "The Great Frame Game," had a weird techno-futuristic look to it. There were a lot of tubes and pipes and fake electricity. The first season had a lot of computer accouterments to it. The buzzers were computer keyboard and there were these games played during "Power Surges" that involved playing shuffleboard with floppy disks or throwing computer chips in a game of toss across. Naturally, seeing all this technology décor from 1991 in the present makes it feel both retro and also indicative of a time that never really existed. That being said, the teams, which consisted of two kids, wore either orange or yellow jumpsuits that felt like they fit in this environment. It reminds me of how movies from the '70s set in the future always seemed to involve jumpsuits, but it also feels like attire that technology repair people would wear. Or somebody doing low-level work at Gizmonic Institute.

I'm going to start by explaining how the game worked in the first season. Primarily, you answered questions for cash and the chance to get clues to figure out the hidden picture on the big screen. Actually, it wasn't just one screen. In the show's lore, it was a video wall of 16 screens, each one hiding a piece of the picture. The first round was a connect-the-dots round. There, you could see the dots making up the hidden image, and when you got a question right you could reveal one piece. It wasn't of the actual picture, but lines connecting the aforementioned dots. Correct answers to questions got you 20 bucks, while guessing the image, or getting the picture as it were, won you 50 bucks. However, if you guessed what the picture was and were wrong, you lost 20 bucks.

In the second round the cash on the line went up. There, you got $40 for answering questions correctly and $75 for guessing the puzzle, but getting it wrong still only cost you 20 bucks. The game was different as well. The image was totally hidden, and now there were numbers in all the corners of the 16 different screens. When you got questions right, you got to connect those dots, and when you fully surrounded a section with lines you got to see that piece of the actual photo. While there was only one game in round one, they would play multiple games in round two. The team with the most money would then move on to the final round, aka Mega Memory.

This was the portion of *Get the Picture* that was clear in my memory, fittingly enough. The kids kneel at the foot of a nine-number keypad. They were shown nine images around a theme for 10 seconds, and then the images disappeared. Then, for 45 seconds, O'Malley would give them clues related to the images, and they had to hit the number corresponding to the picture the clue applied to. The teams were given 200 bucks for every correct answer up to six, seven and eight got them some merch like a backpack or a bike, and then if they got all nine of them they would win the grand prize. This was usually a trip, and that trip was often to Universal Studios. Which, you know, wasn't a great prize. The show was shot at Universal Studios, so the kids had already been there. They were also almost definitely just kids from the Orlando area. When you are churning out 75 new episodes in like a month you aren't pulling in kids from across the country.

There were also the Power Surges I mentioned previously. When you landed on a Power Surge spot, you had to complete a task for a chance at cash and to see a section of the picture. During the connect-the-dots round, you got to see the actual image, not just the lines. In the first season, some of these were physical challenges, but not messy like *Double Dare*'s physical challenges. This is where they played shuffleboard or mini golf or did jigsaw puzzles. These physical Power Surges were eliminated after the first season, replaced with solely cerebral challenges.

Like I said, the show made a lot of tweaks after the first season ended. Most notably, the teams stopped playing for cash and started playing for points before Mega Memory. Also, Mega Memory became trickier, as the time limit was dropped down to 35 seconds. A toss-up round for 20 points began the festivities now as well. Then, there was a revamp of the actual look of the set. The keyboard buzzers were replaced with simple blue plungers. They also changed the look of the podium, the screen, and gave the kids nametags on their jumpsuits. Overall, I think the changes were smart. The show looked better, and the physical challenges honestly didn't fit in with the rest of the show. Everything else was completely mental, and then suddenly you're tossing "computer chips" around?

I don't mind the gameplay of *Get the Picture*. Personally, I'm not a huge fan of the "revealing" an image style of game show. I've tried watching *Concentration* and it's a little dull, but *Get the Picture* is a more eventful show. It's also not easy. I have to admit there were times the kids got the picture before me. Mega Memory is more my speed, anyway. Although, I also don't necessarily enjoy memory-based game shows either. Game shows where you can get ahead of the contestants is always tricky, because once you've figured it out you're just waiting. That's why trivia games or active games make the best televised game shows. You can play along with trivia, and if the contestants are doing something fun to watch that also engages you.

Of course, my favorite game show *Match Game* is neither of those things, but you do get to play along at the pace of the players and it just happens to have a lot of humor and entertainment built into it.

Get the Picture could have lasted another year or two, but to be fair they did crank out over 100 episodes in its one season. Plus, the end of *Get the Picture* opened up O'Malley's calendar to host *Guts*, the show that cemented his legacy in the mind of '90s kids. That show is iconic. *Get the Picture* was not maligned, but its cultural impact was limited. O'Malley has outshined the show that birthed him. *Get the Picture* is not stuck in our collective Mega Memory, but it was a noble effort from Nickelodeon.

Guts

Sometimes, you've got to have guts.
Also, British women are uncommonly trustworthy

As a child, I very much enjoyed the TV show *American Gladiators*. The show pitted two men against each other and two women against each other in a series of fairly intense athletic competitions. These out-there games were designed to test speed, strength, agility and showcase athletic excellence. Part of this involved the contestants having to best the show's collection of "gladiators," super muscular dudes and ladies with names like "Gemini" and "Zap." You could find yourself jousting on a pedestal with a guy named "Nitro" or trying to swing across a field of rings without being stopped by "Siren." There are similar shows in this vein that continue to this day, like *American Ninja Warrior*. People want to watch athletic "regular" folks put themselves to the test in a way that is cinematic and spectacular. It can be impressive to watch a really athletic person overcome obstacles, or opposition, to find televised glory and a sense of accomplishment on a large scale. Watching the kids' version of this? Less impressive as an adult.

Guts was Nickelodeon's foray into obstacle-based competition between "athletes." Maybe it's unfair to put that into scare quotes. Many of these kids were skilled for their age. Comparing them to somebody like, say, Kacy Catanzaro or Wesley "Two Scoop" Berry, though, doesn't do them any favors. Nickelodeon built a massive "Extreme Arena" in a sound stage at Universal Studios and invited children to show up, tackle the competitions, and then finally square off with the Crag. In was unique among Nick game shows, and really played up the whole "sports" aspect of this. To that end, they hired a British actress named Moira Quirk, known to all '90s kids as "Mo," to serve as the "official." The amount of actual officiating she did I am not sure, but it would have been easy enough for her to handle that role. She was mostly there to let the host know who had won each event and how well they had performed. That host? He was a familiar face in the world of Nickelodeon.

Since you just read the *Get the Picture* chapter (unless you read that chapter, set the book down, and went on the first manned flight to Mars) you know that Mike O'Malley got his start hosting that show. While *Get the Picture* didn't last, clearly Nickelodeon liked O'Malley as a host. He was still only in his mid–20s and had a lot of personality. O'Malley was also a big sports fan, and he has what you might call "sports fan energy." There's a reason one of his famous roles is in a series of ESPN ads where he played "The Rick." O'Malley fit the world of sports like a glove, but he also had hosting chops. O'Malley was the perfect guy for *Guts*. Maybe his energy was a little much for some, he had the kind of voice where it seemed like he was yelling even when he wasn't, but this was an ideal match as far as I'm concerned.

Each episode of *Guts* featured three kids going head-to-head bedecked in blue, red, and purple. Do you think the purple contestant ever felt weird that their color was a mix of the other two players' colors? Or did they feel like that made them superior? The show would start with four contests that were "extreme" versions of common sports, but oddly enough no extreme sports. By and large, "extreme" meant throwing on a harness attached to a bungee cord and jumping off stuff to get big air. However, they also had a wave pool and a race track. For an example of a harness-based game, there was "Over the Top." There, all three contestants would take turns jumping off the "Aerial Bridge." They would jump off, hit the ground, and then try and propel their bungeed body over the high bar. If they succeeded, the bar was raised (literally). There were three heights to clear, which were raised over the course of the show's four seasons. Event inflation was commonplace during the history of *Guts*. Seemingly nothing was safe from being made more immense and—theoretically—difficult.

There was an area called the gym, where they only really ever did an event called "Basic Training," which was a six-station obstacle course. Did it eventually become a seven-station course? The answer should be obvious. "Basic Training" was the equivalent of *American Gladiators'* "The Eliminator," but it wasn't the end event. On the track, you might find the kids racing each other in Moon Shoes, which may be the new high bar for the most-'90s thing in this book so far. There was an area known as the field, where they honestly had the best events. A lot of air cannons were used in the field. For example, you might find yourself having soccer balls shot at you out of a cannon and having to make saves. If you made the most saves in the allotted time, you won the event. Lastly, there is the pool, which was a wave pool to make things more difficult. Despite this, they didn't have Plexiglas around the pool until the second season, making the first season a wet mess poolside. In the pool, you could find yourself playing "Boogie Down," where all three contestants kneeled on a boogie board and had to pull themselves across the wave pool. The fastest time won.

I'm not going to list every event. You probably remember most of them. You definitely remember the final event of every episode, which I will get to in a moment. During the first four games, first place got 300 points, second place got 200 points, and third place got 100 points. If there was a tie, both players would get the higher number of points. Well, unless they were disqualified. All disqualified contestants got 100 points as if though they finished third. After all that, the three contestants would face the Aggro Crag, aka the Mega Crag, aka the Super Aggro Crag. As the crag was made more imposing, it got name changes to reflect that. The Aggro Crag, which lasted the first two seasons, was 28 feet tall, while both the Mega Crag and Super Aggro Crag were 30 feet tall.

The Crag was designed to look like a jagged mountain peak and the contestants had to race up the face of the structure, hitting actuator buttons along the way. After they had hit every actuator, and only after all actuators were hit, they could climb to the top of the Crag and hit the final actuator. If you had failed to hit an actuator, you were sent back by a spotter to hit it. This is the most I have ever used the word "actuator." There were other obstacles along the way. Strobe lights simulated lightning. There would be a foam rock "avalanche" in every run of the Crag. "Snow," really confetti, would fly out at you. There were also, stepping away from the elements, "nuclear flying crystals," which were balls shot at the contestants. That was a later addition. As a kid, I could imagine few things more fun than tackling the Crag. As an adult, if I was actually there I imagine it seeming much less imposing, but as a kid it would have absolutely ruled.

Winning the Crag would get you 725 points, while second place got 550 points and third place got 375 points. This meant that as long as you were within 300 points of first place you could in theory win the day by winning the Crag. That score structure also made it almost impossible to have a tie, and indeed there was never a tie in the history of *Guts*. Given the sports motif of the show, third place received a bronze medal, second won silver, and first place won gold and a "glowing" piece of *Guts*' "radical rock," aka a fake piece of the Crag. Which, again, would have been an awesome thing to have. I wouldn't mind having a piece of the Crag right now even. In fact, I just searched for a piece of the Crag on eBay to no avail. This means that winners on *Guts* got less than on most game shows, but it was also probably the most-difficult game show on Nickelodeon to win. Even more impressive were the contestants who had perfect scores. Indeed, after the first season of *Guts* three players had gotten a perfect score of 1,925 points. They faced off in the second-season premiere, a one-hour special called *Nickelodeon Guts All-Stars*. In that event, the kids were competing for college scholarships. They even released a VHS of the special featuring guest commentary from Lawrence Taylor, a Hall of Fame football player with a history of drug abuse and sexual impropriety. Swing and a miss with that choice, Nickelodeon. That will certainly look bad when … people watch that VHS tape from 1994. OK, so they may be able to avoid too much backlash there.

The fourth season of the show became *Global Guts*, which had an international flair. Contestants from all across the world would represent their countries against one another, and also a team of ex-Soviet Republics banded together as the Commonwealth of Independent States. This was the one year of the Super Aggro Crag, and the show ended slightly differently. In the vein of the Olympics, the contestants would stand on a medal podium while the national anthem of the winning competitor was played. Then the three kids would take a victory lap around the arena with their country's flags. Additionally, again taking a page from the Olympics, *Global Guts* kept a medal count for the countries, pitting them against each other.

Outside of the competitions, there would be "Spill Your Guts" sections where the kids got to talk about themselves, the sports they played, their interests, etc. Also, most of the contestants were introduced with nicknames that were used during the episode. These would be nicknames like "The Maniac" or "The Tower of Power" or "The First Lady of American Theater." Actually, they may not have used that last one. Obviously, these kids almost definitely didn't really have these nicknames. When I was a kid, if you had a nickname it was either (A) a play on your name or (B) incredibly insulting. My guess is that they would ask the kids if they had a nickname they wanted to use and if they couldn't think of one (or the one they thought of sucked) they would just give them one. Indeed, in an interview about her experience on the show contestant Anna Mercedes Morris said that the producers gave her the nickname "Roadrunner" because she didn't have a nickname of her own.

Guts was a smart idea for a show for Nickelodeon. Many kids love sports and fancy themselves good athletes. Oftentimes they make their primary point of identity being an athlete. These kids love sports, love competing, and presumably love fake pieces of fake mountains. While building the set of *Guts* was ambitious, after that the financial outlay was limited. After all, how much are you spending on three medals and a plastic statue per episode? They found something kids would do just for the sake of it. They got bragging rights and something to show that, yes, they did indeed rule at sports. O'Malley was an excellent host, though as an adult I would have maybe turned him down from an 11 to a nine. Mo's soothing British accent gave her a level of validity to me as a child. O'Malley was a ball of energy and sports fandom. Mo was the sobering ying to Mike's raging yang.

As a kid who loved sports, I loved *Guts*. The show aired for four seasons from 1992 through 1995 and put 160 episodes on Nickelodeon, including the *Global Guts* season. I must have seen almost all of them. I very much aspired to be on the show myself, though I was too young for it. The kids on *Guts* were tweens and teens and I was only nine when it ended. Alas, Mike and Mo weren't there for me once I was old enough. Watching it as an adult,

as clever—yet simple—as many of the events are, there is an obvious difference. I'm a grown man and these kids do not impress me with their skill.
I have a very different view of watching kids trying to hit tennis balls than
I did when I was younger than them. It's like how when I was a kid I was
so happy to go see indoor soccer. I didn't realize how low of a level of skill
the players had relative to most professionals. Nowadays I can't even imagine watching high school basketball, let alone watching 13 year olds jumping off an "Aerial Bridge" and trying to make baskets. Some Nickelodeon
shows I have never grown out of. *Guts* was built on being impressed by,
and invested in, children playing "extreme" sports games. There is a funda-
mental gap between who I am and what the show is that is nobody's fault. I
don't knock *Guts* for it. This was inevitable. At least I'll always have *American Gladiators*.

Hey Arnold!

Keeping your feelings inside can be toxic

Some comedies, like Barq's root beer, have bite. Others are more about being pleasant, like…. Mug? I believe Mug doesn't have caffeine, so that may sort of make sense. What I mean is there are comedies with a little punch to them. They are dark. They have an edge. Even some comedies for kids have a little more grit to them. They are full of hard jokes and go for the comedic jugular. Think of, say, *Rocko's Modern Life*. Then there are comedies that sort of just wash over you and feel, for want of a better word, nice. You might say things like, "Oh that was fun." Maybe you don't laugh a ton, but the gentility is pleasant to live in for a half hour or whatever. I feel like this is what, say, *The Brady Bunch* would go for. Among Nickelodeon shows, *Doug* sort of falls into this category a lot of the time. In my memory, *Hey Arnold!* was that kind of cartoon. It has some truly devoted fans. Some consider it the best Nickelodeon show. I remembered a pleasant cartoon with a few chuckles that just seemed sweet hearted, the Miss Congeniality of cartoons. Given the love for *Hey Arnold!*, I figured I might be ruffling feathers by telling people it's a decent enough show that doesn't belong on the Nickelodeon Mount Rushmore. Apparently my memories from when I was like 10 aren't entirely reliable.

Hey Arnold! was created by Craig Bartlett. He originally planned to become a painter, but instead after college he got a job at a Claymation studio of all places. Then, in 1987 he found himself working on TV with *Pee-wee's Playhouse*. Now, Pee-wee Herman is another beloved cultural figure of the '80s and '90s. I don't love the show, though I watched it as a kid, but I will definitely step up in support of *Pee-wee's Big Adventure*, a ridiculous but delightful film that brought Tim Burton into our lives. Eventually his films would become about Johnny Depp and Helena Bonham Carter playing dress up, but we'll always have Pee-wee dancing to "Tequila" in a biker bar. While he worked on *Pee-wee's Playhouse*, Bartlett made Claymation shorts about a character named Penny, but she happened to have a friend named Arnold. Three of his shorts showcased Arnold as a character. After his stint with Pee-wee, Bartlett found himself paired off with some former *Rugrats* writers to develop a show for Nickelodeon. It was not going well, so Bartlett figured he'd show them the Penny shorts. Nick wasn't interested in Penny, but the secondary character of Arnold sparked their interest.

Thus, Penny was sidelined like so many Winslow family member's to Arnold's Steve Urkel. Changes were made, obviously. For starters, *Hey Arnold!* wasn't going to be Claymation. That would have been incredible, but it just wasn't going to happen on Nick. Also, Arnold needed personality. He was going from being a secondary character from a few shorts to the protagonist of his own show. Talking to his hometown newspaper the *Seattle Post-Intelligencer* in 1997, Bartlett described Arnold as such: "We came up with a reluctant hero who keeps finding himself responsible for solving something, making the right choices, doing the right thing." That is Arnold in a nutshell, which may be why I remembered this show's primary trait as being "niceness."

Arnold (his last name was not officially unveiled until 2017, so for the purposes of a book about the '90s I will just call him Arnold) is a nine year old in fourth grade who lives in the fictional city of Hillwood. Hillwood is based in part on Seattle and Portland (two Pacific Northwest cities that Bartlett lived in) as well as Brooklyn. To me, the show always had that New York vibe. The buildings and the streets make it feel like Arnold and company live not just in New York, but like New York in the 1920s, only with modern technology. The city has that working-class vibe, and also Arnold lives with his grandparents in the boarding house they run, Sunset Arms. Arnold basically lives in a tenement, and the color palette just screams "East Coast city living" to me. Like Bartlett said back in the day, Arnold is nice and helpful. He seems to truly care about everybody. Also, his head is shaped like a football. Now, cartoon characters with atypical looks are not uncommon. They usually just don't get commented on. It's just an animation decision to make the characters stand out. However, in *Hey Arnold!* it is considered very much notable that Arnold has a football head. He also wears a tiny hat and a sweater over a too-long plaid shirt that makes it look like he's wearing a kilt.

The rest of the show is fleshed out by the kids at Arnold's school and the other people living at the boarding house. Gerald is Arnold's best friend with some impressive Kid 'n' Play–style hair. He's a cool athlete, but it still makes sense he hangs out with Arnold. Arnold seems sort of cool as well. Harold is dumb and kind of a bully, although his bullying tapers down as the show goes on. Again, this is a show with a real "nice" vibe to it a lot of the time. Stinky's name is Stinky. Also, he's from the South. Phoebe is the smartest girl in class and has a crush on Gerald. Eugene is annoying. Then, there's Helga Pataki. I didn't give the other characters their last names, but "Helga Pataki" just rolls off the tongue. Or off the fingers as it were.

Helga needs a lot of unpacking. She has a unibrow, wears a pink dress and a big pink bow in her hair, and looks like she has pigtails even though she doesn't. Helga is complicated. She can be the antagonist here and there. Helga is loud, brash, and high strung. She can be a bully at times. One of the primary targets of her scorn is Arnold, whom she calls "Football Head." However, there is an ulterior motive to Helga's heckling and performative animosity toward Arnold. You see, Helga harbors a deep crush on Arnold. Like, a truly unhealthy and alarming crush. I might even go as far as to say she is obsessed with Arnold and her feelings for Arnold. In Helga's mind, she is in love with Arnold. Now, in reality a nine year old is not capable of romantic love, and either way I don't know if what Helga feels toward Arnold could be considered love anyway. She has multiple secret shrines dedicated to Arnold. One of them includes a bust of Arnold made of gum that she kisses. It's gross as hell. She even has a little locket of Arnold, even though she doesn't want anybody to know about her crush. You'd think she'd be more careful about hiding it. Helga also writes poems about Arnold. She is a talented poet! It also leaves a literal paper trail! Helga is a prisoner of her own mind.

She feels like she can't be vulnerable. If anybody found out she had feelings for Arnold she'd be mortified. And yet, all she wants in the world is to be with him, in whatever way a nine year old perceives that. Holding hands, I imagine. That's a real tragedy. Helga could probably use some counseling.

And not just because of her intense feelings for Arnold. Helga has a rough home life as well. In fact, it was in remembering this, and watching the Patakis in action, that I realized that *Hey Arnold!* is not the Pollyanna show I remembered. Her parents are barely involved in her life. "Big Bob" Pataki only cares about his

Arnold steps up to the plate. Helga is prepared the catch. Gerald seems to be serving as umpire (Nickelodeon).

beeper business. It is heavily implied that her mom Miriam is an alcoholic. She always seems tired and drinks "smoothies" that involve an awful lot of Tabasco and celery. Miriam can also be found sleeping in random places around the house. In short, Miriam is usually too drunk to be there for Helga. She also has to deal with comparisons to her older sister Olga. Olga is the apple of the Pataki parents' eye. Olga is smart and successful. She's considered by many to be beautiful. Olga has a friendly, outgoing personality. Helga cannot live up to her legacy. In fact, Bob often calls Helga "Olga" by mistake. That's just straight-up tragic. Helga is genuinely a complicated, dynamic character. There's so much going on there. You have contempt and sympathy for her at the same time. That's impressive character development.

Arnold's grandparents are a much less sad story that the plight of Helga Pataki. His grandfather Phil may be 81, but he's a cheerful guy who is always there for Arnold. They have a lot of fun adventures together, and if anybody is going to give Arnold advice it's his Grandpa. His grandmother Gertrude, who Phil calls "Pookie," is more of an out-there individual. She does a lot of strange things and seems to take on different personas. Sometimes it feels like maybe she is dealing with dementia, but her sharpness will then return. Mostly it feels like she's just a bizarre woman who likes to pretend she's Calamity Jane on occasion. In the Sunset Arms, there are a few boarders we see an awful lot of as well. Mr. Hyunh is a Vietnamese immigrant who is a music virtuoso, and when he sings country music he loses his heavy accent. Ernie Potts is a demolitionist with a short fuse about being a short man.

Then, there is the tragic marriage of Oskar and Suzie Kokoshka. Oskar is, in short, the worst. He's an Eastern European immigrant, which is not what the problem is obviously. No, his problem is his personality. Oskar is incredibly lazy. He doesn't have a job for most of the show's run, and that's by choice. He can't read English, which given that he's an immigrant is fair but he also doesn't really try. Despite not having a job, Oskar is an obsessive gambler. He's also a pathological liar. He's cheat anybody. He'll tell you he'll do something to get you off his back but has no intention of doing it. Oskar is married to Suzie, and I don't know what she sees in him. Suzie has her stuff together entirely. She's a mature, reasonable, and intelligent woman. She works hard to makes ends meet for their family. Suzie is so supportive of her husband and seems to truly love him. I don't know why. I feel bad for Suzie. She should have kicked Oskar to the curb years ago. Maybe Suzie is happy, but she's trapped in a terrible marriage with a man who is not capable of giving her the support she deserves as a human being. Who knows why she stays with him? Maybe she just likes a challenge. Maybe she's a habitual caregiver. Maybe in a toxic way their dynamic works. It just bums me out.

This is the kind of stuff that made me realize *Hey Arnold!* is far from just being a congenial wisp of a show with no bite and no darkness to it. There is a lot of sadness in the city of Hillwood. People have true problems in their life, not just cartoon problems. I mean, just look at the residents of the Sunset Arms. Look at the Pataki household. There is more substance and depth to *Hey Arnold!* then I gave it credit for. It's not a warm bath of a TV show. I found myself moved sometimes by the show. Arnold and company are indeed often nice people and are kind to each other. That part is true. Arnold puts himself on the line for others to a degree that is admirable. There are those sweet moments. They just serve in juxtaposition to the sour.

Oh, and also *Hey Arnold!* is much funnier than I recalled too. There are a fair amount of jokes in every episode, and some of them are quite silly. They go beyond something just being mildly amusing. I got some real laughs, not just chuckles. I watched an episode I remembered from my childhood that turned out to be a story from only the sixth episode of the series. In it, Arnold and his grandmother set out to save a tortoise named Lockjaw from the aquarium. Gertrude's daffiness really amused me, and there was also a bit in the aquarium with the security guard taunting a shark in a tank. He falls in, and we don't see what becomes of him. I don't recall jokes like that from *Hey Arnold!* I felt like I was watching a whole new show from the one I remembered from my childhood. What else am I remembering incorrectly? Was Stoop Kid, in all actuality, *not* afraid to leave his stoop?

The first look we got of *Hey Arnold!* was in 1996 when the pilot episode aired as a short before *Harriet the Spy*. I saw that Michelle Trachtenberg vehicle in theaters, so that means I assuredly got introduced to *Hey Arnold!* at that time. After that, I watched it for at least its first few seasons on the air. There are many little things from it stuck in my brain, like Dino Spumoni and the aforementioned Stoop Kid. The first four seasons of the show aired in the '90s, and then fifth season was, like so many other Nick shows, kind of a disaster in terms of scheduling. The 24 total episodes aired between March of 2000 and June of 2004. There was no fanfare for the final episode. Also, it's not even all that special. The last story they ever told was about Arnold's grandfather's car being stolen from an antique car show. In 2002, they squeezed in *Hey Arnold!: The Movie*, which is—no joke—about Arnold, Gerald, and Helga fighting to stop an evil real estate developer from turning their old neighborhood into a shopping mall. All that was missing was a breakdancing competition. They also made the TV movie *Hey Arnold!: The Jungle Movie* that came out in 2017. I kind of want to see that, or at least I do now. Prior to revisiting the show for the book, I figured I wouldn't be interested in it. Now that I have seen the quality of *Hey Arnold!*, I feel differently.

Yes, like I remembered *Hey Arnold!* has a lot of nice people doing nice things in it. There is an overarching sweetness. It doesn't just exist on that level, though. There are punchier jokes than I recall, and they get into some serious stuff from episode to episode. Also, befitting a show set in a big (if fictional) city there's a lot of diversity to the world of the show. In addition to the likes of Gerald, Oskar, and Mr. Hyunh, Harold is Jewish, and he even has his bar mitzvah in an episode. I'm not about to put Arnold and company on my personal Mount Rushmore, but I understand it now. There's a lot of good in this show. I just hope you *Hey Arnold!* diehards aren't building shrines in your closet to Arnold. Helga's behaviors aren't something you should be replicating in your own life.

Hey Dude

Sometimes you have to take a chance,
but watch out for that killer cacti

There had to be a first. Nickelodeon had created original programming before. That goes back to the network's debut, when it was really just
the children's show *Pinwheel*. They had created game shows, sketch shows,
educational shows, and shows for preschoolers. When, though, would
Nickelodeon bite the bullet? When would they finally bring us an original scripted show with a narrative? The year would be 1989, and that show
would be *Hey Dude*. Yes, when the '90s began, there was only one narrative show for older kids airing on Nickelodeon, and it was filmed in Tucson,
Arizona, of all places.

While I'm sure most of you remember *Hey Dude*, at least if you are an
older '90s kid, it feels strange that it was the show that opened the door. It's
not a classic Nick series, other than its theme song. You can also kind of tell
this was Nick's first foray into this kind of show. It's a little creaky, and the
budget is clearly low. That's fair. The network was still young. They didn't
know if this was going to work out. Plus, they had to build an entire fake
ranch set on the property of an actual ranch in Tucson. Obviously, in the
'90s original programming took off for the network. It's the decade where
Nickelodeon became *Nickelodeon*. If you were a child of the '80s, Nick was
a channel where you might have watched *Double Dare*. In the '90s, it could
give you a full day of original programming. That all began with *Hey Dude*.
It was the prototype, and that comes will positives and negatives. In 1989,
when the show debuted, it must have felt cool to have a show like this to
watch as a kid, or even a teenager. By the time it ended in 1991, though,
Nickelodeon was an entirely different network. I don't think it is a coinci-
dence that 1991 was the year a bunch of original Nick shows launched and
it's also the year *Hey Dude* went away.

What's *Hey Dude* about? Well, in short, it's about how it's a little wild
and a little strange when you make your home out on the range. All right,
job well done. Time to shut down the shop and end this chapter. Or not.
There's probably more I can do than paraphrase the fantastic theme song.
This is sort of a workplace sitcom, but it's a workplace where everybody
lives as well. The show is set at the Bar None Dude Ranch and focuses on

some of the people who work there. When the show begins, Ben Ernst, known as Mr. Ernst, has bought the Bar None. He was living in New Jersey and working a high-stress job as an accountant in New York City, but decided he wanted to live a simpler, more peaceful life in the desert. That basically makes *Hey Dude* a take on *Green Acres* but for kids. In this case, though, Mr. Ernst's son Buddy is in the Eva Gabor role as the one reluctant to move, as Mr. Ernst is divorced. He's also a bit more of a bumbler and a doofus than Oliver Wendell Douglas in *Green Acres*. Additionally, no pigs get drafted into the United States military during the run of *Hey Dude*.

Since Mr. Ernst is in over his head, the dude doesn't even know how to ride a horse when he buys the ranch, the competent adult on the show is Lucy, who is the ranch hand at the Bar None. She also is the voice of reason and the adult that the kid characters on the show can turn to for advice. Otherwise, the center could not hold. When the show begins, there are four kids working at the ranch, or at least four kids that get focused on. Maybe it's like *Saved by the Bell* where there are other kids at Bayside but we never spend time with them. There's Ted, who is kind of a schemer and, to keep the comparison going, is sort of a Zack Morris type. Only, you know, less of a narcissist and unable to freeze time. Then, we have Danny, who is Native American but, to the show's credit, is not defined by that. It comes up, of course. There is an entire storyline in one episode where Danny bets Ted he can't go a week without using Native American items. All I remember is that it ends with Ted naked. Off camera, of course. However, there is another episode where two of the employees rearrange the rocks that make up the Bar None Dude Ranch sign to make it read "Nude Ranch" and then two nude adults appear looking to book a room. Their nudity is covered by strategically placed items à la *Austin Powers*. I only mention this because I can't imagine something like that happening on a Nickelodeon show from later in the '90s. Again, they were figuring things out as they went along. Also, before I go on too great of a tangent, I do want to note that the actor who played Danny, Joe Torres, was Mexican-American, and not a Hopi Indian like his character. That doesn't mean he didn't have ancestry from pre–European American peoples, of course.

The female characters were a study in contrast, and not just because one was a brunette and one was blonde. Brad was the riding instructor and came from a rich family from Grosse Pointe, Michigan. As a kid, this always stuck out to me, since I was from Metro Detroit and had family in Grosse Pointe. It is indeed a place where a lot of wealthier folks live in mansions both mini and regular sized. It's also were Martin Blank from *Grosse Pointe Blank* is from. I have been to his high school! I do wonder how aware people outside of Michigan were aware of Grosse Pointe as a wealthier place. I'm just too close to it, much as how I just think of Faygo as the cheap pop at the liquor store and not as the drink of choice for Juggalos. Brad is also a bit more sardonic and closed off. On the flip side, there is Melody, who is a lifeguard and the dance instructor. Evidently people going to a dude ranch wanted to learn to dance? Maybe it was all square dancing all the time? Melody came from blue collar Allentown, where there shutting all the factories down, but was also super friendly and bubbly. She was the friendliest person on the staff. Also, Melody was played by Christine Taylor, making her by far the most-successful member of this cast. She played Marcia in those *Brady Bunch* spoof movies—another staple for '90s kids—and also had roles in *Zoolander*, *Dodgeball*, and some other films not made with her then-husband Ben Stiller.

Speaking of acting careers outside of *Hey Dude*, during the third season David Lascher, who played Ted, left the show. He had gotten a chance to star in an NBC sitcom in 1990 that could have taken him to bigger and better things. However, the sitcom had a truly bizarre and grim premise. It was called *A Family for Joe*, and the show is about four kids who were recently orphaned who find a homeless man and have him live with them and pose as their grandfather so they don't get split up in foster care. I mean, *ALF* is a less insane premise than that, and ALF's love of eating cats is less unpleasant than that plot. Also, the homeless man? He was played by Robert Mitchum. Robert Mitchum! Since he also starred in *Night of the Hunter*, maybe he just enjoyed bleak stories that involved him joining a family. This probably won't surprise you, but *A Family for Joe* did not last. That being said, when Lascher left, Ted was replaced by two different new male characters. One was Jake, Mr. Ernst's nephew who was a Los Angeles slacker type. There was also Kyle, who was the son of Lucy's ex-boyfriend, because apparently no new characters were allowed unless they had a connection to the cast. He was a true cowboy type, making him a fish in water as opposed to Jake's fish out of water. When *A Family for Joe* mercifully tanked, Ted returned to the show. Now, though, he had a rival for the heart of Brad in Kyle.

Hey Dude lasted for 65 episodes over five seasons, though the show only aired from 1989 through 1991. It wasn't a season per year. The storylines are what you would expect for a broad sitcom. Literally they only waited until the second episode to do the "Battle of the Sexes" episode. Cartoonish criminals show up to rob the ranch in another episode. Does Ted think one of the guests at the Bar None is a hitman for the mob? You'd better believe they didn't make it through the first season before doing that. There weren't exactly a lot of new ideas on *Hey Dude*, but the entire show was a new idea for Nickelodeon. The only difference here was that the show was happening at a dude ranch. Honestly, that goes ... well not a long way. It goes a little way. Things do feel slightly different when they are happening at a ranch that has a bit of a lived-in feel to it. Besides, there may be nothing new—especially in a sitcom for kids—when Mr. Ernst has to step in and pretend to be a wrestler for a match at the Bar None, but it can still be amusing. It's not like great shows—let's use *Frasier* as an example—don't use well-worn plots. They just execute them to perfection. It's funny when Martin Crane accidentally gets high because the joke writing is so strong and John Mahoney is such a talented actor, not because I've never seen that happen before.

Hey Dude doesn't do that, but it's better that a lot of kids' shows from the era. To bring back up *Saved by the Bell*, this show is way more competent than that one, and *Saved by the Bell* is a constant source of nostalgia content. I could write a book on *Saved by the Bell* and sell copies quicker than the gang sold Screech's spaghetti sauce. Also, I'd love to do that. Buy enough copies of this book and I will. It's not a good show, though. It's funny to laugh at, but it's poorly made. *Hey Dude* is not poorly made. It's hokey and bare bones, but the execution isn't terrible. In truth, it's a pretty low-key show. *Hey Dude* sort of just moseys along, not unlike a cowpoke on their horse trotting along a trail. They don't throw out a ton of jokes, and the ones they do seem designed to only generate a chuckle at most. It kind of feels like Nickelodeon was saying, "Hey, we're taking you into the world of a dude ranch and we have a will they/won't they romance, isn't that enough?" Which, you know, fair enough. For some the answer was assuredly "Yes."

Hey Dude was not an ambitious first foray into scripted storytelling, but it was a marginal success in my eyes. It definitely served as a proof of concept, especially for a show like *Salute Your Shorts*. Yes, several shows that followed *Hey Dude* on Nickelodeon were better, but also some were worse. In the end, there are two things about *Hey Dude* I think are great. One is the opening credits. I'm a sucker for old-school credits, and seeing the characters and actors introduced with their image within a horseshoe is a lot of fun to revisit. The theme song is just so catchy too. It's not the best Nick theme song, but that's only because Nickelodeon has had so many top-notch theme songs. I mean, *Hey Dude*'s unnamed country crooner is no Polaris, but the theme song puts you in the frame of mind for this show, and it's a real earworm to boot. Man-eating jackrabbits and killer cacti will always be in my brain, and likely yours too.

The other great thing about *Hey Dude* is that one of the writers was Graham Yost. He even wrote that episode where crooks show up to rob the Bar None. A show about a crime in a Western setting? That's what I call foreshadowing. *Hey Dude* was Yost's first writing gig, his chance to break into Hollywood, and a few years later he would write the screenplay for *Speed*. Several years after that, he would create the TV show *Justified*.

Justified starred Timothy Olyphant as a lawman in rural Kentucky that is heavy on Western motifs. The fact Yost wrote for *Hey Dude* and then many years later went on to create *Justified* just feels so perfect. There are also definitely worse first gigs for a writer to have.

If you are a younger '90s kid, you may have missed out on *Hey Dude*. Like, say, if you didn't hit TV-watching age until 1995 or so. By then, *Hey Dude* had left center stage for Nickelodeon. In a time before the rise of the internet, that meant it was pretty much gone. Now, no pop culture is really lost forever, at least if it came out in the last 50 years or so. *Hey Dude* was a historical moment for Nickelodeon. It deserves a larger role in the story of Nick. And hey, it's not a bad show either. A little wild? Sure. A little strange? At times. But far from a failure. Get along, little doggies.

The Journey of
Allen Strange

We make our own families.
Sometimes literally out of a mannequin

There have been many sitcoms about aliens coming to Earth. I'm particularly partial to *3rd Rock from the Sun*, and only a little bit because Harry Solomon is a true fashion icon. That's a classic "fish out of water" comedy that may be big and broad, but the cast commits and it's funny if not necessarily substantive. *My Favorite Martian*, a sitcom from the '60s, is mostly a punchline now, but it's actually a better show than you imagine. It too features an alien masquerading as a human, but this time with a human accomplice. This is as opposed to the Solomons, who don't tell any humans they are aliens. Of course, I have to mention *ALF*, which is about an alien living with a family that does not look human at all. He's furry, he loves to eat cats, and he can play a mean saxophone in the opening credits. That show is not good in the slightest, but it's pretty entertaining nevertheless. ALF had a talk show for a minute as well, which I miss dearly. Of course Nickelodeon needed a sitcom about an alien coming to Earth at some point, and that show is *The Journey of Allen Strange*.

The show begins with an extraterrestrial from Xela stowing away on a Xelan research ship on Earth. When that ship has to flee, this young alien is left behind. None of his alien cohorts realize they left him. Maybe they don't have families on Xela? You'd think that this aliens mom or dad or whatever equivalent they have on Xela would be like, "Oh no, my kid has disappeared! I have to find them!" Even the McCallisters eventually realized they left Kevin behind. As an alien, he is big and blue and looks kind of goopy but doesn't seem to be. He has a ton of powers, including the ability to disguise himself as a human. Since the first humans he saw were black men playing basketball, he decided to disguise himself in the visage of a black male himself, in his case a teenager. Down the line, this would lead to a Black History Month episode where he learns about civil rights, slavery, and other aspects of black history. This is nice. However, did the alien really have to see black guys *playing basketball* as his first experience with humans? Basketball is great. Lots of people play it. It just feels like a facile choice bordering on a stereotype.

The alien meets two kids, the Stevenson siblings Roberta, aka Robbie, and Josh. Robbie is 15, while Josh is 11, but it's Josh who is considered a science whiz and a schemer. They live with their father Ken after their parents' divorce. Robbie and Josh are the ones who find the alien and bring him into the world of humans. They also name him Allen Strange, I assume because he is a strange alien. Robbie and Josh invite Allen into their home, but hide him from their dad, passing him off as their friend. Little does Ken know that Allen lives in their attic, hiding himself away inside a cocoon when necessary. Allen's plan is to stay with his only friends until he can return to his planet, but you'd better believe hijinks ensue along the way. You know the drill. Allen has to hide that he's an alien but the way he acts can be incredibly, well, strange. He doesn't understand being a human. Robbie and Josh have to protect him and teach him how to blend in. They have to keep Mr. Stevenson none the wiser. And so on.

Fortunately, Allen seems to have limitless powers, and he didn't even have to take that pill from *Limitless*. When he's in his alien form he can hover. He's incredibly athletic and can master a sport just by watching it. When he wants to read a book he just places his hand on its cover. To me, it feels like his powers go as far as the show needed them to for any given story. If they need him to be able to do something to solve a problem, he can. On the other hand, sometimes his powers fall short to keep the stakes going. Over the course of the series Allen has to worry about multiple alien hunters, which can't be easy when all you want to do is hang out with your two friends and eat a ton of cheese. Oh, and don't think Allen is technically an orphan on Earth. He manages to bring a mannequin to life to serve as his father when necessary. He name is Manfred. Ken calls him Manny and considers him a friend. I don't know if Ken has any other friends. It's kind of sad. I watched an episode where Allen, who is on the wrestling team, volunteers his dad to chaperone, but fills his head with fatherly advice and knowledge first. It goes better than you would expect, especially when Manfred saves the wrestling team from being electrocuted in their bus.

On the alien sitcom scale from *3rd Rock* to *ALF*, *The Journey of Allen Strange* is closer to the *ALF* side of things. At least I imagine the people who worked on *Allen Strange* weren't as miserable as the people who had to work on *ALF*, always worried they'd step into a hole for the puppeteer and break a bone or something. Max Wright was never the same. Arjay Smith, who played Allen, had a lot on his plate for a child actor. He had to figure out how to play an alien who is pretending to be human while also, you know, remembering his lines and conveying them believably. Overall, I think Smith did a solid enough job. He does seem to succeed when it comes to expressing wonder or in little moments where he is just a little off from humans. In an episode I watched, Allen and Manfred are driving in a car, and they both move their heads with the windshield wipers. That was fun. Smith has had a decent career as an actor. He had a role in *The Day After Tomorrow* and has appeared on a lot of TV shows. This includes playing a terrorist in *24* and costarring on the forgotten TNT drama *Perception*. There he acted alongside one of my personal most-underrated actors ever, Rachael Leigh Cook. I once wrote a pilot about Cook trying to reinvent herself as an Andy Kaufman–style performance artist. Nothing came of it.

Other than Smith, most of the main actors leave a lot to be desired. The kids who play Robbie and Josh aren't bad, but they certainly seem to struggle with the craft. Even the dude who plays Ken is kind of a dud as a performer, though, and he's a grown man. I will say I enjoyed the work of Robert Crow, who played Manfred. The plots that I saw all felt a little overly convenient as well. Somehow I feel like they lean on Allen's alien powers both too much and not enough. Maybe I just wish they had made stronger choices. Or stranger choices. It's just a very by-the-numbers sitcom. Why watch this when I can watch *3rd Rock*? Hell, even a kid would be better off watching the Solomons, because Tommy is a better version of an alien posing as a kid. Granted, he was played by Joseph Gordon-Levitt, a much strong actor than Smith, but that doesn't make my statement any less true.

The Journey of Allen Strange was buzz marketed on Nickelodeon where they would show one of their usual promos before blue ooze would seep in and fill the screen, declaring, "Something strange is coming to SNICK." Weirdly, I remember these ads more than the show. *The Journey of Allen Strange* debuted on SNICK on November 8, 1997, just as was promised by the mysterious ads. It would last for three seasons on the channel's Saturday block for older kids, airing 57 episodes in total and ending in the year 2000. I don't know if Allen was able to return to Xela. My guess is not, given Nick's track record and the fact the show didn't seem terribly popular. Hey, ALF never made it back home either. It would have been strange if Nickelodeon had never done a show about an alien on Earth adapting to life on this planet. Thus, they gave us Allen Strange. He's a fun enough character, but this fish out of water is flopping around, unable to adapt to life on land. That's kind of a grim analogy for a show like this. Sorry about that.

KaBlam!

Variety is the spice of life

There is a ton of animation out there. That's impressive, given how time consuming it can be. Due to this fact, there are a lot of short animations out there. After all, think of how many Nickelodeon cartoons did two 11-minute segments per episode. That's much easier to handle from a storytelling perspective, but even that can be daunting. You may not always have enough story to handle a full 11 minutes, or handle doing dozens of episodes in a season. No network may be willing to get that invested in you as well. Can there be a happy medium? Is there a way to showcase a variety of animation to the world, and also potentially see what has legs? Obviously there is. The thing to do there would be to create a show which aired different cartoons of varying lengths by different creators. It's a clever idea, and one Nickelodeon eventually jumped on. They'd done sketch shows before. Why not do an animated sketch show? Although, of course, in certain ways every animated show is a sketch show. That includes *KaBlam!*, the Nick show that introduced us to an abundance of characters, artists, and shorts for four seasons and 48 episodes from 1996 through January of 2000, barely tipping over into the new millennium.

Many people contributed to the creation of *KaBlam!*, though three names stick out two me. Two of them are Will McRobb and Chris Viscardi, the men who brought us Nick's crowning glory, *The Adventures of Pete & Pete*. They were joined by Robert Mittenthal, who had previously created the live-action sketch show *Welcome Freshman* for Nickelodeon and had played a role in the creation of *Double Dare* and *Think Fast!* as well. They were joined by Michael Pearlstein, Cote Zellers, and Albie Hecht, to name check all the listed creators. The premise of *KaBlam!* was simple. Well, the real-world premise was. The premise of the show itself was a little more convoluted. There were two hosts, Henry and June, who would turn the pages of a comic book to introduce us to each animated short, which were I guess within the world of the show part of some living comic book? Henry and June had their own personalities and would have little stories themselves in between segments. This gave the wraparounds more personality and freshness to them. It wasn't just the hosts throwing to comics. Did I mention Henry and June are also animated?

And one of the people who works on the show is named Mr. B. Foot and is a sasquatch? Henry and June had their own dynamic going on, though it fluctuated over the years. Henry pulled a Homer Simpson and got a little dumber as time went on, while June got smarter and more mature. I don't know what reference to pull here. Kimmy Schmidt maybe? It doesn't matter. Henry and June were their own thing. Also, Henry was voiced by a young Noah Segan, who is good friends with filmmaker Rian Johnson and has at least a small role in all his films. Julia McIlvane voiced June. She has done some other voiceover work and is not friends with Rian Johnson near as I can tell.

So that's the premise within *KaBlam!*, but what the show was really about was having a place for Nick to try out some different show premises and animators. It also was a show that would cater to less traditional styles of animation or storytelling. The different shorts were all fairly distinct from each other, making *KaBlam!* feel like a real mix of influences and styles. That's pretty cool, and I'm sure some of the show creators preferred that. Sure, it would be nice to have your own Nicktoon, but only having to make a handful of five-minute cartoons in a year is much less taxing, and not all artists are in it for the money. In fact, several cartoons on the show were one offs. Whether that was because the creator had made only one short with intent or Nick was not interested in more I do not know. I do know that there were several sketches that were regulars throughout the years, and even a couple that ended up becoming shows of their own.

There were only three cartoons from *KaBlam!* I remembered distinctly. Two of them were regulars that aired in almost every single episode through all four seasons. The other I was stunned to find only aired twice. It must have made a huge impact on me. No, it wasn't in a positive way. That show is *Angela Anaconda*. The premise is simple enough. It's just about a girl, Angela, who is an outcast and somewhat awkward. I just could not stand the way it looked. I have strong feelings about animation aesthetics. There are shows I enjoy almost entirely because of how they look and shows that I simply cannot bear to watch because of the style. *Angela Anaconda* is one of the latter. It was made through animating cutout photos and literally I could not tolerate it as a kid. I genuinely remember turning the show off as quickly as possible when I first saw it, and swiftly turning the show off when I heard the name *Angela Anaconda* in reruns of *KaBlam!* It would not be unfair to say I lived in dread of accidentally seeing *Angela Anaconda*'s viscerally displeasing visual style. You know those people who can't, like, look at a fruit cut in half with all the seeds in all the holes? I don't want to look up what it's called because I have a tinge of that sometimes. I had that kind of reaction to *Angela Anaconda*.

Apparently this was a rare reaction, because *Angela Anaconda* is one of two shows that aired on *KaBlam!* and ended up being turned into their own shows. The series version was produced in Canada and aired on the Fox Family Channel in the United States, making the move away from Nickelodeon. *Angela Anaconda* aired for three seasons and 65 episodes, of which I watched zero. Still, it speaks to the value of a show like *KaBlam!* It gave Joanna Ferrone and Sue Rose, the creators of *Angela Anaconda*, a showcase for their work and then they were able to turn their shorts into a whole show thanks to Canada's love of cheap animation.

The other show that got spun off from *KaBlam!* also happened to be my favorite of all the segments. This is not going to be an unpopular opinion either. I'm talking about *Action League Now!*, which was basically the centerpiece of *KaBlam!* It's the only show to be a part of every single episode and was almost assuredly the most popular. It was definitely the best of the bunch to me. The premise is already pretty great. The Action League is a quartet of superheroes, but those superheroes are all well-used, off-brand action figures. There's Thunder Girl, who flies like thunder. She's just some generic superhero, the kind of toy your grandmother bought you to save a few bucks. The Flesh is super strong and super naked. Like many a doll or action figure, The Flesh's clothes he surely originally came with have been lost to history. Stinky Diver is a toy diver, but being a child's toy he has spent a lot of time diving in the toilet. Then, there's Meltman, with the power to melt. He's the poor toy that has been treated like garbage and misused by some kid. Shout out to the Stretch Armstrong that got his arms ripped off by me when I was a child because I wanted to know what was inside.

Action League Now! is not a cartoon, but is instead live-action animation. The style was called "Chuckamation," which is basically low-fi stop-motion animation. Instead of intricate movements, the characters move in herky jerky ways. Sometimes they are clearly just being thrown from off camera. Their mouths don't move at all. Their faces don't move at all. It's so bare bones, but that just adds to the charm. It's just funny to watch this in action, a brilliant mix of ambition and a clear lack of ambition at the same time. This was also the most comedic of the shows on *KaBlam!* While other creators were more interested in showing off their animation and their original visions, the people behind *Action League Now!* were comedy writers first and foremost, and it made for a regularly entertaining little short every time around. Eventually *Action League Now!* was turned into its own thing, but the episodes were just the shorts packaged together into episodes. Still, it qualifies as a show spun off from *KaBlam!* and the greatest success Nickelodeon had from the *KaBlam!* universe.

The other shorts I remembered are the *Prometheus and Bob* ones, which were more traditional stop-motion animation. They told the story of a super intelligent alien, Prometheus, and a caveman, Bob, with Prometheus trying to teach Bob basic things. In short, Prometheus is trying to speed up human evolution in a way, but Bob is just too dumb to catch on. It's all very slapstick, given that neither of them speaks English. These were always fine, and I never minded when *Prometheus and Bob* popped on. They are still utterly fine to me. I'm not a diehard stop-motion animation or Claymation person, but if I was I bet I would love it.

Among the other shorts, which I had to refamiliarize myself with, there were some regulars. *Sniz and Fondue* was about two ferrets getting into adventures. Once I checked this one out again it started to come back to me. I thought it was fine as a kid, if I recall correctly. To me, it feels like it's doing a *Ren & Stimpy* style thing, in that it is subverting old-school mismatched animal cartoons, but with less of a fetishization of the grotesque. *Life with Loopy* is another one whose look I can't stand. The characters are puppets with metal heads and magnetic features. *The Off-Beats* is notable because it actually predated *KaBlam!* on Nickelodeon. These shorts started airing during commercial breaks on Nick to promote *KaBlam!*, so they must have thought highly of it. While Nick must have thought highly of *The Off-Beats*, it only aired in the first two seasons of *KaBlam!*, because creator Mo Willems made the move to the rival Cartoon Network.

Of the many one-off cartoons that aired on *KaBlam!*, the one that sticks out to me most is *The Girl with Her Head Coming Off*, though that's mostly due to the title. I was afraid about searching that one online, not knowing what would come up if I searched for "the girl with her head coming off." Everything turned out all right in the end. One of the one timers, *Untalkative Bunny*, actually became a show in the 2000s as well. Like I said, though, part of *KaBlam!*'s role on Nick was to allow them to show other styles of animation and let avant-garde animators stretch their legs. There's a reason why it was the first animated show created for SNICK, and it even ended up with a Y7 rating.

Live-action sketch shows are hit-or-miss. That's also true of animated sketch shows. In fact, it's even truer. After all, these animators weren't part of a staff or a cast. *Saturday Night Live* has the same writers and cast week in and week out. Also, it's not like suddenly one sketch is going to be in black and white, or one sketch is going to be filmed entirely differently. Well, that does happen occasionally, but the look from sketch to sketch doesn't change as much as with animation. If a short was not up your alley, it could be a massive miss. You know, like *Angela Anaconda* for me. You could get whiplash watching *KaBlam!* However, I'm glad that *KaBlam!* existed. It introduced kids to more experimental animation (even if most of it wasn't any good). It showcased a lot of clever and interesting creators. Most important to me, then and now, it gave *Action League Now!* a home. There are shorts from *KaBlam!* that I would happily watch as full shows and shorts I wish had never seen the light of day. Also, I don't know if I made enough of a deal of the fact a sasquatch canonically worked on *KaBlam!* That's as strange as anything else the show ended up doing.

Kenan and Kel

*Never underestimate the power of
friendship ... or orange soda*

Saturday Night Live exists as a sketch show, but in a way it exists just
as much as a source of talent for the entertainment industry. Since the very
beginning that's been the story of *SNL*. Unknown actors and comedians
show up on *Saturday Night Live* and a few years later they are either TV or
movie stars. Chevy Chase left after the first season to become a movie star
and then, later, a guy with a personality so toxic nobody wanted to deal
with him. Adam Sandler got his start on *Saturday Night Live*. So did Will
Ferrell, Kristen Wiig, and many more. Hell, even lesser sketch shows, such
as *MAD TV*, gave us people like Keegan-Michael Key and Jordan Peele.
Nickelodeon had a sketch show of its own in the '90s that was quite popular, namely *All That*. It didn't quite serve as the jumping off point for future
stars it could have, but it did leads to two notable spinoffs. One was *The
Amanda Show*, a sketch show designed to showcase the precocious Amanda
Bynes. Then, there was the sitcom built around the two biggest standouts
from the earliest days of *All That*. Watching that show, you could see the
potential in Kenan Thompson and Kel Mitchell, and so it was fitting they
were given their own sitcom that was built off their personalities and popularity. I mean, why else call it simply *Kenan and Kel*?

The show was created by Kim Bass, who had written on *In Living
Color* and created another sitcom based around kids, *Sister, Sister*, starring
Tia and Tamara Mowry. However, how much work Bass contributed to
the show beyond its creation is unclear to me. Bass co-wrote the pilot with
Dan Schneider, the now-disgraced Nickelodeon legend who had served as
the original head writer of *All That*. Schneider served as the co-executive
producer of the first two seasons, before Kevin Kopelow and Heath Seifert, writing partners who were also writers and producers on *All That*,
took over as co-executive producers on seasons three and four. Schneider,
Kopelow, and Seifert wrote a ton of the episodes as well. I'm not diminishing the role Bass played in the creation of *Kenan and Kel*, and for all I
know his work beyond the scenes in ways not directly credited on screen
was vital. It just ultimately feels like *Kenan and Kel* was more of an exten-
sion of the *All That* creative crew, which makes sense given that the two

stars came from that show as well. Hey, Matt Groening gets credit for creating *The Simpsons* and he only has solo writing credit on one episode and hasn't been running the show since the second season, and even then he shared that role.

You aren't here for me to parse behind-the-scenes credit for *Kenan and Kel*, though. When you were a child in the '90s, you likely barely thought about that sort of stuff. You just want me to talk about orange soda and who may or may not have dropped the screw in the tuna. *Kenan and Kel* is about two high school friends living in Chicago. Thompson plays Kenan Rockmore and Kel plays Kel Kimble, swapping out their own last names for fictional ones to make them more like characters. Bob Newhart played Bob Hartley in *The Bob Newhart Show* and Mary Tyler Moore played Mary Richards on *The Mary Tyler Moore Show*, so that's more than fair. Although, it would have been kind of fun if Thompson's character had been named Kel and vice versa. That would have probably gone over the heads of kids, though.

Kenan's got a classic sitcom family, namely a stern dad named Roger, a loving and patient mother named Sheryl, and a mischievous younger sister named Kyra who has a crush on Kel. As for Kel, well, his family is irrelevant. Kel exists on this show as a pure agent of chaos. What are his origins? We don't know. There is something fantastical about his character in a way. He's an extreme oddball, while Kenan serves as his straight man. It's the dynamic that they both showcased on *All That* and served as the heart of the film *Good Burger* as well. Kenan was the brains of the operation, always with a scheme or a plan up his sleeve. Kel is happy to go along for the ride, though he's also likely to screw it up either due to a lack of intelligence, or perhaps more a lack of awareness. It is noted during the series that Kel does well in school, better than Kenan even, making him more of a social oddball than a classic sitcom dumb guy. Kel almost feels like he has more in common with characters like Jeannie from *I Dream of Jeannie* or ALF from, well, *ALF*. He's not supernatural or otherworldly, but his character is so much a collection of tics, quirks, and bizarre behavior he barely feels moored to our reality. However, he's just restrained enough for the show to not completely lose the plot and seem entirely insane.

Most of the action, at least in my memory, takes place at Rigby's, the store where Kel works. It's called a grocery store, but it feels more like a bodega. That may be more because of the fact the set is relatively small. This was a multi-cam sitcom, after all. Maybe we were supposed to imagine more store beyond what we could see, but what we saw was very much like a bodega, or a liquor store without the liquor. Kel is hanging out there all the time, even though he doesn't work there. He mostly just screws things up or annoys Kenan and the store's owner Chris. Chris was played by Dan

Frischman, who was previously best known for playing Arvid, the most stereotypical "nerd" on *Head of the Class*. You may recall that '80s sitcom from
the *All That* chapter, as it was the show where Schneider and Brian Robbins met as actors. They would eventually join forces to create *All That*, and
they were both producers on *Kenan and Kel*. Clearly, they were giving an
old friend of theirs a shot, and it's not like Frischman didn't have experience doing multi-cam sitcoms. It's also worth noting that when Frischman
started on *Head of the Class* he was already 27. Kenan and Kel were much
more age appropriate as high school actors.

At its core, *Kenan and Kel* was a very traditional and classic multi-cam
sitcom. The show was built around a mismatched pair of friends who
brought different personality elements to any storylines. There were only a
few regular sets we saw. Each week there would be a new adventure, things
would go awry, and in the end everything would go relatively back to normal. The only difference is that I don't know any other sitcom characters
with Kel's undying love of orange soda. If anything sticks out from this
show, it's Kel's defining trait of loving orange soda, and even dedicating a
song to it. Who loves orange soda? In short, Kel loves orange soda, and it is
indeed true. He does, he does, he duh-uuuuus. In terms of sitcom quirks,
there are ones that are way worse. It's distinct and odd, which is fitting for
the character, but doesn't go over the top.

I remember liking *Kenan and Kel* quite a bit as a kid, but there are a
lot of shows I enjoyed as a kid that do not hold up now. I figured *Kenan and
Kel* would fall into that to some degree. It was a multi-cam on a network
for children, after all. And yet, *Kenan and Kel* was unexpectedly enjoyable.
Take, for example, "The Tainting of the Screw," the first episode after the
pilot. It's one of the most-memorable episodes, mostly for the courtroom
scene at the end where Kel loses it on the witness stand. Kenan chokes on a
screw in a tuna sandwich and sues Luna Tuna over it, not knowing Kel had
dropped the screw in the tuna. On the stand, Kel completely freaks out,
repeatedly and hysterically exclaiming, "I dropped the screw in the tuna."
He flips out, climbs into the judge's box and does a ton of physical comedy. It's broad, but I was genuinely laughing. Mitchell's performance in that
scene is so strong, but Thompson does a good job as well. Watching other
episodes, and many an online clip, I was impressed with the relative quality of this show.

It would be a stretch to say that Thompson and Mitchell were "good"
actors, at least in the first couple seasons. However, they are perfectly capable, and for teenagers that's nothing to sneeze at. They have comedic timing, even though they can play up to their sketch sensibilities and go overly
big at times. That's especially true for Mitchell, but that's also how his character was written. Mitchell is supposed to go insane and do all sorts of big,

goofy physical comedy. He had a skill for that, and Thompson makes a solid straight man. However, he can also be funny within that role. The adult actors on the show, including Frischman, are also capable. I was impressed with the quality of the writing, as there are many good, hard jokes in the scripts, and the delivery of these jokes amp up the humor. Sometime the plots are a little cheesy or broad. In one episode the President of the United States stops into Rigby's for inexplicable reasons. I'm not sure if he's supposed to actually be Bill Clinton or merely a Bill Clinton type. All I know is that the guy playing him is doing a bad Clinton impression. He goes to grab a can of orange soda off an unstable stack job and Kenan "saves his life" by tackling him before the cans fall on him. The problem is that the cans are all clearly empty in real life and they don't come close to falling on "Bill." It's a bit much for a plot, and also the execution in the directing really failed the show there.

Nevertheless, *Kenan and Kel* holds up to a high degree. It reminds me of many an old-school sitcom that is pretty good and fun enough to watch when you come across it. I'm not surprised that Thompson has gone on to success in comedy as an adult, though he did return to his sketch roots and become the longest-serving cast member of *Saturday Night Live*. Mitchell's career hasn't gone as well, though in recent years he's been appearing more and returned to Nickelodeon, the channel that made him famous. At least the legacy of *Kenan and Kel* holds up and will keep Mitchell in the minds of '90s kids forever. He's a star to us. It's not like I watch Thompson on *Saturday Night Live* these days anyway. I'd much rather watch an old episode of *Kenan and Kel*. And, of course, it's worth noting that it was a sitcom built around two black stars—and a predominantly black cast—which was not a thing Nickelodeon had done before, and was barely happening on TV in the '90s in general.

Kenan and Kel aired from August of 1996 through July of 2000, ending with a made-for-TV movie that is also technically considered three episodes of the show, giving it 65 episodes total. That movie (slash collection of episodes) was called "Two Heads Are Better Than None" and featured the final acting role of Milton Berle. I don't remember seeing it, probably because by 2000 I was done watching Nickelodeon. I kind of want to see it now and may try to track it down. It's on YouTube, but I'd like to try and find a better, more legitimate version if possible. *Kenan and Kel* will also always have a place in my memory because when I went to Nickelodeon Studios down in Orlando I saw them rehearsing an episode of the show. It was the episode "Clowning Around," the second episode of the second season. A clown robs Rigby's and cause Kenan and Kel to develop a fear of clowns. The only scene I got to see was the clown robbing the store. That was enough for me. I got to be part of the television creation process in some small, insignificant way. Kenan Thompson and Kel Mitchell got to star in their own sitcom for several years and make an indelible mark on an entire generation. I'd drink an orange soda in their honor, but gave up on drinking soda many years ago. Unlike Nickelodeon, I left that in my childhood.

Nick in the Afternoon AKA
Long Live Stick Stickly

One of the ZIP codes of New York City is 10108

In the summer, when I wasn't out playing street hockey or what have you during the day, my TV was glued to Nickelodeon. To be fair, that was true when I was home during the spring, fall, and winter. Summers, though, were special on Nickelodeon. That is, they were special from 1995 through 1998. During this time, the channel ran a programming block they called Nick in the Afternoon. To me, and many others, it was known as the Stick Stickly block. Of all the personalities affiliated with Nick, one of the ones that sticks out to be most is, well, a popsicle stick. To borrow the parlance of a different era, we stan a wooden king.

Nick in the Afternoon started off as just a branding of their regular-schedule programming airing during the summer. The only difference was that Stick Stickly was the host, introducing the shows and talking to the audience. Stick Stickly was a popsicle stick, seemingly never truly encased in a popsicle, with googly eyes (red in color), a yellow jelly bean nose, and a little black mouth. He was supremely simple, but distinct. Stick Stickly was a puppet without arms or legs or a mouth that moved. He was voiced by Paul Christie, who did a falsetto voice akin, but legally distinct from, Mr. Bill. Christie's New York accent comes through in Stick's voice. Indeed, Stick Stickly had some Mr. Bill to his personality, and lot in life, but he had the added charm of being a little popsicle stick person. You knew what would be airing, and could plan accordingly, but Stick Stickly would be around to make things a little extra fun. That stick had some personality to him.

After the first summer, though, Nick in the Afternoon changed. Now, the whole day of programming was up in the air. While there were still shows that had been selected by the network to air, you didn't know what would air when. You found out what was airing by Stick Stickly being used as the pointer on a spinner, with different shows on different segments of the spinner. This was fun in concept and also kept you on your toes. When a show you dug that you didn't get to see very often was airing it was extra exciting. I knew sometimes the spinner would throw a curveball and I'd get psyched. There was also "U–Pick," which was when viewers got to pick the show, and the episode, that aired. I don't know how much legitimacy this had. It's kind of how like *Total Request Live* would tweak the voting results on occasion. Still, we felt involved, especially as kids. The U–Pick also gave Nick a chance to show something totally unexpected. Shows long out of reruns, such as *You Can't Do That on Television*, would air. They would also show Nick at Nite shows, but obviously always the ones that traditional appealed to kids, like *The Munsters*. We weren't getting any episodes of, say, *The Bob Newhart Show*. Unfortunately, from my perspective. I'll get into that more in the Nick at Nite chapter.

I'd get excited when the spinner would give me a traditional Nick show I enjoyed, like *Rocko's Modern Life*, but Nick in the Afternoon was responsible for my brief fascination with *Batfink*. While most of the shows on Nick in the Afternoon were Nick originals, they would also occasionally include *Batfink*, a supremely cheap Hal Seeger cartoon for the '60s. The episodes were only like five minutes long and the animation was done as cheaply as possible. Batfink was something of a parody of Batman, or at least he was inspired by Batman. He was an anthropomorphic bat superhero with metal wings. In fact, his wings were a veritable shield of steel, which I think he said in every episode. He also used supersonic sonar radar in his superhero activities. His sidekick was named Karate, a parody of *Green Hornet's* Kato. Karate was dumb and drove Batfink's car, the Battillac. If you're wondering if he was a problematic character, he is. Although, the white guy who did Karate's voice eventually stopped doing an Asian-style voice and starting doing a Don Adams parody. Since the animation was so bad at that point Karate could probably pass for not being Asian.

Like Batman, Batfink had a rogue's gallery, though his own personal Joker was a mad scientist named Hugo A-Go-Go. There were also villains like Manhole Manny, Greasy Gus, and Professor Hopper, who has trained fleas to commit crimes. It was not a good show. I did not think it was at the time. However, I was always rooting for *Batfink* to air on Nick in the Afternoon. I can't quite put my finger on it, but it delighted me to no end to see it on Nick. I think it was the fact it was a random '60s cartoon I had never heard of before. Also it helped that it's so cheesy and goofy. While I didn't enjoy the show traditionally, and I wasn't necessarily laughing at it either, I just liked knowing that it aired on Nick and kids were seeing *Batfink*.

However, I have ulterior motives for wanting to talk about *Batfink*. Evidently a political message was hidden in two episodes of the show. While it sounded like gibberish on the show, when slowed down the secret message, split across the episodes "Spin the Batfink" and "Bride and Doom," was as follows: "The most dangerous force in America today is Walter Reuther and his political machine. It's time we realized that they intend to run this country. When the smut publishers put a dirty cover on a clean book, let's take it at face value and call it trash and dump it in the river." As a native of Detroit, I am quite familiar with Reuther. He was President of the United Auto Workers union from 1946 until 1970. Reuther was considered progressive politically and was even considered for vice president by John F. Kennedy. Both Barry Goldwater and George Romney called Reuther one of the most dangerous men in America, so you know he was doing something right. After surviving two assassination attempts Reuther died in a plane crash at the age of 62. Coretta Scott King spoke at his funeral. The I-696, one of the vital highways in the Detroit area, is named the Walter Reuther Freeway. Anyway, it's incredibly funny to me some lunatic snuck a secret message slagging him off into *Batfink* of all shows.

The other big segment of Nick in the Afternoon was "U–Dip," which I always thought of as "Dip Stick" due to the theme song. This was where a viewer would suggest a substance, or mixture, for Stick Stickly to be dipped into (blindfolded, of course) so that he could guess what he was being dipped in. It was often something that would be gross, and Stick would be grossed out by what he was feeling. Sometimes it might be mayonnaise or mustard or something else you'd put on a hot dog. Occasionally things would be mixed. I don't remember specifically shampoo and cranberry juice being used, but that's an example of the kind of weird, apropos of nothing mixture that Stick might be dipped in. Literally one time he was dipped in popcorn and strawberry sauce mixed together. Also, Jonathan Taylor Thomas suggested he be dipped in yogurt.

On the one hand, the whole point of these segments on other shows is seeing a person experience something weird or gross. If a person steps in yogurt you can laugh at their experience as a human being standing in yogurt. Stick, of course, is a stick. He has no physical sensation. He's not actually sentient. That makes this whole thing almost avant-garde. The joke is that we know this is all fabricated and Stick feels nothing. It's funny because it's so pointless. I was always delighted when it was time to dip Stick. The theme song also ruled.

Speaking of songs, or rather jingles, if you watched Nick in the Afternoon even once I'm sure that Stick's iconic jingle is forever burnt into your brain. Stick would ask you to write to him, and because of his song I will never forget the address P.O. Box 963, New York City, New York State, 10108. This will be with me on my deathbed. Stick's run was pretty much perfectly aligned with my childhood. He was on the show from 1995 through 1998, the summer before I went to junior high school and wouldn't really want to be watching Nickelodeon anymore. It wasn't cool enough for a junior high school student. I know now as an adult that was false. Stick Stickly rules. He was a great host. He was a sport. How many other hosts let themselves be dipped in guacamole for my amusement? I would rather watch a talk show hosted by Stick than any man named Jim, Jimmy, or James. Nick in the Afternoon was a great block of television for a kid, and a big reason for that was a charming little popsicle stick with a jelly bean for a nose.

Legends of the Hidden Temple

*Teamwork makes the dream work ... until
you run into a silver monkey*

Welcome to the jungle. Or, at least, to a poor approximation of a jungle built in a studio in Orlando, Florida. Not that I am going to knock *Legends of the Hidden Temple* much. This game show ran for three seasons and 120 episodes, debuting in September of 1993 and running until November of 1995. Of all the Nickelodeon game shows, it's probably my favorite, both now and then. I feel like it was the game show I wanted to be on the most as well, though I wanted to be on pretty much every game show for kids. Of course, now I want to be on pretty much every game show for adults. I've had the chance to audition for *Jeopardy!* twice, but have not been on the show. I did tell a producer during the interview that I won Most Desirable Male at the 1994 *MTV Movie Awards*, and then told him that I had briefly confused my life with William Baldwin's. He did not seem to realize the first part of that statement was a joke. Sadly, I was not in *Sliver*, but they can feel free to call me for a reboot.

Legends of the Hidden Temple was a busy game show, in that it requires brains and athleticism and had a few different parts to it. Interestingly, the original premise was going to involve monsters in a haunted house, but that was exchanged for the milieu we are familiar with, which is an approximation of ancient ruins that mixed together different American civilizations with made up stuff. This aspect of the show maybe doesn't hold up great. The titular hidden temple is purported to be Mayan ruins, but the show's star—no offense, Kirk Fogg—is a talking Olmec head. Those are different civilizations. Also, the temple guards were presumably played by dudes who just graduated from Florida State and needed a little cash from an acting gig. There's a bit of squeamishness to that element of pantomimed culture, but *Legends of the Hidden Temple* isn't a major offender, especially by '90s standards.

As I mentioned earlier, Kirk Fogg was the human host. He had a decent energy to him, and he knew how to rock a denim shirt and khaki shorts. This whole show was big for the khaki shorts industry, an industry that I personally have nothing but contempt for. Fogg did the actual hosting, the explanation of tasks, the interacting with the kids. He was joined by Olmec, who was a giant stone head. Evidently he was a cheap creation. Mostly he was just a statue, but with a rubber bottom lip attached to a two-by-four. Dee Bradley Baker, who voiced Olmec, would stand there with a microphone and move the lip while he talked. Baker, by the way, has gone on to an extensive voiceover career. He also apparently excels at doing animal sounds which is good, because Frank Welker won't live forever.

Olmec was the keeper of the knowledge and the lore. Every episode had an artifact at its center, though they weren't real artifacts by and large. They would be something like Ben Franklin's electrified key or Catherine De Medici's golden pepperoni. These treasures were always somewhere in the temple, which raises questions about how this civilization had such a vast array of treasures. Maybe they had a working relationship with Carmen Sandiego? After this treasure, and the prizes for the actual game show, were six teams. They were the Red Jaguars, the Blue Barracudas, the Green Monkeys, the Purple Parrots, the Orange Iguanas, and the Silver Snakes. Yes, I've been able to rattle those off the top of my head for years. Why do you ask?

Each team had shirts to designate who they were, and those shirts were awesome. In fact, *Legends of the Hidden Temple* had a great aesthetic overall. The show had a fun look, and it was totally distinct in that it took place in a "world," even if the production didn't seem to be flush with cash. Compare it to, say, the big blue void of *Double Dare*. I'll take *Legends of the Hidden Temple* any day of the week, especially those shirts. It would be worth it to be on that show just to get one of those shirts. Especially the Orange Iguanas shirt, which was my personal favorite as a kid.

Each team was comprised of two kids, one boy and one girl. They were between 11 and 14 years old, and evidently were basically just kids from around Orlando. Who's traveling to be on a game show like this, I suppose? The first round was the moat, where all six teams had to race to get across a body of water. There were different ways it was done. Sometimes by pulling a raft. Sometimes they had to swing on ropes. The water was apparently quite shallow, so being able to swim was not a necessity. The first four teams across went on to the next round, which means two teams saw their day end after, like, two minutes. Bummer.

Next was the Steps of Knowledge, which was Olmec's time to shine. He would tell a little story about the artifact of the week which was pure nonsense. This was not an educational show. I didn't realize when the show debuted how much of it was just straight-up made up, but by the time it ended I had grown up enough to realize it was heavy on the creative license. The kids had to listen and remember what Olmec was talking about, because they were asked questions about his story. To answer, you had to stomp on your step to ring in, which kids would screw up on occasion. When you were right, you moved down a step. The first two teams to answer three questions won. Yes, this was the least-interesting part of every episode, and I was a brainy kid who liked to read and stuff. When you jam it in the middle of a bunch of action and stunts, though, it feels like it drags.

Thus began the Temple Games. These were three contests in every episode. Each member of a team would have a solo challenge for half a pendant of life, and then the teammates would compete together for a full pendant in the final game. I will explain pendants of life more momentarily for those of you who aren't fully on board yet, but since you bought a book about '90s Nickelodeon I'm betting you are. For whatever reason, the primary memory I have of these games involve kids trying to climb up slippery surfaces. I feel like a lot of Velcro balls were also thrown at targets. If a tiebreaker was needed, they would ask a question, but in my memory that happened infrequently. The winning team would then move on to the highlight of the episode, the Temple Run.

The temple was a pretty sizable obstacle course consisting of 12 rooms that would rotate. Within the temple was the artifact that needed to be collected. Some doors would be locked, which partially chose the path for the kids. To get out of a room you had to complete a task. Some of them were physical, like either swinging across a chasm (or failing to do that and then plummeting into a pile of foam and having to crawl across the room to get out). Others were puzzle based. I had my favorites. You have your favorites. Personally I liked the rooms like The Pit of Despair and The Mine Shaft.

Standing in your way of getting the artifact were the temple guards. They hid in certain rooms and would jump out to startle the kids and grab them. If you had a pendant of life, you could give it to the guard and continue. If you didn't, you were booted from the temple and your teammate entered. If they didn't have a pendant and got caught, the game was over. Basically, you really wanted two full pendants, which meant either crushing the Temple Games or picking up the extra piece in the temple itself. Once you grabbed the artifact, all the rooms unlocked and it was a race to get out of the temple before time ran out. Teams got a small prize for making it to the temple, they got a bigger prize for getting the artifact, and got the grand prize if they made it out in time. Considering that this was Nick in the '90s, it probably meant going to Space Camp.

This was just so much fun to watch as a kid. I was always curious what rooms we would get to see and how well the contestants handled them. Where would the guards be? How freaked would the kids be when the guards jumped out? Would they crush the obstacles? Or would they completely screw it up and keep themselves from getting that sweet, sweet Space Camp trip? It was fun to see the rooms in action, and to see the teams race against the clock. For a game show for children, it was an engaging watch. There was true complexity to it, and a lot of fun to be had, even just watching. Would have been a lot more fun to actually run the course, though.

Speaking of screwing it up, even broaching the subject makes me a basic '90s kid, but it must be done. I must discuss the Shrine of the Silver Monkey. It is the room that stands out in people's minds. You never hear people talk about, say, the Viper's Nest. I have heard so much talk about the Shrine of the Silver Monkey and had multiple conversations about it. It seemed simple enough on the surface, which is partially why it has become such a topic of conversation and controversy. A silver monkey statue was broken into three pieces. You had to put them on its pedestal and get them all in place. Once you did, the door would unlock. No room was screwed up more by contestants on *Legends of the Hidden Temple* than the Shrine of the Silver Monkey. They made a TV movie in 2016 about the show, with the premise that the temple was real. This included a Shrine of the Silver Monkey, and the entire bit in the movie is that the kids think it will be easy but it takes them forever to do it right.

And yet I share the frustration with my fellow *Hidden Temple* aficionados when it comes to this task. It shouldn't be that hard! There were two primary problems. Either kids could not figure out which way the middle portion was supposed to go or they didn't get the head on straight. Of course, that's the classic rub of game shows. It seems so easy at home when the pressure and stakes are low. Let's see you sweat it out in the Shrine after getting jumped by a temple guard with a ticking clock.

Games shows based on physical challenges were big on Nickelodeon. *Legends of the Hidden Temple* had the added quality of doing a bit of world building. Sure, that involved a tinge of cultural thievery and a cheap fake Olmec head. This show was just so enjoyable as a kid. I can't enjoy it as much now. The challenges are less impressive to me as an adult and the seams show a bit more. Why not just watch game shows for adults instead? You're never that far from a *Match Game* rerun being on TV, after all. Still, there will always be a place in our hearts for Fogg, Olmec, and those dope t-shirts. Plus, now as adults we can haughtily claim that we would have nailed the Shrine of the Silver Monkey and nobody can call us on it.

Make the Grade

You should have paid attention in school.
And apparently watched the Little Rascals

I enjoy watching *Jeopardy!* because it is designed to be able to play along at home. There's very little filler to it. The show is all about answering trivia questions, and they are tough enough to challenge you even if you are a trivia fan such as myself. The contestant picks a question, Alex Trebek asks it, watching along at home you can read it and think of your answer before they get to the contestants, somebody answers, we see the result, and the next question is asked. Downtime is kept to a minimum. The half hour breezes by, and if you had a strong day in term of your answers you end up feeling good. There is beauty in the simplicity of *Jeopardy! Make the Grade* is the closest Nickelodeon has ever come to having their own version of *Jeopardy!*, but it's far less beautiful, and definitely less simple.

While many a Nick game show has had a trivia element, none go as far down that path as *Make the Grade*, which debuted in 1989 and lasted for three seasons and 160 episodes. Given that it aired five days a week, though, that means it just tipped into the '90s, and was even out of reruns by the end of 1991. There is no other chapter in this book where I feel more daunted about explaining the premise. Getting through all the lore of *100 Deeds for Eddie McDowd*, wherein Richard Moll turns a teenage bully into a dog and also makes the boy's parents disappear until he can do 100 good deeds (as a dog) was easier than explaining all the business that goes into an episode of *Make the Grade*.

Three contestants sit at different color-coordinated desks, one red, one blue, one green. Maybe the episodes I watched just had short kids, but they all seemed dwarfed by the desks they were sitting at. They were all like that Lily Tomlin character who sits in the giant rocking chair, but funnier. No, they aren't trying to be funny but being funnier than Edith Ann (I looked the name of the character up because I'm a professional) is about the easiest thing you can do. It's definitely easier than some of the questions these kids get asked. In front of the kids are 14 different icons, and to explain those I need to talk about the board.

The game board for *Make the Grade* is a 7 × 7 collection of squares making up a grid. Going down the left-hand side vertically are the subjects for the day. Those subjects are usually things you would find in school, such as math, geography, science, etc. In the second season the seventh subject would be a "special elective," which allowed them to throw a curveball. In one episode I watched, the elective category was *Little Rascals*. You know, those short films from the '30s with Alfalfa and Buckwheat? This was 1990, mind you. We were years away from the *Little Rascals* reboot movie that came out and bored us '90s kids to tears. Going horizontally along the top of the board were the "grade levels" for each question. There was an elementary level, and then grades seven through 12 were also represented. When it was a kid's turn, they would choose a subject and grade level. If a kid answered a question right, their color would appear on the square. If nobody got it right, a black square would appear in the spot.

That's how most of the squares went, but there were also wild card squares. A free square is what you are imagining. You just got that square. If a take square showed up, you could take somebody else's square. A lose square cost you a square. Lastly was the fire drill square. Because this was Nickelodeon, they still had to have a physical challenge element to their game shows. The fire drills all seemed space based, as far as I can tell. They would be simple enough. You'd play ring toss or mini golf or operate a claw machine. If you won the fire drill, you could choose which desk you would take. That means if you had been losing and some other kid was killing it, you can take their desk and get all their squares. The player in second would get second choice, and third place would be left with the remaining desk. What this has to do with a fire drill I don't know. It seems to have more in common with a certain kind of "fire drill" I will not name explicitly, and that definitely sits awkwardly with me. To win, you had to get one question right in each difficulty level and each subject. Or, if time didn't allow that, you just had to have the most squares of the three kids. If you won, you got 500 bucks and would be off to the "Honors Round." Now, to me, getting 500 dollars in 1989 or 1990 as a kid sounds incredible. Maybe it's the adult in me who isn't interested in a new bike or Space Camp but would love some straight cash in my pocket.

For the Honors Round, you picked one of three categories, and then you have seven questions to answer, one from each of that day's subjects. You had 45 seconds to answer as many questions as possible. In the first season there were only seven questions and you could only answer each question once. For the second and third seasons you could get a question wrong or pass and then you could go back to that subject and answer a new question if time permitted. I think that is a better way to go, personally. In all seasons you got $100 for your first six correct answers. Meanwhile, in the first season getting all seven right meant you won $1,000 while in the later seasons it meant a trip to Universal Studios in Orlando, Florida. Ah, that's more like the Nick I know and love.

Honestly, trying to parse the game was a little trickier than a lot of the questions. Doesn't that sound overly complicated? It is! The board is super busy. They didn't make things easy on themselves, the viewers, or the contestants. I can't imagine being a kid trying to watch this. As for the trivia questions, I like the level they went with. There wasn't a single question I didn't know the answer to as an adult (save for that *Little Rascals* category), but they weren't super easy. Although, the kids didn't always seem like the biggest trivia buffs. In one episode, I watched all three kids get stumped by the elementary math question, which was the fewest number of triangles needing to make a square. The answer is, of course, two. Also, one kid in the Honors Round said that Alfred Nobel invented the explosive product known as "plastic." Now I'm ragging on 11-year-old kids, so I'll cease this digression.

The first season of *Make the Grade* was shot in a little studio in New York without an audience. It looks so cheap. The set is basically empty and the canned audience sound is so artificial. This season was hosted by Lew Schneider, who wasn't great but also had little to work with. There was no audience to play off of, it was just him and three kids. Then, for the second season they moved the production down to the brand-new Nickelodeon Studios in Orlando. They had a studio audience now and a new host, so I presume Schneider didn't want to move from New York to Orlando. Instead, a guy named Robb Edward Morris took over as host. This was his first gig and, as far as I can tell, pretty much his only gig of note. According to his IMDb profile, he is "known for" the projects *Kill God* and *Road Killer*, though, as of this writing, those projects don't actually exist. Morris may have been a nice guy, and he seems friendly to the kids, but as a host he is a total zero. Not that he was given a lot to work with either. The first I saw of him on my screen he was taking a terribly-written joke and somehow making it worse with his delivery.

I wish, in hindsight, Nickelodeon had put together a strong trivia show for kids. Then again, I also can't imagine then trying that in the '90s. Everything had to have more pomp and circumstance to it. It's *Double Dare* that set the course for the future of Nick, not *Make the Grade*. To be fair, that may be in part because of the execution. Everything seems designed to make *Make the Grade* feel dull. The set, the hosts, the eerily quiet audience in the second and third seasons, it all drags on you. Again, I really enjoy playing trivia. This was not a difficult show for me to play along with— though no easier than *Celebrity Jeopardy!*—but it was not so easy I was not engaged in the game play at all. If you were a kid and didn't like playing trivia, there was zero reason to watch *Make the Grade*. They brought it back for Nick GAS in the 2000s, but I have no clue why. Much like *Little Rascals*, *Make the Grade* belongs a forgotten relic of the past.

Mr. Wizard's World

What's old can be new again

I said I was covering every show that aired original episode on Nickelodeon in the '90s, and I meant it. That includes a show like *Mr. Wizard's World* that stopped airing in 1990. It still counts, and 1990 was the end of a long journey for Mr. Wizard. Seriously, it's a long, long journey that goes back to the 1950s. You know, back when Marty McFly invented rock music.

Don Herbert was born in 1917 and aspired to be an actor after college. Then, World War II happened. Herbert enlisted in the army, and then joined the Air Force. He ended up flying the B-24 bomber and flew 56 combat missions during the war. When the war ended, Herbert was honorably discharged as a distinguished captain. What is a man to do when his life is disrupted by war and now has to basically start his life anew? He gets into children's programming, of course.

Hebert moved to Chicago, where he acted on the radio and had a role in the show *It's Your Life*, a documentary show about health for kids. This was in 1949, when television was a new medium. Herbert apparently saw the potential in the medium, because he came up with the idea for a show where he would teach science to kids through experiments that he thought would excite them and interest them. The character of Mr. Wizard was born, as portrayed by Herbert himself. This is 1951. Bear in mind this story ends in 1990.

Mr. Wizard was basically your friendly neighborhood scientist. He did experiments in his home and his door was seemingly always open. Each week, a kid from the neighborhood would show up at his house to see what Mr. Wizard was working on. Ah, the days when the idea of a kid randomly wandering into an adult's home wasn't considered disconcerting. Mr. Wizard always had a concept he was working on. He would show the kid his experiment, which would amaze the child, but then Mr. Wizard would explain that—in reality—the experiment was simple enough to do at home. More importantly, it was safe enough for actual kids to do at home with adult supervision. At least, it was safe by the standards of the '50s. Let's not forget that lawn darts used to be a popular toy. They used to literally sell at-home chemistry kits with radioactive material in them. However, Mr. Wizard had a noble goal. He wanted to teach kids science in a way

126

that would draw them in, but also be easy enough to understand. I mean, remember the first time you saw a volcano made of baking soda and vinegar? As an adult, that's something you do to unclog a drain. As a kid, that mixture is a wild experience bordering on magic.

Herbert's *Watch Mr. Wizard*, the name the show was given, proved quite popular. It swiftly moved from airing in Chicago to airing in 14 markets. In the early days of television, being in 14 major markets was huge. Thousands of kids were watching every week. Mr. Wizard became a beloved figure. By 1956, there were over 5,000 Mr. Wizard science clubs for kids across the country. There were books and science kits and other tie-in products. Herbert was a huge star in the early days of television. His work was recognized by adults as well. *Watch Mr. Wizard* won a Peabody in 1953.

In 1955, Herbert moved the show from Chicago to New York, and he kept chugging along. *Watch Mr. Wizard* aired until 1965. That's 14 years of early television, producing a staggering 547 episodes. What an incredible number of episodes, and what an incredible number of experiments. There had to be repeats, right? It's not like reruns were a thing back then. The kids of 1953 gave way to the kids of 1963. A new generation needed to see how balloons generate static electricity. The show was briefly brought back in the '70s as *Mr. Wizard*, with 26 episodes produced in Canada and airing on NBC in the United States. Herbert was in his fifties at this point. He could have easily hung up the beakers. Instead, Herbert persevered, thanks to the rise of cable television.

Once Nickelodeon became its own network, it needed programming. Herbert was champing at the bit to bring Mr. Wizard back to the world. A whole generation of kids had missed out. In 1983, *Mr. Wizard's World* debuted. The show was a bit less lackadaisical than the original version. It was the go-go '80s, after all. Between 1983 and 1990, Herbert made 78 more episodes of television, this time in color. By 1987, Herbert had turned 70, and yet he kept going for a few more years. In fact, he didn't even stop there. In 1994 he created 15-minute shorts called *Teacher to Teacher with Mr. Wizard* that highlighted elementary school science teachers. The man dedicated almost his entire life to teaching kids science. Herbert passed away in 2007, just before turning 90. His legacy was already established. Bill Nye, a guy with affinity for science, wrote in his obituary that Herbert changed the world. That doesn't qualify as hyperbole.

Indeed, Herbert has an incredible legacy. Mr. Wizard has been name-dropped in pop culture many times. How many people get a shout out in song from both Weird Al *and* Smashmouth? On *The Big Bang Theory*, Bob Newhart plays a character named "Professor Proton," a riff on Mr. Wizard. Both Bill Nye and the folks on *Beakman's World* gave Herbert love for paving the way for their shows. You can honest say that Herbert changed television. He also gave Nick programming at a time when it was still a fledging network. *Mr. Wizard's World* aired three times a week in the early days of Nick, and remained a part of the lineup for many years after. However, you had to be up at some odd hours to catch it. This is my personal relationship with Herbert.

Mr. Wizard's World aired in reruns on Nick at Nite until 1995, but usually as one of the last things on the air before Nick at Nite became Nickelodeon again in the morning. After that, it aired in reruns on Nick until 2000, but in the incredibly early hours of the morning. It was only aired as paired of the "Cable in the Classroom" project, which I go into greater detail on in the *Nickelodeon Launch Box* chapter. Nick did not expect kids to watch *Mr. Wizard's World* when it aired. It was on because something had to be on, and they had the rights to it. I only ever watched *Mr. Wizard's World* when I was up extremely early for some reason, usually for going on a family trip. Indeed, all my distinct memories of watching the show come from when we would get up early to drive down to Cedar Point—America's Roller Coast—for the day. Before I rode the Magnum and the Gemini I was checking out Mr. Wizard doing science experiments.

I liked seeing *Mr. Wizard's World* on those mornings, but mostly because of the novelty of it. It was the voracious TV junkie in me that was enjoying watching something I normally didn't get to see. The show was totally fine, and I was interested in science. However, it definitely felt like a show from a bygone era. I was watching an old man lacking what you might call a "TV personality" calmly doing science experiments. It may have been paced faster than *Watch Mr. Wizard*, but it was still slow by the standard of kids' programming in the '90s. Mr. Wizard was a throwback. He was from a different world of television. The man had been at the forefront of TV. He just refused to ever go anywhere.

What did that get him? In the end, airing at six in the morning to barely anybody. I didn't know anything about Herbert at the time. I didn't know I was watching a TV legend in action. He was just a nice-enough-seeming old man doing science experiments I could see in school. Mr. Wizard may have aired in the '90s, especially when it comes to reruns, but he was not of the '90s. He was tangential to our childhoods. I'm an adult now, though. My worldview is not what's in my immediate vicinity. I can look at Herbert's work in the big picture and feel tremendous respect for what he did. Mr. Wizard spent more time on television than anybody else from Nickelodeon's history. I bet he could have told me how those roller coasters I was riding at Cedar Point worked. He just never got the chance.

My Brother and Me

Some people are bad at their jobs

We learn many lessons in our childhoods. Sometimes it is less that we learn something new than we finally have the mental capacity to realize something that was in front of us the whole time. You know, like when you figured out that Santa wasn't real, or that your childhood pet probably isn't living on a farm upstate. Another thing that we learn is that some people are bad at acting, but they still get acting jobs anyway. I learned this from watching *My Brother and Me*.

Needless to say, I had seen bad acting before *My Brother and Me*. I had been watching Nickelodeon and other kids' shows for years. When *My Brother and Me* debuted in 1994, I had just turned eight. Suddenly, I was able to pick up things I hadn't been able to when I was younger. Like the fact some people, especially kids, are truly terrible actors. Not long after this, I started watching *Mystery Science Theater 3000*. That opened up a whole new world of bad acting and bad movies being fun. Unfortunately, there is nothing fun about how bad *My Brother and Me* is. It's just a lousy, boring show that, naturally I watched every episode of as a kid. What else was I going to do? It was on television!

There's not much of a premise to *My Brother and Me*. It's a show about the Parker family living in Charlotte. Naturally, the show focuses on the two brothers in the Parker family, Alfie and Dee Dee. Now, who was the "brother" and who was the "me" of the title? I always felt like Alfie was the ostensible main character, maybe because his best friend Goo showed up more often than Dee Dee's friends. Plus, Alfie was the older brother, and it felt like more stories were about him. Perhaps the title was supposed to be able to be read both ways. Also, why did Alfie and Dee Dee's sister Melanie get left out of the title? Sure, she was a secondary character, but she's part of the family! She's a Parker sibling!

The stories were about pretty basic stuff. Your typical family sitcom, but dumbed down for kids. Dee Dee got bullied, and it turned out the bully was a girl. Alfie tries out for the basketball team (coached by Dennis Scott!) and gets cut because he's a ball hog. Alfie won't play Robin Hood in the play because he doesn't want to wear tights, but then realizes tights are not, in fact, for girls. *My Brother and Me* leaned into imparting lessons quite a bit.

It was not from the *Seinfeld* school of "no hugging, no learning." There was lots of hugging and learning and overly simplistic lessons delivered with some of the most wooden performances I can recall.

It was notable that the Parker family was black, and that many of the secondary characters were black as well. It would have been nice for *My Brother and Me* to be a good show. Unfortunately, it wasn't. This show was boring to me as a kid, and it was apparent to me when I was only eight that it was a bad show. Not in the way where I didn't like it. For the first time I can recall, I could see that it was poorly made. These kids were such bad actors by and large. I explicitly remember Dee Dee's friends Harry and Donnell being awful. Granted, they were like eight years old, but they simply could not give a proper line reading to save their lives. The kids on this show would even move woodenly. Everybody who wasn't awkward was way over the top. That extends to the adults in the cast. The dad of the Parker family, Roger, definitely chewed the scenery. So did the kid who played Goo, but Goo was also the only memorable character on the show. He managed to stand out, but I am damning him with the faintest of praise here. Being the best character on *My Brother and Me* is akin to being the most-successful villain on *Scooby-Doo*.

There are few things I remember about this show beyond the bad acting and stale performances. If anybody took anything from *My Brother and Me* into their adult lives, it's probably "Goo Punch." In the basketball episode, Goo is dreaming of what will happen once he's a star on the middle school basketball team, and it's him shilling his own titular punch. I still remember the song, and it was, I must admit, mildly amusing. I also recall the dad being told by Melanie that what she was wearing was "fly," and Roger went on a long, purposefully (I think) unfunny riff about how if somebody had worn that in his day they would have been "swatted." This bit is driven into the ground. I also remember "Fuzzy Wuzzy," which was stupid then and is annoying now.

Shockingly, there were only 13 episodes ever made of *My Brother and Me*. I'm not being sarcastic. I genuinely was surprised to see that they only made 13 episodes. That short of a run was rare for Nickelodeon shows in the '90s. This show definitely looked cheaply made so it's not like they were spending a ton of cash on it. They hopefully had saved money by hiring bad actors. Nobody seemed to care about quality. And yet, kids still watched, because it was on the air. I watched reruns of *My Brother and Me!* That's the primary reason I felt like there had to be more episodes. This speaks to the experience of being a TV-loving kid in the '90s. Even though I didn't like *My Brother and Me*, even though I knew it was bad, I watched it repeatedly. It reminds me of when I watched *Simpsons* reruns every day until I was in my early twenties, because it was always on and that was what I usually did.

The routine didn't change. This is something the kids of today will never comprehend. They will never sit there and watch a lousy show like *My Brother and Me* simply because it was on. No eight year old today is going to watch a sitcom, realize that they could do a better job than the actors that were actually hired, and then keep watching the show anyway.

Not surprisingly, none of the actors from this show, especially the kid actors, went on to do much else. In fact, most of the people from *My Brother and Me* don't even have Wikipedia pages, and that is a low bar to clear. Alfie, Dee Dee, and Goo all disappeared. The only kid actor who ended up with a notable career is Amanda Seales, who played Donnell's older sister Dionne, a character I don't really remember. She has gone on to make music and have a role in *Insecure*. She rose above these humble beginnings.

Is *My Brother and Me* the worst show from the days of '90s Nickelodeon? It's definitely in the running. *100 Deeds of Eddie McDowd* and *Animorphs* are just as bad, maybe even worse. However, they are also funny in how bad they are. You can laugh at *100 Deeds of Eddie McDowd*. You don't laugh at *My Brother and Me*. You're just bored. The worst thing a show can be is boring, and I definitely have never found any Nick show I've seen as dull as *My Brother and Me*. It also has the worst acting, or at least has to be considered tied for that dubious honor. One "Goo Punch" segment can't make up for 13 episodes of child actors in over their head, facile stories, and clumsy punchlines. We were lucky that we did not get a second season of *My Brother and Me*. Because I know I would have ended up watching it because I had no better way to spend my time apparently.

The Mystery Files
of Shelby Woo

Life is full of mysteries, and some of them
can be solved by a teenage girl

I am not going out on a limb to say mystery shows are popular. I am including under this umbrella most procedurals. In fact, maybe it is more apt to say people like seeing cases get solved and smart folks figuring stuff out. After all, you know who the killer is during an episode of *Columbo*. It's Patrick McGoohan. Well, not always, but you do always spend time watching the murderer plan their crime and commit the deed. Then, you watch Columbo put the pieces together and catch the killer with one of his clever ploys. Actually, some of his ploys are less clever and more "oddly convoluted but luckily panned out against the odds anyway." Not that I'm knocking *Columbo*. It's a lot of fun, but it's mostly because it's great watch Peter Falk do his thing.

Pop culture, and literature, is full of sleuths, detectives, and amateur crime solvers. Jim Rockford is out there in his Pontiac Firebird cruising all over LA to try and make a buck. Sherlock Holmes is using his incredible intellect to solve nearly impossible mysteries between cocaine binges. There are plenty of child mystery solvers too, naturally. There's the Hardy Boys, who were the sleuths of record of my childhood. Although, in hindsight, it's weird that they seemed to only have two friends, Chet and Tony, and each Hardy boy was dating one of their sisters. There's Nancy Drew, Encyclopedia Brown, the list goes on. Of course, throwing her hat in the ring of young amateur detectives (children rarely draw a paycheck for their crime solving) is Shelby Woo, the protagonist of *The Mystery Files of Shelby Woo*.

There are not many procedural mysteries for kids, which makes *The Mystery Files of Shelby Woo* an intriguing program to delve into. Among Nick shows, it stands out as an original idea. It also stands out because they shot the show in a single-cam style, which was not common for Nick shows filmed at their studios in Orlando. Simply put, they couldn't shoot this show in a multi-cam style. What, were all the mysteries going to keep happening in the same three places? We needed to see Shelby Woo out in the world, pounding the pavement like a true gumshoe.

If you have ever seen a procedural mystery show, you don't really need me to tell you the gist of how every episode went. A crime occurs, and make no mistake there are crimes committed in each episode of *Shelby Woo*. Yes, it was a show for kids, but Shelby wasn't out there figuring out who stole a pie off a windowsill or who broke Old Man McClintock's window. You know, window-based crimes. Primarily, Shelby seems to get involved in thefts, but there are also kidnappings, arsons, and even a hit and run. Shelby pokes around. Suspects arise. Some of them are red herrings. The tension builds. Maybe Shelby is in peril. In the end, she figures out who the culprit is, even though she's a teenager and not a trained detective or police officer. Lather, rinse, repeat. That's the beauty of the procedural. You can just luxuriate in the formula.

In terms of the details of this particular procedural, Irene Ng stars as Shelby Woo. She's a Chinese-American teenager who lives in Cocoa Beach, Florida, with her grandfather. Speaking of Cocoa Beach, I would be remiss if I didn't mention another show that took place in the same city, the seminal '60s sitcom *I Dream of Jeannie*. Funnily enough, I imagine I was mainlining *I Dream of Jeannie* on Nick at Nite around the same time *The Mystery Files of Shelby Woo* was airing on Nick. *I Dream of Jeannie* is a silly high-concept sitcom, but a pretty fun one. At the very least, it's got a striking visual palate, not to mention the presence of the ultimate wacky sitcom sidekick actor Bill Daily.

Speaking of iconic actors, Shelby's grandfather Mike is played by Pat Morita. Yes, the one-and-only Pat Morita, an Academy Award nominee, spent years on a Nickelodeon sitcom as the wise and well-meaning father figure. He's an innkeeper, and he doesn't agree with Shelby poking around in all these police cases. Shelby has two best friends, Cindy and Noah. Cindy likes to be part of the detective work and Noah doesn't. The usual dynamic. There's also, of course, the police detective who doesn't like Shelby getting involved in open police investigations but can't help but worry about her regardless. Oh, and his name is Whit Hineline, which is amazing. I should also say that this all only applies to the first three seasons. For the fourth season, which was shot in Montreal, the Woos ship up to Boston. Evidently Canada could not pass for Cocoa Beach. Once that happens, we lose all the Cocoa Beach characters, but the replacements are pretty much more of the same, though the new police detective is a woman, and she's a bit friendlier than Whit, but only a bit. Shelby still had the required one male and one female friend, though.

Since the show was for kids, there was a bit of outward prompting to get the viewer to try and figure out which of the three suspects really did it. There were recap moments where Shelby and her crew would go over the suspects and clues, giving possible motives and other hints. The actual clues are laid on pretty thick, but that may just be me as an adult watching in hindsight. In rewatching episodes for this book, it was always clear who the perpetrator was. Although, in one episode I watched a key clue involved a middle-aged man's scrapbook including a news story about a seven-year-old girl losing her skirt on a local kids' show, so frankly there really needed to be two arrests that day.

The single-cam shooting definitely made *Shelby Woo* a more kinetic show than much of its Nick brethren, and I also find the surf rock score pretty delightful. That being said, in rewatching my favorite element was probably the computer interface that shows us the suspects and the clues. It's a retro '90s look that reminds me of watching movies like *Hackers* and *The Net*. At the time, this was not something I could envision as being a positive, because my kid brain wasn't thinking of future kitsch charm. Now I love it. If only I could have seen her rollerblading too. Or hanging out with Matthew Lillard.

The Mystery Files of Shelby Woo was a good stepping-stone show. It kept you engaged and trying to solve puzzles like shows for little kids in the vein of *Blue's Clues*. However, it was less obvious and involved an actual story. You were watching crimes being solved and detective work being done, which felt more "adult," something kids strive for at a certain age. The clues aren't totally spoon-fed to you. I can imagine that being really engaging to a preteen. Then, of course, it also served as an introduction into the world of procedurals and mystery shows. First you spend time with Shelby Woo, and then you grow up and watch *Law & Order* or one of the literal hundreds of procedural mysteries that have graced television since back in the '50s. I doubt this was fully the intention, but regardless I admire the show for that. It also is a reasonably decent show, all things considered. Ng was in her twenties when she played the teenaged Shelby Woo, which probably helped. There were also more adult characters, which meant more adult actors, and they weren't all broad comic relief.

Look, are the mysteries engaging enough for me to really want to watch *The Mystery Files of Shelby Woo* as an adult? Not really, and it's not quite funny or well-crafted enough to be anything more than adequate programming. That being said, I feel like this show hasn't gotten enough love in hindsight. What other show for kids was like this? Not to mention that the protagonist was a Chinese-American girl. The only shame is that they didn't get to make more episodes. The first season of *Shelby Woo*, which debuted in 1996, was only a six-episode test run. It went well enough they added seven more episodes in a second season they aired on SNICK. The third season was supposed to be 13 episodes, but a strike limited it to eight. Then, they moved to Montreal and made a 20-episode fourth season. Four seasons, 41 episodes, and a whole lot of mysteries.

That being said, I really wish somebody had poked around into that dude with the scrapbook more. Shelby Woo really dropped the ball on that one. Fortunately, she helped out plenty on many more cases, and introduced a generation of kids to the joys of watching a sleuth unpacking a mystery while you try and figure out whodunit before they tell you.

Nick Arcade

Life isn't always what it seems

Writing this book has made me realize how many shows on Nickelodeon were burned into my brain by reruns. Take, for example, *Nick Arcade*. It only aired for one year in its initial run, before reruns took over and were shown through 1997. Seriously. The show debuted in January of 1992 and ended in November of the same year. Sure, they shoved two seasons and 84 episodes into that time, which must have meant they were doubling up episodes. In fact, in that old-school game show style, they probably were doing four or five episodes a week. It was good enough for *Match Game* in the '70s, and it was good enough for *Nick Arcade*. I assume Phil Moore was less drunk than most of the *Match Game* panelists, though.

Moore was a familiar face on Nickelodeon in the '90s. He made frequent appearances as himself on multiple Nick shows, and was a host for a couple of their game shows, including *Nick Arcade*. This was basically his television debut, and you can see why Nickelodeon liked him so much. Honestly, now that I think about it, Nickelodeon really nailed it when they hired their game show hosts. I can't knock any of them, save for maybe Summer Sanders. That may be because she was more in the vein of the modern game show host. She was a celebrity who got a gig as opposed to a performer who had honed the skills required to be a host. Sanders wasn't bad, but she couldn't hold a candle to somebody like Moore, who had been a standup and done warm up for another game show, MTV's *Remote Control*.

Nick Arcade had an awesome premise for a game show in the early '90s. It would still be pretty cool now, but the technology felt fresh at the time. Although, the technology that isn't fresh now appeals to me more than it did then. I am a big fan of old-school video games. In fact, I only play the retro games. If it's newer than Nintendo 64, I'll politely decline. The aesthetics and game play of '90s video games are perfect. At the time, though, the games on *Nick Arcade* were cutting edge. In fact, they had the honor of unveiling a prototype of *Sonic the Hedgehog 2*, to give you a sense of what the video game world was like in the early '90s.

Each episode of *Nick Arcade* featured two teams of two kids, a red team and a yellow team. They would earn points, and victory, through a mix of video game skills and knowledge. Each round would begin with a video game faceoff between one member of each team. The show had actually commissioned their own original arcade cabinets for this round, which was pretty cool. Sure, the games were simple, and strikingly reminiscent of existing games, but that showed the level of commitment that *Nick Arcade* had to its production value. Also, apparently they only played the games for 30 seconds, which feels so short when I read it but when watching the show it definitely did not feel short. Surprisingly, the professional game show producers knew best.

Then came the Mikey round. Here, an everyboy named Mikey was moved around the board by the two teams. There were several different worlds that he could be dropped into. There was a medieval level called Camelittle and an underwater level known as the Specific Ocean. There was a haunted house near a swamp, and the swamp felt like overkill. Then, sometimes, he'd just be in his neighborhood or the mall, which felt a little underwhelming after all the fantastical worlds. All the graphics on this part of the show was pretty limited, but I chalk that up to the era. I certainly had my favorite levels, and I'm sure you did as well.

Mikey rounds were built around what Moore called "The Four P's," which were points, puzzles, pop quizzes, and prizes. If you landed on a points spot, you got points. It was that simple. Prizes were simple too. You won yourself a prize that you could keep whether or not you won the overall game. Pop quizzes pitted the two teams against each other for points and control of the board. There were a lot of different kinds of puzzles, and looking back a lot of them were pretty awesome. Yeah, you would get the occasional rebus—those were boring on *Concentration* and they are boring now—but they had fun little puzzles like "Video Repairman" and "What Was That?" In particular, "What Was That?" would show video of an object being destroyed in reverse, and you had to buzz in to answer what the object is. "Video Repairmen" involved music videos, and since we're talking 1992 you know they were awesome.

Also on the board were Video Challenges, which is when a team would get a chance to play games like *Toki* and *Sonic the Hedgehog 2*. One player had the chance to play for 30 seconds to beat the score of the "Wizard's Challenge." They changed that to "Expert's Challenge" for season two, which is garbage. Wizard's Challenge is 10 times better. One team member would play, while the other would write down a wager on a Magna-Doodle. If the game player beat the challenge, that wager was added to their score. If they failed to beat the challenge, they lost those points. That's a lot of pressure to put on a kid, but *Nick Arcade* did not care. In the end, you were just watching a kid playing a video game, but as a child I guess I thought it was worthwhile to watch. I mean, you spent half your time as a kid in the '90s watching friends or siblings playing video games. It was just business as usual.

Unfortunately for the contestants, and Mikey, it wasn't all fun and games on the board. For you see, Mikey had enemies. Powerful enemies. Depending on the level, a different enemy would pop up if you ended up on the wrong spot. All you lost, as a player, was control of the board. Mikey, though, suffered greatly. In Camelittle a dragon would breathe fire on him. Pirates would come after him, and so would genies. There was a bully named Game Over in a few different levels. I assume he took on that moniker as sort of a nom de bully, and also he may have been an omnipotent demigod, because why call yourself Game Over if you don't realize you exist in a video game world? As a kid, I found either some or all of these upsetting. I have a vague memory of looking away from the screen when an enemy space was landed on. The ominous music would warn me and I'd look away. I do not recall if that was for all of them or just some of them. I am confident I did not like when the hammerhead shark would smash Mikey and turn him into a coin. It goes without saying, but now none of them really bother me. Except the Smooch Aliens. Those are still weird, and they kiss Mikey vociferously without his consent.

There was a goal spot on the board that the teams tried to get Mikey to, but usually time ran out before that could happen. That would mean a pop quiz for the points. There were two rounds of the face off, and of Mikey, and then we got to the part of the show that was the most exciting, and which I couldn't wrap my head around as a kid. It was time for the winning team to enter the Video Zone.

When the kids entered the Video Zone, the premise was that they were getting brought into the video game world. They would have 60 seconds to clear three levels. The first two levels were solo challenges. The player would have to collect three of something, be it bananas or statues or coins while avoiding various hazards and enemies. Players had health bars and if you ran out of health you'd have to start the level all over again. Then, in the final level, the teammates would join forces to face one of the three main bosses. There was Merlin, living up to the show's preoccupation with wizards, Scorchia, a lady who threw fireballs, and Mongo, who punched out a horse in *Blazing Saddles*. Wait, he was a monster who threw balls of "energy" at you. That was a mix up. If you touched three orbs before time ran out, you won the grand prize, which was typically a vacation to some place that Nickelodeon had a partnership with.

I hate to burst your bubble, but the kids were not actually placed into a video game world. That would not happen until the documentary *Jumanji: Welcome to the Jungle*. The Video Zone was all done on blue screen. I watched video of behind-the-scenes footage from the show, which really robs you of any of the mystery. Not that I haven't seen blue, or green, screen in action. It just can't help but jar you to watch a kid run up some stairs wrapped in a blue covering, banister and all. Knowing that, a lot of my questions from when I was a kid were answered. No, I did not think that they were actually in a video game. I just didn't figure out how they made the illusion happen. Also, now as an adult I feel like that must have been so jarring as a kid to figure out. You had to avoid fireballs that weren't actually there or grab gems that you can't see in front of you. I have memories of contestants waving their hands around trying to activate something they just couldn't quite hit. It must have been immensely frustrating. It was certainly entertaining to watch.

There are elements of pop culture gone by that are said to "scream '90s," or whatever decade you're talking about. *Nick Arcade* screams '90s like Bobcat Goldthwait, both because he was prominent in the '90s and because he did an awful lot of screaming as part of his shtick. The video games are retro, and so are the computer graphics. Blue screen technology wasn't close to what they can do now. For the time, though, this was a conceptually strong game show, especially for kids. Many kids loved video games, and loved the idea of being in a video game. Yes, watching other people play video games, or swinging their arms in front of a blue screen, is passive, and passive viewing can be a problem for game shows. Fortunately, it proved interesting enough, especially when I was a kid and I could marvel at real human beings interacting with Merlin on my screen. Moore was a charming host, and he still comes across that way. If not for the fact you have to be famous now to host a game show, I bet he could still handle that gig. Instead, Snoop Dogg gets to host *Joker's Wild* and Alec Baldwin is fronting *Match Game*. It's not a surprise that technology has moved well past what they were doing on *Nick Arcade*. It's a bit of a surprise, and a shame, that the world also moved past people with Moore's skill set. He was hit with the proverbial pie in the face by Game Over. At least he has the legacy of *Nick Arcade*, a game show that was perfect for its era.

Nick News with
Linda Ellerbee

It can't all be fun and games

If I was trying to make this chapter reflective of my childhood experience with *Nick News*, I would be doing the writing equivalent of changing the channel or going to play video games. Throughout this book, I have
noted that part of being a kid in the '90s was watching whatever was on.
Many of us of the Gak Generation would just put on Nickelodeon and
watch it until we went to bed. There were many days I did that. However,
one thing that could get me to try and change the channel or turn off the
TV would be *Nick News with Linda Ellerbee*. Although, it usually aired on
Sunday nights, which was when my family would usually be watching TV
together. We were probably watching *The Simpsons* or *The Critic* or some
other Sunday night network primetime programming. There were plenty
of reruns of *Nick News*, of course, because Nickelodeon loved reruns. These
reruns were an excuse for me to think to myself, "You know, it seems like a
nice day to go play some street hockey."

Which, you know, as an adult doesn't feel great. The fact of the matter was that, as a kid, watching TV was about having fun, and almost everything on Nickelodeon was at least conceptually fun. There was nothing
fun about *Nick News*. It was serious and informative. It felt like school, and
that's not what you want on a Sunday night. I'm sure there were some kids
who were watching *Nick News* because they were already engaged in issues.
It's not that I didn't care about stuff. I read the newspaper as a kid. Did I
mostly just read the sports section and the comics? I fail to see how that
was relevant. By the time I got into news programming, I was watching *The
Daily Show with Jon Stewart*, which I started watching as a teenager. Before
that, I got my information from school.

Now, as a grown man, of course I'm happy that *Nick News* existed and
that they were trying to talk to kids about important issues. A news program that kids could comprehend, but that didn't talk down to them, was a
smart idea. They also found a great host in Linda Ellerbee. She is the only
host *Nick News* ever had, though they did a one-off special in 2020 hosted
by Alicia Keys. Ellerbee got the job in 1992, and for decades every time *Nick*

News came on, there she was, keeping it chill but dropping knowledge. She was a newscaster who just happened to be primarily working on a news show for kids. That didn't make her work any less valid.

Nick News wasn't a week in and week out show. It was specialty programming. Between 1992 and 2015, they made 178 episodes of *Nick News*. That's a handful of episodes per year, and apparently episodes were only in half-hour blocks. In my memory it was a longer show, but that again is probably because I just wanted the fun shows back on TV. Instead, if I had watched, I could have learned about topics like equality, global warming, political matters, and all sorts of important stuff. I would have been more informed, but, if I am being totally honest, how informed does an eight year old need to be? It's not like I could vote. What I'm saying is that my desire as a preteen to just watch fun TV shows was forgivable. I doubt I missed out on learning anything important in the '90s from skipping *Nick News*, because anything they would talk about I imagine I would have learned in school.

That being said, *Nick News* was very meritorious, and television professionals agreed. The quality of the program was often lauded. It didn't merely perform a valuable service, and also have politics I happen to agree with as an adult. I just had a horrifying flash of a conservative news program for kids. Thankfully, *Nick News* was far from that. The show won a Peabody in 1994, and Ellerbee won a Peabody for his work on the show in 1998. Ellerbee had previously hosted another Peabody-winning special for Nickelodeon from 1991 called *It's Only Television*, which was dedicated to espousing how television could be used as a tool to educate children. That seemed to presage the ethos of *Nick News*. The show was also nominated for a whopping 22 Emmys in the category of Outstanding Children's Program, which it won nine times.

As I mentioned, Ellerbee retired as the host of *Nick News* in 2015 with an hour-long special. Do I wish I had spent more time as a kid watching *Nick News*? Truthfully, not really. It's not like my lack of *Nick News* has somehow hindered my adult life. Everything I would have learned from *Nick News* I learned eventually. I became an informed person. I had other avenues for learning that engaged me more than *Nick News*. As capable of a host as Ellerbee was, the show simply did not grab me. It wasn't engaging to my child's brain, even though I was a kid who didn't mind going to school and didn't have attention issues. I don't know if any of my friends watched it. I don't know what became of kids who grew up avidly watching *Nick News*. What kind of teenagers did they become? What kind of adults did they become? In the long run, did it really make a significant difference?

Regardless, Linda Ellerbee was a presence on Nickelodeon for as long as anybody. She dedicated her life to helping inform kids in a way they could appreciate. The show didn't shy away from serious subjects. I admire all of this, and Ellerbee earned her Peabody. I respect *Nick News*. I respect Linda Ellerbee. The show simply had a daunting task to overcome for an audience of children. It had to give them their proverbial medicine sans a spoonful of sugar. Some kids were never going to be into that. I was one of them. For everybody else, though, *Nick News* was an important, valuable piece of television. It isn't all just mindless entertainment, after all. Ellerbee would end episodes by declaring to the kids watching, "If you want to know, ask!" That alone was a lesson for kids to take to heart, even kids who wanted to ask "What else is on?"

Nickelodeon
All-Star Challenge

You have forgotten a lot of celebrities from the '90s

This may be a brief chapter, as I am discussing a one-time event that lasted for three episodes. However, the *Nickelodeon All-Star Challenge* was so momentous I figured it was worthy of covering nevertheless. After all, it had four different Nick hosts and six different child celebrities involved. Plus, it was all for a good cause. Well, it was designed to get kids watching Nickelodeon during an event that was a good cause. That counts, right?

The event in question was the 1994 edition of The Big Help. The purpose of The Big Help, which Nick held multiple years in the '90s, was to get kids involved environmentally. There was a telethon vibe to it all, with stars of Nickelodeon appearing in ads or hosting television events to get kids to help out the planet. Usually, this meant calling and pledging time to environmental tasks and community service. You know, planting trees and things of that ilk. In turn, Nickelodeon would also offer to refurbish local parks across the country. For the purposes of this chapter I watched some of the old Big Help bumpers. Unsurprisingly, the *Pete & Pete* ones were the best in my mind. While I never volunteered for The Big Help, I do remember it showing up on TV and obviously I'm all for it. The smart thing was getting kids to donate time, which is something a kid can do reasonably. Plus, if they fell short they were off the hook. Mike O'Malley wasn't going to show up at your house if you pledged 15 hours but only did 12.

To try and get kids watching during The Big Help, the better to feed them the pledge breaks and calls to action, they would have events such as the *Nickelodeon All-Star Challenge*. Although, near as I can tell this is the only time this actual event occurred. It was one of those events where a superteam forms for a larger goal, like the Avengers or when all the cartoons taught kids not to do drugs. In this case, the *Nickelodeon All-Star Challenge* combined several of Nick's iconic game shows and brought in celebrities to up the ante. The three-episode event involved games from *Guts, Double Dare, Legends of the Hidden Temple,* and *What Would You Do?* That last one is a weird choice, which I will get to in that chapter, but it is what it is. There were also four hosts. Mike O'Malley was there, naturally.

Marc Summers was nowhere to be found, but Robin Marrella, Summers' foil on *Double Dare* and *What Would You Do?*, was. Joining them was Phil Moore, a Nick staple who did not have any of his shows being represented, but his hosting skills made him a wise addition to any Nick event. Last, but definitely not least, Olmec was there. Yes, Olmec the statue from *Legends of the Hidden Temple*. Talk about breaking out the big guns. You try telling Olmec you aren't interested in helping the environment. The dude is made of stone!

Six teams competed in the event. Sadly, they were only represented by colors. You couldn't have broken out the *Legends of the Hidden Temple* teams for this? Why have Team Purple when you could have had the Purple Parrots? Way to drop the ball, everybody. All six teams featured somebody who had won a gold medal (and a glowing piece of their radical rock) on *Guts* and one person who had won the grand prize on *Legends of the Hidden Temple*. They were all joined with one child celebrity from 1994. Who were these celebrities? I'm glad I prompted myself by pretending you asked. First we have Christopher Castile, who was repping *Step by Step*. You may also know him as Ted from the *Beethoven* movies. God, I wish Charles Grodin had been involved in this. Michael Fishman, the once-and-future D.J. Connor from *Roseanne*, was probably the biggest name at the time. Joanna Garcia, now Joanna Garcia-Swisher after marrying baseball player Nick Swisher, was the only one there from a Nick show, in this case *Are You Afraid of the Dark?* Jeremy Jackson played Hobie, the son of David Hasselhoff's character on *Baywatch*. Nicholle Tom was on *The Nanny*, where she was nannied. Lastly, there was Adam Wylie, who was on *Picket Fences*. Name a more iconic sextet. The cast of *Friends*? Not a chance!

The first two episodes saw three teams going head-to-head. In the first round they competed in games taken from the aforementioned four Nick game shows. Maybe you found yourself in the *Guts* game slam dunk, jumping off the Aerial Bridge and trying to make baskets. Or you might have been playing the *Double Dare* game where you catch pies in oversized pants. There's something fascinating about seeing *Legends of the Hidden Temple* games outside of the context of that show. It's the only one of those shows with a lore to it. That creates a little dissonance when the games are just being played like they are any other contest. The magic—such as it is— is lost. *Guts* scoring rules were used, which meant 300 points for first, 200 for second, and 100 for third.

Then came round two, aka the "Gakfest Question Round." Here, one team would ask a trivia question to the other two teams. A player would buzz in and if they were right they would get 100 points and their opponent would be slimed. If they were wrong, they got slimed. If the other team then got the question wrong as well they too were slimed and the questioning team got 100 points. The team that answered the question right got to ask the next question, which to me is weird. I would want to stay in the game and keep answering questions to try and get points that way, but then again I enjoy playing trivia. Then came the final round, which they called the "Action Finale." Before this event, you could recruit audience members for your team, but if you did that it cost you 100 points per person. The events used in the first two episodes were Big Ball Volleyball, a weird three-way version of volleyball with, well, a big ball and Gak Gauntlet, where teams had to run the gauntlet while the other two teams tried to hit them with balloons filled with Gak. First place won 1000 points, second place for 750, and third place won 500.

The winners of the first two episodes, plus the runner up with the most points, moved on to the finals. There the rules were slightly different. For starters, one team was eliminated after the trivia round. Second, if you wanted audience help for the "Action Finale" you had to give up all your points. The final game of the *Nickelodeon All-Star Challenge* was called Gakheads, where teams had to grab Gak-filled balloons being launched at them and pop them on their helmets. The team with the most popped balloons won it all. They would be the true Nickelodeon All-Stars. I won't spoil who won, in case you want to check out this game show event from 1994 for whatever reason. However, I do want to tell you the three teams that made it to the final, so I guess that spoils the first two episodes to some degree. Too bad. It's my book. The finals pitted Team Pink, led by Jeremy Jackson, against Team Purple, Christopher Castile's team, against Team Red, helmed by Michael Fishman. Is it fair for me to say that the celebrities were the team leaders? Because the kids who had actually won Nickelodeon game shows brought more to the table.

Nick only did this once, and since it happened in 1994 I bet some of you reading this book missed it. You never got to see worlds collide. The glorious combo of Mike O'Malley and Olmec is something you never knew was possible. I don't know why there was only one *Nickelodeon All-Star Challenge*. Maybe it didn't work as well as they wanted. Soon thereafter, most of these game shows were off the air. That could have been it as well. Still, in that case they could have come up with some other challenge, if only to support The Big Help. One time only did we get to see multiple Nick hosts, multiple former Nick champions, and a hodgepodge of '90s child celebrities participating in a series of physical challenges and slime-centric trivia games. As an adult, the most enjoyable thing about this is the fact that I can say things like, "Oh yeah, that's the kid who played Hobie on *Baywatch*. What a random thing to stumble upon over a decade later." It's amusing as an artifact of 1994. Back then, it was a massive once-in-a-lifetime event. Once upon a time we looked upon Michael Fishman's works and despaired.

Now, he's just two vast and trunkless legs of stone. Or something. I guess he's on that *The Connors* show. What seemed immense once becomes forgotten. The *Nickelodeon All-Star Challenge* is the thing that needs some Big Help now. Also the planet still very much needs help. Maybe go plant a tree in Mike O'Malley's honor.

Nickelodeon Launch Box

We are floating in space, and Nickelodeon
just would not shut up about it for some reason

Don't sweat it if you don't remember *Nickelodeon Launch Box*. There were only nine episodes of it and they aired from 1991 until 1994. Granted, the show stayed in reruns until 2000, but it would run super early in the morning after Nick at Nite ended but before morning cartoons. You know, the time of day when *Mr. Wizard's World* episodes would air. The shows you were never up early enough to watch unless you had to get up early to go camping or to drive to an amusement park in the summer. *Nickelodeon Launch Box* was a joint venture between Nick, NASA, and the Astronaut Memorial Foundation. In fact, it's even under the "joint ventures" category on Wikipedia. There are good odds you never saw this show air on Nickelodeon.

On the other hand, you may have seen it in school some day when your teacher needed to kill some time or nurse a hangover. This was an educational program, and the explicit intent was for teachers to tape the episodes as their aired, in the old-school VHS way, and then show the taped episodes to kids as part of the curriculum. Yes, instead of distributing tapes to teachers, Nickelodeon and fricking *NASA* said, "Hey teacher, how about spending one of your blank tapes on our show? We get some free advertising and you get to eat up a half hour?" This was all part of the Cable in the Classroom initiative, which I certainly remember. Its logo is burnt in my brain, though I will never understand why there is a pencil in said logo. Does a pencil represent education? Diligent note taking? It's an eternal mystery.

The premise of Cable in the Classroom was that cable channels would air shows deemed educational commercial free and then Cable in the Classroom would maintain a master list of when they were going to air, so that teachers could check the list and then, as previously mentioned, record episodes. They also waived any copyright claims for the sake of the teachers. As noble as that may sound, these programs were almost entirely aired early in the morning on weekdays, when basically nobody would be watching TV. *Mr. Wizard's World* was one of these shows, as was *Nick News*. Also, apparently *The Twilight Zone* was included in the Cable in the Classroom

147

oeuvre. Looking into this further, I found myself on the website of the Rod Serling Memorial Foundation. Serling, of course, created and hosted *The Twilight Zone*. They had a letter from a teacher who wrote at length about how he had used *Twilight Zone* in his teaching and highlighted some episodes. Naturally, "The Monsters are Due on Maple Street" was one of them. I did indeed watch that in my 10th grade English class, though I don't know if that was a Cable in the Classroom taping. I just like to imagine a seventh-grade glass sitting there in 1996 watching Rod Serling puffing on a heater as he introduces some morbid, ironic tale.

So that's Cable in the Classroom, the entire reason that *Nickelodeon Launch Box* existed. Each episode was 30 minutes long—against these shows were commercial free—and was about the space program and space technology. Each of the nine episodes covered a different subject. They filmed *Nickelodeon Launch Box* at their studios down in Orlando, naturally, in front of a live audience. They made use of other sets down at Universal Studios sometimes to save a few bucks, so you could learn about space while thinking to yourself, "Is that the *What Would You Do?* set?" Spoiler alert: It was!

I found exactly one episode of *Nickelodeon Launch Box* for research purposes. Sadly, I couldn't get my hands on a well-worn VHS copy from some embittered retired teacher. This episode was more about space itself than about space travel. For example, the first few episodes were about spacesuits, life on the space shuttle, and astronaut training. The show would feature a mix of NASA employees and space veterans and Nickelodeon personalities. One episode featured Robin from *Double Dare* and also Ren and Stimpy. Phil Moore, game show host extraordinaire, showed up quite often. Then, there's the episode I watched, which was about the inner planets. It was hosted by Ferguson Darling himself, Jason Zimbler.

Rocking a cardigan with such a deep V it seemed primed to fall off his shoulders, Zimbler played host and narrator for our journey into the world of Mercury, Venus, Earth, and Mars. Standing in front of a green screen, Zimbler did his best old-school weatherman impression as he read somewhat clunky dialogue. Although, I must say that even I learned some new stuff about these planets. It was genuinely educational. Zimbler's monotone monologues were, at least. They also had a *Star Trek: The Next Generation* parody shoehorned in called "Space Trip," which was supposed to be both fun and educational. I feel like it failed on both fronts. Here is all I have to say about Space Trip. One, Phil Moore plays a LaForge parody named "LaF-ridge." Two, the captain of the ship is Jean-Lukewarm Pecan. That's a sweaty double pun. I understand NASA not having the best sense of humor, but I imagine that Nickelodeon was handling the entertainment. That being said, when the Space Trip segment began there was a clarifying statement flashed on the screen in a front style that screamed '90s. It simply read "A PARODY," which honestly made me laugh more than about 75 percent of the TV I watched for this book. The idea that they felt the need to explicitly state that Space Trip was a *Star Trek* parody was just so funny to me.

At the end of every episode there was a teacher's section that wasn't to be screened in the class. Instead, it was designed to help teachers plan their lesson. This part involved a space program professional going through key information in what was, apparently, a condescending way. They treat the teachers like they are completely clueless. At the end of the Inner Planets episode all of a sudden a shuttle pilot shows up and is like, "OK morons, listen up!" Literally, he says, "If I'm going to fast, you can pause the tape to catch up," and then he starts talking about how Mercury is the closest planet to the Sun. Which is weird, because they did not talk down to kids at all during the part for students.

So that's *Nickelodeon Launch Box*. It's nobody's favorite Nick show, especially not the teachers who had to remember to set their VCR to tape it at five in the morning. The interesting conversation to have here is about how much space and NASA had a foothold in our childhoods because of Nickelodeon. How many times did kids win a trip to Space Camp on game shows? It was usually the grand prize. Space Camp was ubiquitous in my youth, and it was entirely as a game show prize. It definitely intrigued me, but probably in part because it was always treated as the ultimate thing for a kid in the '90s. It's all tied to trying to be educational to some degree. Yeah, Space Camp may have been fun, but you were also going to be learning stuff. Nick also may have figured space was a "cool" thing to learn about for kids. It was fantastical and such a massive thing to wrap your head around. As Jose Marti once said, immensity brings joy. Or was that Jason Zimbler? I always confuse the two.

I am left to wonder what those who missed out on being '90s kids feel about space. Do they have any sense of Space Camp? Was that purely a Gak Generation preoccupation? Is space cool to kids any longer? Nickelodeon could have come up with all sorts of different educational programs to include in Cable in the Classroom. They created a show about outer space. Space was part of Nick's brand in the '90s, right up there with Marc Summers and slime. We learned a lot about space as kids in the '90s. Some of us even got to go to Space Camp. And none of it was A PARODY.

Oh Yeah! Cartoons

Everybody has to start somewhere

Earlier in this book, I wrote about the cartoon cornucopia that was *KaBlam!* This was the show of my personal youth on Nick that was dedicated to showing a variety of animated shorts. Some of them were recurring, while others only showed up once. That show spawned a couple of spinoffs during the '90s, though one was merely the "Action League Now!" shorts repackaged as half-hour episodes of television. Then, there was also the waking nightmare known as *Angela Anaconda*. This may have been Nick's first foray into being a cartoon clearinghouse, but not its last. The second time around, it was more successful as well. This show was called *Oh Yeah! Cartoons*, because if you are going to be a Nickelodeon showcase for animated shorts apparently you need an exclamation point in the title. Maybe this book should have had an exclamation point in the title as well.

Oh Yeah! Cartoons, which began life in 1998, was a collaboration between Nickelodeon and Frederator Studios. Frederator is an animation production studio founded by—and presumably named after—Fred Seibert. Seibert had been the creative director of MTV previously and then took on the role as President of Hanna-Barbera. You may also recall Seibert from earlier in the book, because he and Alan Goodman basically created the initial branding of MTV. They were then commissioned to overhaul Nick in the '80s, as well. Seibert was in charge when they came up with the "splat" logo and all that stuff. He is a hugely underrated figure in the history of Nick, and *Oh! Yeah Cartoons* is a part of that as well. After Seibert was done with all that impressive handiwork, he founded Frederator to get into the animation production game to help create new shows. In the interest of full disclosure, and also maybe this is one of those so-called "humble brags" as well, I have written pilots for consideration at Frederator, though none of them ended up being produced. I don't hold it against them.

In essence, *Oh Yeah! Cartoons* was an incubator for animation. Dozens of creators put together seven-minute cartoon shorts, three of which aired in every episode. That was the entire gist of it. The show didn't have any real premise beyond that, a la *KaBlam!* Additionally, they didn't have nearly as many recurring animated shorts. I mean, "Action League Now!" appeared in every episode of *KaBlam!*, while no cartoon aired more than a handful of times during the three-season run of *Oh Yeah! Cartoons*. That being said, as an incubator it was certainly the more successful of the two, although to be fair *Oh Yeah!* was an overt and unabashed attempt to create series, while I am not so sure that was what *KaBlam!* was looking to do.

All three seasons of *Oh Yeah! Cartoons* had a different host, or rather hosts. The first season was just hosted by a gaggle of school kids. That must have not worked out terribly well, which isn't shocking, so they turned to Kenan Thompson. At the time, Thompson was still acting on his sitcom *Kenan and Kel*. In the third season they turned to Josh Server, another *All That* alum. That third season was a sporadic one, as there were only six episodes and they aired intermittently between 2000, when Server was still on *All That*, and 2002. There seems to be a history of Nick shows getting all wonky in terms of scheduling in their final season. Animation production can also be tricky, to be fair. Part of me wonders if Server recorded all his interstitials on one day in 2000 and then they were just still being used two years later. However, I will give the show credit for this: They aired 32 episodes and 96 segments. They stuck to every cartoon being a seven-minute short and to doing three per episode. That's a level of consistency and reliability I appreciate.

The first season of *Oh Yeah!* was truly noteworthy, as over the course of 13 episodes they aired 39 different shorts. No show got a second episode that first year. We were introduced to 39 separate worlds, which is kind of amazing. I did not watch *Oh Yeah! Cartoons* as it aired, or at least I don't remember doing so, so I don't remember all these shows. Obviously, they aren't all available to watch now and it would be daunting to try and watch 39 separate shorts anyway. One of them was "Zoomates," which was about an animal activist who helps zoo animals adapt to living a human life. It was created by Seth MacFarlane. One year later, *Family Guy* debuted on FOX. Now that's an animated show I was definitely watching around that time. Because I was in junior high school, which is the perfect time in your life to think Seth MacFarlane is funny.

Some of these shorts were surely good, and some obviously didn't work. However, for Frederator and Nick this was intended to be an incubator for potential series. In that sense, three of the cartoons stand out, because they all did indeed eventually became full series on Nickelodeon. Two of them aired multiple shorts on *Oh Yeah!*, while one actually only aired one short. That being said, they all did indeed become their own shows, fulfilling the wishes of Seibert and company. In fact, I would say one of these shows—to the best of my knowledge—became one of the premier Nicktoons of the 2000s.

One of these shows was *ChalkZone*, which was born out of the very first short ever to air on an episode of *Oh Yeah! Cartoons*. *ChalkZone* is about a kid named Rudy Tabootie (not a fan of that name) who has magic chalk that takes him into another dimension whose name you can probably guess. In the ChalkZone, everything you draw and erase becomes real. Rudy goes on a lot of adventures in the ChalkZone, and is also voiced by E.G. Daily who also voiced Tommy Pickles on *Rugrats*. It's a little like the "Little Girl Lost" episode of *The Twilight Zone* combined with *Green Lantern* combined with an old-school adventure serial. However, I feel like *ChalkZone* skews a little young for me. Still, it lasted for 40 episodes from 2002 through 2006 on Nick, though I had never heard of it before this book project.

The last of the three shorts turned series, and the one that only aired one short, to debut was *My Life as a Teenage Robot*. However, on *Oh Yeah!* it was a short called "My Neighbor is a Teenage Robot." Apparently they realized it's a little more interesting to build a show around a teenage robot as opposed to focusing on their neighbor. It's kind of like how they didn't call *ALF* something like "Willie Tanner," and also like how in retrospect they would have just called the show "Urkel" instead of *Family Matters*. The show focuses on XJ-9, aka Jenny Wakeman, a robot who is apparently the protector of all of Earth but also wants to be a normal teenager despite the fact she is a robot and not, in fact, a teenage girl. Interestingly, the creator of the show, Rob Renzetti, created 11 different shorts for *Oh Yeah! Cartoons*. Only "My Neighbor is a Teenage Robot" clicked apparently. The first two seasons aired on Nick, but the show was cancelled before the third season. That final season debuted in 2006 on Nickelodeon's subsidiary channel Nicktoons.

Finally, there is the most-successful show in the bunch, *The Fairly OddParents*. The show, created by Butch Hartman, aired 10 seasons and a whopping 172 episodes between 2001 and 2017. There was a hiatus in there, but the show proved popular enough to return. Here is a grand reveal for you folks. In a bygone era of channel flipping, one day when I was in high school I flipped onto Nickelodeon while going through channels. *The Fairly OddParents* was airing. I stopped to watch it, and found myself enjoying it. Nick, like when I was a child, would air new episodes of cartoons on weekday afternoons after school. Hey, I would be home in afternoons. Soon enough, I found myself actively watching *The Fairly OddParents* and becoming a fan. I really dug the show. After many years of not watching Nickelodeon, I had my post–'90s show on Nick that I was watching. It is the only new Nickelodeon shows of the 2000s I have ever watched with any regularity. *The Fairly OddParents* really grabbed me. I thought it was a good show, and I still think it is.

The show is about a kid named Timmy Turner with two fairy godparents named Cosmo and Wanda. They would grant his wishes, though they would often go wrong, because it's a comedy show. Also, because Timmy is a short-sighted child and Cosmo is a big ol' dummy. Timmy's parents are usually out of the loop, and there is also a teacher, Mr. Crocker, who believes in fairies and is obsessed with proving they are real. Naturally, Timmy, and his fairy godparents, have to hide Cosmo and Wanda's existence. That means an awful lot of pink and green animals. *The Fairly Odd-Parents* is a genuinely funny show with a lot of great voice performances. Timmy's dad is a perfect doofy sitcom dad character. It caters to an adult audience a bit without going over the top. I have to admit it has been over a decade since I was a regular *Fairly OddParents* watcher, but revisiting the show it is still funny, and I like the animation style as well. Had this show aired in the '90s it would have probably been a favorite of mine. Then Cosmo and Wanda had a kid and it was lame.

Yes, dozens of the shorts that aired on *Oh Yeah! Cartoons* didn't become anything. If the show was a baseball player it would be sent down from the majors. However, TV shows are not baseball players. Sorry if I just blew your mind. The goal of *Oh Yeah!* for Frederator and Nick was to find shorts that could become their own shows. Three did just that. One, *The Fairly OddParents*, became incredibly successful. It's a better show than anything that aired on *KaBlam!* I think you have to call *Oh Yeah! Cartoons* a huge success. So I will.

100 Deeds for
Eddie Mcdowd

Every bully turned into a dog has their day

During the 1932 World Series, Babe Ruth was at the plate for the New York Yankees against the Chicago Cubs. He made a pointing gesture of some kind and then proceeded to smash a home run deep into the stands at Wrigley Field. The Yankees took the lead with the Babe's homer, and they ended up winning the game and the series. Legend now considers this home run Babe Ruth's called shot. It is one of the most-storied pieces of baseball lore, right up there with Willie Mays' catch and the time Dock Ellis pitched a no-hitter on LSD (allegedly). Ruth wasn't the only one to ever call his shot. The creators of a Nickelodeon show that debuted just before the end of the '90s did it as well when they decided to give the world *100 Deeds for Eddie McDowd.*

When you create a television show, unless you see it as a finite story, you dream of it lasting a while. Not everybody is like Phoebe Waller-Bridge, where you do 12 episodes of *Fleabag*, get lauded with critical praise, and then end the show definitively so you can spend more time doing stuff like voicing a droid in a movie that made a lot of people's favorite *Star Wars* super boring. Steven H. Berman, Mitchel Katlin, and Nat Bernstein were not content to imagine 12 episodes of their show. In *100 Deeds of Eddie McDowd*, the titular Eddie is cursed to perform, as you may have guessed, 100 good deeds. He's not exactly cruising through deeds, either. Each episode is essentially dedicated to one good deed being done, though there was some elasticity there. Now, take a moment to do the math. Yes, before their show even debuted, the trio behind *100 Deeds of Eddie McDowd* was basically saying that they were going to have 100 episodes of their show. At the very least.

Maybe they were trying to speak 100 episodes into existence. Hey, Rhonda Byrne's *The Secret* wouldn't be published until 2006. Maybe Berman and company were ahead of the curve. To be fair, they had nothing to lose. What was the worst-case scenario? Their show got cancelled? Would anybody really care? Was anybody going to point and laugh and say, "Look at those fools! Eddie McDowd didn't get to do those 100 deeds!" Not very likely. In a way, the fact that the show asserted the existence of 100 episodes before they even aired one is one of the only reasons *100 Deed for Eddie McDowd* is remembered and talked about. The other main reason, though, is a doozy.

If you aren't familiar with this show, I have very much buried the lede with intent. You know that whole curse thing? There's an added layer to that. When the show begins, Eddie McDowd is a 17-year-old bully brimming with arrogance. He's played by Jason Dohring, who is probably known best as Logan on *Veronica Mars*. Then, one day he runs afoul of a man known only as "The Drifter." Now, it'd bad enough to mess with somebody who goes by "The Drifter." It's an even bigger error when they are played by Richard Moll. The towering Moll—he reportedly stands 6'8"—is memorable for his role in the sitcom *Night Court*, where he played the bailiff Bull. I also remember him from his appearance as Genghis Khan—yes, *the* Genghis Khan—in an episode of the nightmarish misfire *The Munsters Today*. Moll looks extremely menacing as The Drifter, but he's not merely going to, say, bash the bullying Eddie over the head with a jug of wine. Like many a mysterious drifter in popular culture, Moll's character is supernatural, and he turns Eddie into a dog.

That's right. Eddie goes from teenage bully to dog in the blink of an eye. He maintains his human brain, but he's stuck in the body of an Australian Shepherd/Siberian Husky mix. Eddie won't be made human again until he performs 100 good deeds. That seems like a daunting task for a dog. How many deeds can a dog really do? Then again, he doesn't have to do 100 different good deeds. He could just drill down on, say, barking to keep people from walking into traffic. This is just the beginning of Eddie's problems. Until he does all 100 good deeds, Eddie's parents are gone. Just, like, straight-up gone. Trapped in some netherworld, presumably lacking any sentience or awareness. This seems particularly cruel and unfair of The Drifter, unless he is blaming Eddie's parents for his behavior. Maybe we know the side of the nature versus nurture debate that The Drifter falls on. I do wonder how the show would have handled this had Eddie completed his task and become human again. Would time have reverted back to when Eddie was turned into a dog? Or would his parents just appear out of nowhere years later, having lost their jobs, presumably their home, and so on. What a nightmare.

Of course, the fact that they made Eddie an anti-hero played a role in this being considered acceptable, at least for kid brains. Yes, it would be awful to be turned into a dog and to have your parents disappear. However, the children at home could sit there and think, "Well this happened to him because he was mean and a bully. I'm not a bully. I'm in the clear." There is a quasi moral justification to all this as such. Also, Eddie had to be a flawed protagonist to even justify the plot. Otherwise, why would he be cursed, and how hard would it be to do 100 good deeds? True anti-heroes are rare in children's programming, so in a way it's kind of cool that *100 Deeds for Eddie McDowd* went this rout. Although, this was more a story of redemption as opposed to, say, a *Breaking Bad*–type show about an unredeemed villain. Shows for kids often have morals, and the moral here was clearly "People can change. You should work to be a better person. Also, if you see a scary-looking dude that reminds you of Richard Moll, steer clear."

Then again, it was hard to avoid The Drifter, because he didn't always look like Moll. In addition to having the power to turn teenagers into dogs, The Drifter could shape shift and appear out of nowhere. The Drifter also talked in rhyme—I would have liked to see him in a musical improv game—and would always let Eddie know magically how many good deeds he had remaining. Basically, after turning this dude into a dog The Drifter gave over a lot of his free time to watching said dog go about his business. Must have been a dull life for him before all this. Another of the supernatural rules is that only the last person who Eddie bullied, in this case a kid named Justin, can hear him talk. As such, Justin's family takes in Eddie as their new dog. Eddie did need a home, after all, since The Drifter wished his parents into the cornfield.

As you can imagine, this is kind of a bonkers show, but not necessarily in a fun way. The novelty wears off fast. That being said, if you have not seen *100 Deeds of Eddie McDowd* a little morbid curiosity is justified. They made the decision for Eddie to truly "talk" as a dog, which means visual effects to make it look like the dog is actually talking. For decades-old special effects it holds up better than expected, but it still looks weird, especially paired with the icy eyes of Rowdy, the dog who portrayed Eddie in canine form. Helping to bring this dog boy to life were the voices of Seth Green, yes, the famous Seth Green, and Jason Hervey, who took over for Green after the first season. Hervey is best remembered for playing the jerk of an older brother in *The Wonder Years*. You know, the kind of teenager that The Drifter would have turned into a dog. Hervey got out of the acting game and got into public relations. He's also apparently good friends with Eric Bischoff from professional wrestling circles, and the two had a production company together. Are you wondering who to blame for *Scott Baio Is 45 … and Single*? It's Hervey and Bischoff.

I would say that *100 Deeds for Eddie McDowd* went off the rails quickly, but in truth it was never really on them. Eddie would get good deeds rescinded by The Drifter, who brought a whole mess of overcomplicated stuff to the table. In the final episode that aired, we find out that there is a whole council of Drifters who seem to have dedicated themselves to reforming kids in a *Scared Straight* by way of David Cronenberg sense. It should be noted that this final episode I speak of was not when Eddie performed his 100th deed and returned to human form. No, it was only the 40th episode of the show. *100 Deeds for Eddie McDowd* fell well short of its goal. The show ended with Eddie still a dog and his parents still gone. You can't watch five minutes of this show and imagining it having the stamina to make it 100 episodes, though.

Since *100 Deeds of Eddie McDowd* debuted in August 1999, I was too old for it, and I didn't watch it as a kid. I have no attachment to it from my childhood. My view of it is unsullied by nostalgia or memory. This was a bad show. It was a messy premise executed poorly, and not just because they made the terrible idea of having the dog's mouth move when Eddie talks. They may have hoped kids would learn lessons about self-improvement from this show. The only lesson I learned? Richard Moll can rock a killer beard.

The *Ren & Stimpy* Show

It's important to be able to recognize toxic relationships

I will admit something up front, because if I do not I imagine it will rattle a few cages and ruffle a few feathers. It may even rattle some feathers and ruffle some cages. Of all the "classic" Nickelodeon shows of the '90s, that is to say the memorable ones that have made inroads in our collective consciousness, The *Ren & Stimpy* show is the one I least wanted to revisit. It is not all to my sense of taste or my style of humor. Now, I'm not saying that to try and praise it in some weird way. If I don't like something that means I don't think it is good. Some people will say "It's not really my style" to avoid giving a real criticism or saying anything negative. That's not how I roll. I will say that *Ren & Stimpy* wasn't good. It wasn't fun to watch. I do not like it at all. The experience is unpleasant in a very visceral way. It's kind of like how people will talk about an Oscar bait movie by saying it's a "tough watch" or it's "hard to get through," because the content is brutal or sad. That means it's a bad movie. If something is tough to watch it means you don't like it and you don't think it's good. Saying something is "not to your taste" means you think it's bad. Let's not kid ourselves here. I'm already worked up. Did I mention I don't like this show? Of course, it's very specific style makes it a cult hit and one of the more adored Nick cartoons. They lost me from the audience, but they gained a devoted following. Then, eventually, they lost that following as well.

There is a time period in these United States called the "Golden Age of American Animation." It is roughly considered to have started in the late '20s, which cartoons with sound first started to pop up, until some point in the '50s or '60s. It's always harder to pinpoint the end of things. We're talking the time when characters like Mickey Mouse were starting to debut and Warner Bros. began making their cartoons. Tom and Jerry were there for MGM. Fleischer Studios brought us the likes of Betty Boop and Felix the Cat. Tex Avery made his name during this time. Then, Jay Ward showed up with Rocky and Bullwinkle and William Hanna and Joseph Barbara started to make cheap animation with minimal movement and repeat backgrounds. This is roughly when the Golden Age ended. Think of the animation style that was showcased in *Who Framed Roger Rabbit?* This is the style of animation I'm talking about.

Stimpy and Ren engage in their traditional level of civil discourse (Nickelodeon).

Why did I start here? Because *Ren & Stimpy* is, in many ways, a perversion of the Golden Age of American Animation. It takes that style of animation, and those types of characters, and twists them into something grotesque and horrific. *Ren & Stimpy* was designed to make something ugly out of people's childhoods, and the man behind that design was a distressing individual by the name of John Kricfalusi. Kricfalusi first designed the characters of Ren, a bug-eyed Chihuahua, and Stimpy, a doofy-looking cat, way back in 1978 just for the sake of drawing. He was years away from making a career out of animation. Eventually, he got himself a meeting with Vanessa Coffey, Nick's Vice President of Animation, when they were working on buying their first Nicktoons. Kricfalusi was pitching a cartoon riff on a different staid genre of a bygone era: Shows like *Our Gang*. One of his pitches including a peripheral cat and dog. Coffey didn't like Kricfalusi's overarching idea, but she liked the dog and the cat, so *The Ren & Stimpy Show* was born. Like the two other original Nicktoons, *Doug* and *Rugrats*, it debuted on August 11, 1991. Unsurprisingly, it debuted latest in the evening. It would never again have anything in common with those two cartoons, especially the mild-mannered *Doug*.

Ren & Stimpy isn't really about anything. It seemed mostly to serve as a vessel for the things percolating in Kricfalusi's brain, or at least that was the case at first. Ren and Stimpy would have different adventures and experiences, but continuity didn't matter. The show was all over the place. One week out of nowhere Ren and Stimpy could be plopped into space. Another week they were professional wrestlers. There was little to grab hold to. All you knew was that Ren would be angry to the point of violence and Stimpy would be largely cheerful and oblivious. Mismatched animal pairs were quite common in the Golden Age of American Animation, but even Wile E. Coyote and the Roadrunner didn't have a relationship as toxic as Ren and Stimpy. The violence there was also less visceral. "Visceral" is probably the watch word for *Ren & Stimpy*. It's a show that luxuriated in creating a perverted version of Golden Age–style animation. Everything looked just off from something soft and safe and without maggots. However, Kricfalusi was always primed to drag you through the muck.

My main beef with *Ren & Stimpy* is not the darkness or the bleakness or even the violence. It's the grossness. The show is just so gross. Bodily fluids and functions abound, in as graphic of detail as Kricfalusi could get away with. It's unrelentingly unpleasant. Even when he's not being overtly gross in some way, and this show loves to be gross and push the envelope on that front, the animation can be quite unpleasant. This was with intent, I'm sure. Nothing about *Ren & Stimpy* seems designed to be pleasant. It defies you to like it. I, for one, don't feel like putting up a fight to enjoy a show.

It's perhaps unsurprising that Kricfalusi had a lot of beefs with the brass at Nickelodeon. Much of that was about censorship and standards and practices, sure, but Kricfalusi also proved an unreliable individual. Episodes would routinely arrive after deadlines, and Kricfalusi would fight tooth and nail for the content he wanted. Eventually, he turned in an episode called "Man's Best Friend," wherein the character George Liquor appears in the role of an abusive father to Ren and Stimpy. Then Ren beats him with an oar. Nickelodeon refused to air it, perhaps unsurprisingly. This was pretty much the end of Kricfalusi on *Ren & Stimpy*. In 1992, he was fired off the show he created, refusing to stay on as a "consultant." The show was moved from being animated by Kricfalusi's own studio "Spumco" to Games Animation. He also no longer voiced Ren, who he based on Peter Lorre. Instead, Billy West—who was already voicing Stimpy—began doing both for the remainder of the show's run on Nickelodeon. Now, West is an incredibly talented voiceover actor, so this wasn't a problem. And yet, fans started to turn against *Ren & Stimpy* without Kricfalusi. It wasn't the same, they claimed. They were just going through the motions. The comedy remained crude and the animation remained gross, but was it only because that was the show they were supposed to be making? They were just trying to live up to another man's vision in hopes of appeasing his dedicated fans.

The Ren & Stimpy Show would end up airing until October of 1996 over five relatively short seasons. No season had more than 14 episodes, and overall only 52 episodes (and 93 segments) were produced. It's weird to think that Kricfalusi, the man responsible for the show, only worked on 18 of those episodes. To many, only his episodes count as "true" *Ren & Stimpy*, which means they are devoted and dedicated to a mere 18 episodes of TV. Not that I don't understand that. There are plenty of one-season wonders out there that I am a fan of. I will talk extensively about the pilot of *Lookwell*, a show created by Conan O'Brien and Robert Smigel starring Adam West, and that's the only episode that ever saw the light of day. I'm just saying I think time has given us a skewed vision of what *Ren & Stimpy* was. Not for me, though. My vision was always crystal clear, and it's a vision of a show I do not enjoy.

Although, I must admit it wasn't all bad. The "log" ads are somewhat clever. Powdered Toast Man has a funny name at the very least. I can't completely write off "Happy Happy Joy Joy." There is something I admire in a skewed way of a man including the words, "I told you I'd shoot, but you didn't believe me. Why didn't you believe me!?" in a show for children. Or, at least, a show on a children's network. I don't feel like Kricfalusi ever thought of his audience. I think he just did what he wanted and figured Nick would air it. A little darkness in a show for kids isn't a bad thing, though. A smidge of subversion is healthy. A heaping helping of grotesquery, violence, and sexual innuendo? Maybe a little less admirable. I'm not clutching my pearls here. Children's minds weren't warped and lives weren't ruined. That doesn't make some of this stuff anything less than weird and inappropriate, though.

In the end, Kricfalusi probably needed the folks at Nick reeling him in. In 2003, Kricfalusi brought Ren and Stimpy back for *Ren & Stimpy "Adult Party Cartoon"* for Spike TV, the network for dudes. It's the place that brought us *Stripperella*, the cartoon where Pamela Anderson voices a buxom stripper superhero. Spike TV sucked, in short. And you know what really sucked? *Ren & Stimpy "Adult Party Cartoon."* Don't just take my word on it as a noted *Ren & Stimpy* critic. Billy West refused to provide his voice to the show saying it "wasn't funny." Critics agreed, and so did fans of the original show. Nobody seemed to like it, save for Kricfalusi himself, who was back with his baby and back voicing Ren. He could do what he wanted, and what he wanted was a bunch of female nudity and even more bodily fluids. Only three episodes aired of the nine that were ordered. Fittingly for the end of Kricfalusi's time with *Ren & Stimpy*, those were the only three episodes he delivered on time.

And yet, Ren and Stimpy will not die. People can't get enough of the angry dog and the dumb cat. Another revival has been announced, this time for Comedy Central. If I had to guess, it will land somewhere between the Nick show and the Spike show in terms of content. I will not be watching, and John Kricfalusi will not be working on it. In 2018, he was hit with accusations of sexual misconduct and was not invited to be part of the show. He lives on as a pariah now separated from his most-famous creation. Billy West may be returning, though, which is nice for him.

I'm sure some of you were more excited for the *Ren & Stimpy* chapter than any other chapter in this book. I feel like it's a show that is either one of your favorites, perhaps your all-time favorite, or one you didn't really enjoy. Unfortunately for you, I am one of the latter. As a kid, I watched *Ren & Stimpy*, but in part because it was considered a little rude and mature. That enticed me as a kid, which is the case for many kids. I wanted to see something I wasn't "supposed to," but within the safe confines of a cartoon on Nickelodeon. I wasn't out looking to, say, see a dead body or some crazy stuff like that. I also watched some of those Golden Era shows, mostly *Looney Tunes*. You know, I never really cared for those either. A twisted version of that style of cartoon could have potential appealed to me, especially now. Instead, *Ren & Stimpy* falls flat. It's delivering something I'm not looking for. I do not feel happiness. I do not feel joy. No sir, I don't like it.

Rocket Power

Sometimes you need to go to the extreme

The year 1999 was big for extreme sports. *Tony Hawk's Pro Skater* was released, and it remains the ultimate skateboarding video game series. The first game is loaded with charms that still remain, even if the levels are small and the graphics are a little basic. I'm still happy to visit the school or the mall, or even the warehouse, while "Superman" by Goldfinger is blasting on repeat. It turned out to be a great year for that game to come out, because at that summer's X Games Hawk became the first person to ever land a documented 900 on a skateboard, which is two-and-a-half revolutions. It would be five years until anybody did that again. Between Hawk's 900 and the release of *Tony Hawk's Pro Skater*, though, came another big moment for extreme sports. In August of 1999, the world was introduced to *Rocket Power*.

Yes, *Rocket Power* was just able to eke into this book by dint of debuting in 1999. As you have probably surmised by now, that means I didn't watch it when it was airing. I was certainly aware of *Rocket Power*. Nickelodeon was still on the televisions in my house at the time as I had two younger siblings, but I was not watching the channel of my own volition. *Rocket Power* must have been on occasionally, but I do not recall spending any notable time with it. All I knew was its premise, which was that the show focused on kids who were into extreme sports. Skateboarding, BMX biking, and the like were having a moment at the turn of the millennium. I was part of that as well. I had a skateboard and a BMX bike, and I watched the X Games, but I had no interest in cartoon children partaking in those activities when I could it myself.

Rocket Power came from the duo of Arlene Klasky and Gabor Csupo, much like *Rugrats, Aaahh!!! Real Monsters*, and *The Wild Thornberrys* before it. Of course, in 1999 the *Rugrats* machine was still churning, but that's for a chapter soon to arrive. You can definitely tell *Rocket Power* comes from Klasky and Csupo, because it bears their distinct animation style. However, the look isn't exactly the same as, say, *Rugrats*. The animation is more colorful and the characters look more distinct. *Rocket Power* looks more like traditional, or maybe the more apt term is run-of-the-mill, animation. People look more like people, and there seems to be more detail

163

in all the drawing. My guess is more time and money went into the animation for *Rocket Power*, and of course technology had advanced since the early '90s as well. Mark Mothersbaugh was back as the composer as well, but the theme song to *Rocket Power* is hot garbage and so is most of the music in the show. It feels like it all comes from a CD you get from the library called "Xtreme Sportz!"

The show focuses on four friends who live in the fictional beach town of Ocean Shores, California. It's the perfect place for extreme sports, what with the beach and the warm weather. You can surf, you can skate, you can even play roller hockey. Yes, apparently in the world of *Rocket Power* roller hockey is an extreme activity. It even makes the opening credits. I played a lot of street hockey as a kid, and it did not feel extreme at any point. The name of the show comes from the Rocket family. Otto Rocket is the best athlete of the bunch but also the most brash and overconfident. These are the sort of things that cause complications in stories from his perspective. His older sister is Regina "Reggie" Rocket, who still spends a lot of time hanging out with her younger brother and his friends for some reason. Well, I suppose if she didn't have anybody else to skate with it makes some sense. When I was a kid, if I wanted to play sports sometimes I would have to see what my brother was up to even though he was too young for me to really hang out with at the time. Still, Reggie could use some more friends her own age from what I can tell. Their dad Ray Rocket is a single father who co-owns a restaurant/surf shop called Shore Shack. He seems like kind of a jerk. Also, he doesn't look like Otto or Reggie at all which has led to people on the internet claiming he isn't their biological father. The internet is weird.

In the first episode of the series, Sam Dullard—that's a tough last name to get saddled with—arrives to town, the product of divorce. He's brainy and a technological genius, but he's relatively new to the whole "extreme sports" thing. Sam is a fish out of water, and yet he ends up with the nickname "Squid." Lastly, there's Twister, aka Maurice Rodriguez, who is kind of dumb and just videotapes everything the Powers do. This is probably the most accurate thing about *Rocket Power*. If you see a group of skater kids hanging out you'd better believe there is going to be one kid who sucks at skating but is kept around because he's willing to just stand around filming what everybody else is doing. Twister has an older brother named Lars who is something of a bully and antagonist in the series. Now, having not watched the show prior to writing this book I do not know if any explanation is given for why two Latin kids with the last name Rodriguez have the names "Lars" and "Maurice." The other notable character is Ray's business partner, sage surfer Tito Makani, who is seemingly Hawaiian, though I am basing that in part on the fact the actor who voiced him, Ray Bumatai, was Hawaiian.

Like Klasky Csupo's other shows, *Rocket Power* episodes usually consist of two segments. They involve the kids going on various adventures, usually involving extreme sports. Conflict happens, conflict is resolved. If the kids are mad at each other, by episode's end they are the best of friends again. The same goes for family conflict. Does this all sound generic? Well, that's because it kind of is. It's your usual themes and tropes of shows for kids, only with skateboards in them. Oh, and one time they decided to try the cool, new sport of street luge. That makes me laugh, because I remember when X Games tried to make street luge a thing. It didn't work. I do like the number of stories that seem to involve zines, though. I'm all for zines, which are basically self-published magazines that are usually super low budget and are for somebody who is a super fan. This is from a time before blogs and social media, though zines still exist as a throwback treat. *Rocket Power*'s zine love is another place where this show rings kind of true.

Alas, I don't have much else positive to say about the show. It's not funny at all. I didn't laugh once while watching it. The jokes are kind of baffling sometimes, in terms of what exactly is supposed to be funny. Despite the extremeness of the sports involved, the stories are rarely exciting or interesting. Mostly, the directing just seems so poor. I mean that in terms of the animation and the voice acting. They do some really cheesy stuff with the animation that makes it feel like it was made with a 13 year old using video editing software for the first time. I would say it was like a kid like Squid was doing the directing, but I have no idea how old these kids are supposed to be. They look young, and the voice actors sound like young kids, but then also they work at Shore Shack? Also they do extreme sports without supervision? While wearing a ton of safety equipment, of course. You have to set a good example for the children. They could be anywhere between 10 and 14 and I would believe it.

As for the voice acting, it just always seems off. Nobody seems comfortable with it, but that can't be true. I mean, John Kassir—a voiceover acting veteran—knows what he's doing. It might just be the pacing of the animation and how those lines of dialogue are being laid over the visuals. As an illustrative point, when I was watching the show I was wondering if the voices of Twister, Lars, and Tito were being done by white people because they sounded so inauthentic. They weren't, so my best assertion is that what I was hearing was hesitancy and uncertainty from the voiceover actors. Why is that happening? It boggles my mind.

And yet, *Rocket Power* was a success. It ran from 1999 through 2004 with 71 episodes and 132 segments produced. There's a video game, *Rocket Power: Beach Bandits*, and they even released a soundtrack album. Only *The Adventures of Pete & Pete* can say that as well among Nick shows. By the way, on that soundtrack is a cover of "99 Red Balloons" by Goldfinger, the band from the *Tony Hawk's Pro Skater* soundtrack. If you were a young enough kid that was into extreme sports when *Rocket Power* debuted I'm sure you were into it. I was just a few years too old to be gripped by Otto, Reggie, and the gang. In 1999, I skateboarded, played street hockey, and rode a BMX bike. I also could not find *Rocket Power* entertaining. At the time, I would have said I was too old for it. Now, I just say that it wasn't good enough to be enjoyed. I will not be making a *Rocket Power* zine, needless to say.

Rocko's Modern Life

Day-to-day life can be stressful,
even if you're a wallaby with a dope shirt

We're all familiar with Goldilocks, that adorable little criminal who broke into the house of a bear family and figured she would just eat their food and sleep in their beds like a true maniac. The concept that the story is built on, other than illegal trespassing, is the notion of things being "just right." Why we would care that this delinquent found exactly what she was looking for I don't know. Still, the notion has remained in culture for an exceedingly long time. I feel like, for some, *Rocko's Modern Life* was that "just right" cartoon on Nickelodeon. It was a little more mature and risqué than the tamest 'toons, but it did not simply devolve into the grotesquery of *Ren & Stimpy* that could be quite off-putting. When you got a little older, but were still watching Nick, *Rocko's Modern Life* could help you feel a little more "grown up."

Delving into the creation and production of the show it doesn't surprise me that *Rocko* ended up turning out this way. It was made by a group of individuals who seem like genuine oddballs that weren't interested in children, children's programming, or, frankly, television at all. That definitely seemed true of the show's creator Joe Murray. In fact, he's been quite upfront about this over the years. Murray had created a comic that didn't get off the ground and was looking for funding for a film called *My Dog Zero*. Murray had not worked in TV, and he wasn't really interested in it. However, he figured if he could sell a show, he could fund his movie, and he ended up in conversation with Linda Simensky, who was in charge of Nickelodeon's new animation department.

Murray was skeptical, and flat out said he had no interest in writing for children. The executives at Nickelodeon were fine with this. They were still relatively new when it comes to original programming. They wanted to cultivate an edge. After all, they hired John Kricfalusi, which is not a decision a network makes if they don't want to make waves. Mostly, Nick wanted adults, or at least college kids, to consider watching the network. More eyes meant more ad sales which meant more profits. Murray still needed a concept for a show, though, and then he just so happened to see a wallaby at the San Francisco Zoo. This stoked the idea for Rocko, and then he made his pilot. Murray remained apathetic about television though. He figured the pilot would fail, he'd get a payday, and then it would be back to his movie. Obviously, that didn't happen. Instead, *Rocko's Modern Life* got the green light, debuting in 1993 as the fourth Nicktoon, and the first since the original three all debuted the same day in 1991.

You can understand why *Rocko* might appeal to adults, certainly more than, say, *Doug*. Rocko has an adult life. He owns a home and he has a job at a comic book store, Kind of a Lot O' Comics. His job is stressful at times and his boss is a jerk. We spend a lot of time with Rocko, and his dog Spunky, as they deal with adult things in and around O-Town, the city where he lives. Rocko goes grocery shopping. He has beef with his neighbors the Bigheads, especially Ed Bighead. As he's an Australian immigrant, Rocko even has to worry about being deported in one episode. Rocko has two good friends. Heffer is a steer who is in a state of arrested development. He seems childlike, but maybe that's just because he's dumb and enthusiastic. Then, there is Filburt, who is a neurotic turtle. He's neurotic in a way that speaks to adult anxieties. There is a weird level of maturity to the themes of *Rocko's Modern Life*, at least when you think of it as a cartoon on a network geared toward children. Like Murray said, though, he had no interest in writing for kids. The potential adult audience was just as important to him, and also the writers and storyboard artists he surrounded himself with. They were a group with a shared goal, and that goal was to push the envelope and to think outside the box. Given that, they would probably be really unhappy I just describe their goal with two profoundly banal clichés.

There is a heaping helping of satire in *Rocko's Modern Life*, but much of it is aimed toward adult matters. How many cartoons on Nickelodeon have had such a disdain for corporate culture? Mr. Bighead works for a massive company called Conglom-O and their slogan is literally "We Own You." Not the most subtle of jokes, but pointed nonetheless. Also, the boss at Conglom-O, Mr. Dupette picks his nose and flicks boogers all the time and it is so gross and has always truly revolted me. Save that stuff for *Ren & Stimpy*, guys. Nevertheless, so many of the storylines on *Rocko's Modern Life* are much more geared toward adults. The kids watching would enjoy the slapstick comedy and big, broad voice performances. Characters are yelling on *Rocko* all the time. Rocko deals with a lot of stress, and when he does he really lets loose. Ed Bighead seems to be aggravated all the time. You may not have "gotten" the story, at least not fully, but you could still laugh at what was happening.

Given Murray's lack of television experience, and his seeming apathy about the whole process, it's also not surprising that there was a lot of satire about TV in *Rocko*. In fact, Murray seemed to be taking down his own show, and the process of making animated television, at times. For example, some episodes of the show are built around two parasites that live on Spunky, Bloaty the Tick and Squirmy the Ringworm. They seem to exist in a sitcom in the vein of *The Honeymooners* or *The Odd Couple*. Then, of course, there is "Wacky Delly." It is, without a doubt, the most-memorable episode of *Rocko's Modern Life*, and probably the most popular. Certainly it is the most meta, which is something that I love about it as an adult. Within the world of the show, Rocko and his friends love a TV show called "The Fatheads." It is a crude, broad show that basically features a married couple yelling at each other and hitting each other with parking meters and what have you. The joke is how broad and inane it is, basically taking slapstick cartoons and turning that up to 11. Also, the Fatheads are based on the Bigheads, because the show was created by Ed and Bev's estranged child. During the show's run in the '90s, this was Ralph Bighead, but in the Netflix movie that came out in 2019, *Rocko's Modern Life: Static Cling*, it is revealed that Ralph has transitioned and is now known as Rachel.

The scion of the Bighead family ends up in the world of cartooning, but hates it. In fact, in "Wacky Delly" we find out that Ralph just wants to be an artist. The apathy toward animation, despite the success it has brought, definitely makes Ralph feel a bit like Murray himself. Fittingly enough, Murray—who was not a voice actor—voiced Ralph. Ralph gets the idea to let Rocko, Heffer, and Filburt have the chance to create their own show, with the presumption it will get Ralph out of his contract because the show will be terrible. The trio of friends creates "Wacky Delly," which is about Betty Bologna, Sal Ami, and the Cheese, who is a better character than Betty and Sal combined. Just ask him. "Wacky Delly" is terrible animated and should be a disaster, but instead it is a hit. It's also maybe the funniest thing the show ever did. There is something so difficult about creating something so bad it's good. That is a hard line to walk, especially if you aren't doing straight-up parody like *Black Dynamite*. *Rocko's Modern Life* nailed it with "Wacky Delly" though. The tricky thing is you can't recommend it as the first episode people should watch, because it is so specific and different from much of what the show does otherwise.

Rocko's writers openly desired to write jokes that only adults would get, and they definitely did that. They also did jokes that both kids and adults could understand but were not really appropriate for kids. There is a bizarre amount of sexual content in this show given that it is both on Nickelodeon and involves a bunch of anthropomorphic animals. Rocko has a job working as a phone sex operator for a bit in one episode. Most notably, the fast food chain that Rocko and his friends go to began life as Chokey Chicken. This not-so-thinly veiled masturbation joke was eventually excised, and the restaurant became Chewy Chicken. As a child, I believed the joke was simply on the idea of a restaurant having the word "choke" in its name. Little did I know. Hell, or rather Heck, also plays a role in the show. In one episode Heffer goes to Heck, where he meets Peaches, who is I suppose Heck's Satan? Additionally, I remember seeing the word "Hell," as in the place of damnation, in at least one episode as a kid, which floored me then. Once TV ratings came into existence, *Rocko* would sometimes get the Y7 rating, which you never saw for *Rugrats* or shows like that.

I'm not one of those people who go gaga for adult jokes snuck into family programming. I have never tried to convince people that the priest in *The Little Mermaid* has an erection, because obviously he doesn't and please shut up. What I care about is if jokes are good or not. *Rocko's Modern Life* had plenty of really clever jokes. It's a funny show. It definitely resonates more as an adult than other Nicktoons. Murray and company's effort to have some edge and keep adults in the intended audience definitely paid off. Some of it is inappropriate for kids, but the show isn't just trying to be raunchy or "naughty" just for the sake of it. They just wanted to be funny, and they usually were. Sometimes things could be a bit gross or off-putting, but mostly the look of the show is fun. The voiceover work is strong. Tom Kenny, the voice of *SpongeBob SquarePants*, got one of his first voice acting gigs in Heffer. Carlos Alazraqui, perhaps best remembered as a member of the *Reno 911* ensemble, voiced Rocko. Filburt was voiced by a writer on the show known professionally only as "Mr. Lawrence." *Rocko's Modern Life* was exactly the kind of show that would hire a guy who called himself Mr. Lawrence professionally. They actually had quite the crew on *Rocko*. Jeff Marsh, billed as Jeff "Swampy" Marsh, went on to co-create *Phineas and Ferb*, another cartoon that considers its adult audience, but with a bit less bite and transgression. Most notably, Stephen Hillenburg, who basically took over the show in season four at Murray's request, went on to created the most-successful Nickelodeon cartoon ever, *SpongeBob SquarePants*.

Murray planned to leave the show entirely after season four, but instead the show ended up being axed. Between 1993 and 1996 they created 52 episodes and 100 segments. While Murray, unsurprisingly, seemed burnt out by the experience, he is happy with the show's output. I do not know the man, but everything I have read about him, and every interview I've seen with him, seems to indicate a restless spirit. Murray did, however, eventually return to animation. In 2005, his show *Camp Lazlo* debuted on Cartoon Network. In a stunning development, Murray also created a show called *Let's Go Luna!* in 2018. It airs on PBS in the United States and it's … an educational show for children. Yes, the man who once refused to write for kids is now educating small children on public television. We are not static characters in the stories of our lives.

As I mentioned previously, there was also a special one-off movie made by Nickelodeon that ended up on Netflix after a long, circuitous path.

Rocko's Modern Life: Static Cling began life in 2016 but did not actually arrive until August of 2019. It was a chance for the crew to make some jokes about Rocko and friends in the modern world. In the film, Rocko, Heffer, and Filburt return from space (it's a long story, but it involves a banana being found in the driveway) to a modern world. Heff and Filburt love it, but Rocko can't stand the change. He just wants to get "The Fatheads" back on television. Fitting to the acidic ethos always percolating under the surface for *Rocko*, the movie has a bit of an anti-nostalgia theme to it, but mostly it's about not being afraid of change. At first, Ed won't accept his daughter Rachel's personal identity, but eventually he comes around. Don't worry. There is no treacle here, even if Murray has now created a show where Judy Greer voices a moon. After this happen, Rachel debuts her first new "Fatheads" episode in years, and there are new characters. Rocko, who had been pushing Mr. Bighead to accept change and accept his daughter, flips out at this difference. "The Fatheads" isn't the show he remembered, and desperately wanted, and it makes him have a total mental breakdown.

There is a lot I admire about *Rocko's Modern Life*. If the grossness and weirdness was cut down just a bit it would be a great show. Even so, it's my favorite Nickelodeon cartoon from the '90s. It truly is the "just right" animated show. As a kid it was my favorite, because I thought it was the funniest cartoon of the bunch, even with all the jokes I didn't get. Now I get those jokes, and I have lived an adult life and understand Rocko's adult experiences. *Rocko* accepted people's intelligence and played up to it, while also being gross and telling masturbation jokes in a cartoon on Nickelodeon. A bunch of eccentrics with an edge got to play in their own sandbox and this was what they came up with. *Rocko's Modern Life* is a testament to what can happen when you let creative people do what they want. You get "Wacky Delly." You get a musical episode about spring cleaning. *Rocko's Modern Life* was a hoot. I'm still a fan, and I imagine Joe Murray would be glad that it's not because of simple nostalgia.

Roundhouse

We can go anywhere from here

My parents kept an eye on what I watched as a young child. They weren't overly strict, I've been watching *The Simpsons* since I was about eight or so, but they didn't necessarily approve of everything I tried to consume. When it came to Nickelodeon, they were fine with pretty much the entire lineup of the '90s. I don't recall them clucking their tongues at *The Ren & Stimpy Show*, though if they did I would understand that with hindsight. The one show I distinctively remember them not liking me watching was *Roundhouse*. That didn't stop me, granted, but I also do not recall watching it every time it was on SNICK. It feels possible to me I simply didn't really "get it," or didn't find it funny, but I may have also been listening to my parents' declarations. I had exactly two memories of *Roundhouse* prior to this book, other than remembering the theme song and that people danced sometimes. I remembered a sketch about a fake game show where every answer was "You're not my real father," save for the last answer, which was "yams." I also remembered a sketch that involved a bra stuffed with balloons and when one of the balloons was popped another one inflated. This led me to believe it was probably some cheesy sketch show starring teenagers, like a slightly older, slightly earlier *All That*. Indeed, *Roundhouse* is a fairly cheesy sketch show, but it's so much more than that, and I was genuinely taken aback by much of it.

Roundhouse was created by Buddy Sheffield, who had been a writer on *In Living Color*, alongside his ex-wife Rita Sheffield Hester. They were joined by musician Benny Hester, who produced the music for the show and co-produced the show. He's apparently a pretty big wig in Christian music, a genre with which I am strikingly unfamiliar. The title *Roundhouse* is in reference to a railway roundhouse, which is something used to turn trains around and get them on the right track. I have never seen one of these to my recollection, but the name is certainly distinct. The cast of *Roundhouse* was always extensive and multicultural. Given Sheffield's history with *In Living Color*, you might expect a sketch show like that. Instead, *Roundhouse* is something decidedly different. In fact, it feels way more like a stage sketch show than a TV sketch show. I can honestly not recall seeing anything like it on television before.

Each episode is built around a theme, and all the sketches are to that theme. There was an episode on divorce and step families (the one I recalled from the "yams" joke), one about the environment, one about popularity, etc. Ostensibly at the center of the show were the Anyfamily, Dad, Mom, and two kids. The dad of the family was played by John Crane, but he would be in other sketches as well. He had a recliner like a regular Martin Crane (no relation I'm sure, since Martin is a fictional character). The mom was played by Shawn Daywalt. While the family is revisited during the episodes, there are a ton of other sketches going on. And I do mean a ton. The number-one thing that struck me about *Roundhouse* is how frenetic it is. I hope you like blackout sketches, because *Roundhouse* has a bunch of them in every episode. They get in, they do their bit, and then they immediately throw to the next sketch. One sketch will end and the next one will start adjacent to it. The camera movement is so kinetic. There are no down periods in an episode of *Roundhouse*. The energy is genuinely impressive.

Granted, to make this happen things are pretty ramshackle. Costumes are minimal if not entirely eschewed. Props are hastily thrown together. I hope you can accept improv space work and object work, because you get both of those in *Roundhouse*. Maybe it's the comedy performer I me, but I was willing to accept that, especially from a sketch show that is moving so fast. Like I said, it feels like you're watching a stage sketch show, and I was able to buy into that and therefore accept everything on its face value. I know what they were doing was impressive in terms of staging and editing, all while doing it for a live audience. This was not an easy undertaking. And that's just the sketch comedy!

Roundhouse also has music and dance numbers. Here's the thing: While the show has a band, it's the cast members that do the singing and dancing. One minute they are doing a silly comedy bit, the next they are doing an elaborate dance number or *singing* an original song. The ambition of this show! Thing about watching a lesser episode of *Saturday Night Live* with a bunch of recurring sketches and a host that is staring daggers through the cue cards. They look positively lazy compared to any given episode of *Roundhouse*. Now, I'm not really a dance fan, and I don't enjoy the dance numbers, but it is really impressive that the cast can do that. The singers are clearly hired for their singing skills, but then they can do comedy as well. You almost had to be a triple threat to be on *Roundhouse*.

As for the quality of the comedy … well like I said this is a sketch show. More than that, it's a sketch show that shoved seemingly over a dozen sketches into any given episode. There are some misses. Overall, there's a little corniness to some of the comedy. You'll hear some lazy puns in every episode, usually in a parody of some kind. There are a ton of parodies on *Roundhouse*. Farts are a punchline (and in some cases effectively the whole sketch) on many occasions, which I groan at. And they aren't fart jokes like you might find in some children's programming these days. They do skew a little older, which speaks to my parents' concern about me watching the show when I was six or so. *Roundhouse* was one of the first shows on SNICK shows when it debuted in 1992, and it definitely was testing the horizons of what Nickelodeon could handle contest wise. It was very rare to hear the word "panties" on Nickelodeon in the '90s. I assume it still is now. Some of the dances are also what one might call suggestive. *Roundhouse* was far from raunchy, but it is to my memory the most "mature" and risqué live-action show to air on Nickelodeon.

That being said, there are also good sketches on *Roundhouse*. What most impressed me was the pointed nature of some of the show's satire. When I was looking for episodes to watch I noticed that there was one about war. I had to give that a chance. Would a kids' show in 1996 do war satire on television? Indeed, they would, at least if that show was *Roundhouse*. There was straight-up anti-war satire in that episode. Also, a joke about a cleaning solution called "Napalmolive" that was surprisingly dark. Two characters get their hands blown off in another sketch. I have to give genuine credit to *Roundhouse* for doing an episode like this. The overall quality of the comedy is merely pretty good, but the ambition—as always with this show—I can get behind.

One other thing that surprised me about the show is the cast, and specifically the age of the cast. Having not seen a single second of roundhouse in almost 15 years I had just assumed they were teenagers. Sure, maybe older teenagers, but I figured nobody on this cast was going to be older than 20. Of course, when you are a little kid you are a terrible judge of age. Looking back I'd bet my first grade teacher was like 24, but at the time she was indistinct to me from a 40 year old. Instead, all the *Roundhouse* cast seemed to be adults upon this watching. Most of them seem to be in about their mid-twenties, and in fact John Crane, who played Dad, wad 30 when the show began. Crane had actually been in Groundlings alongside the likes of Will Ferrell and would eventually become the head writer of *MADtv*. In hindsight, this makes sense. No kid was going to be able to manage being on a show like this. Doing fast-paced sketch comedy, singing, and dancing? You need the time to learn all those skills. I don't think Nick would have built a sketch show around adults, even somewhat young adults, later in their run. They seemed to eventually get preoccupied with the idea kids only want to watch other kids. Or cartoon sponges.

Roundhouse brought its envelope-pushing (for Nick at least) humor to SNICK from 1992 through 1996. They aired 52 episodes over four seasons. Overall, 19 different people were in the cast. None of them other than Crane when on to particular success. Although, Crystal Lewis, who was only on the first season, went into a career in Christian music. Jennifer Cihi apparently sang the original Hot Pockets jingle, so you've been hearing her voice in your head for years. Obviously, *All That* is the quintessential Nickelodeon sketch show. It's the one that birthed other stars and helped define the network in the '90s. Kenan Thompson and Amanda Bynes have had better careers than any *Roundhouse* cast member, even with Bynes' troubles in adulthood. That may be true, but after watching both shows for this book I have a declaration to make: *Roundhouse* is a better show than *All That*. It's more ambitious, it's more impressive, and in fact it's also funnier as well. My parents may not have wanted me to watch it back then, but they can't stop me now. Oh, and to answer the other big question: yams.

Rugrats

Everybody's gotta go sometime

Was *Rugrats* for six year olds who were nostalgic for being two? Or for six year olds who saw two year olds and thought, "Man, I'm glad I'm not that young and naïve anymore?" This never occurred to me as a child, but as an adult it has baffled me. The premise of *Rugrats* is strange when you think about it for more than two seconds. That didn't keep it from having a great deal of success, at least in terms of its lifespan. *Rugrats'* original run went from 1991 through 2004, with spinoffs and movies thrown into the mix. And yet, is it anybody's favorite cartoon from '90s Nickelodeon? We all watched it, but does anybody love it? It was a huge part of your childhood if you grew up on Nick at this time, and it definitely made a cultural impact. *Rugrats* was ubiquitous, but quantity and quality are not the same thing.

Rugrats is one of the three original Nicktoons, as you know at this point. This has already been established at this juncture of the book. On August 11, 1991, the first three Nicktoons debuted, with *Rugrats* airing right between *Doug* and *Ren & Stimpy*. *Rugrats* was the first major original program produced by the animation studio of Klasky Csupo. The company was named for the founding duo, then-couple Arlene Klasky and Gabor Csupo. This was not the animation firm's first brush with greatness, to be fair. The studio was called upon to animate some shorts for *The Tracey Ullman Show*. It was about a family of five. One of their kids, the only boy in the family, was a bit of a rapscallion. I'm talking about *The Simpsons*. Klasky Csupo also helmed the animation for the first three seasons of mankind's greatest creation, before moving on to their own productions. Also, apparently Dr. Nick on *The Simpsons* was partially inspired by Csupo. In terms of his look, that is. Csupo has never performed surgery with a knife and fork from a seafood restaurant ... as far as I know.

Klasky and Csupo joined forces with Paul Germain, who had more experience with writing and producing and was able to bring those skills to the table. The trio started working on the pilot back in 1989, which was when *The Simpsons* debuted, and they finished the pilot in 1990. They were joined by Peter Chung for that, who directed the pilot and helped design the characters. According to Chung, Csupo's desire was to make the babies look "strange" as opposed to "cute," which I think is basically the only way Klasky Csupo animation can operate anyway.

The animation style of Klasky Csupo's shows is quite distinct, and not necessarily good. Everything seems squiggly and a little amorphous. Characters seem off model even when they aren't. When they really go all out, characters can look downright bizarre and seem like caricatures. That didn't always serve them well, especially when it came to a couple of Jewish characters from the show. I am a bit particular about my taste in animation, and *Rugrats* isn't necessarily my style. It works for creating a distinct world, and the way settings and backgrounds look I do like. The way the characters look, on the other hand, is a little off-putting.

Who are those characters anyway? *Rugrats* focuses on a group of toddlers who are friends that go on adventures. The ostensible protagonist is Tommy Pickles, a one year old who rarely if ever wears pants. You know, because he's basically a baby and that's how you know he is a baby by pop culture terms. Was this a pre-onesie world? I do not have children and I do not know (or care). He's adventurous and bold, even though he is the youngest of the main characters. His best friend, to the extent a one year old can have friends, is Chuckie Finster, who is two and is afraid of everything. There are the twins Phil and Lil DeVille, who I guess are "gross?" Is that their characteristic? They do fight a lot, and when they do they call one another "Philip" and "Lillian" like an infant sibling version of *Who's Afraid of Virginia Woolf?* The antagonist of the show is Angelica Pickles, Tommy's cousin who is a bully despite only being three. Being a three year old who bullies a one year old is pretty psychopathic behavior, but what three year old isn't towing the line of psychopathy on a day-to-day basis? Susie, who lives across the street and is also three, shows up sometimes as a friend. There are other kid characters but I don't care about them because they aren't from my childhood. Even Dil, Tommy's younger brother, didn't debut until 1998, at which point I wasn't really watching *Rugrats*.

Then, there are the adults, who bear much more relevance to me as an adult now myself. Stu and Didi Pickles are Tommy's parents and now my favorite characters on the show. That's only partially because Stu was voiced by Jack Riley, who played Eliot Carlin on *The Bob Newhart Show*. Mr. Carlin was the most frequently seen of Bob Hartley's patients, and definitely the best of the bunch. He was a misanthropic cynical man who hated everybody, most of all himself. Jack Riley was great as Mr. Carlin, and he's great as Stu Pickles, who is much nicer but just as crushed by life. He's a toy inventor who must have enough success to have a pretty sizable house and raise two children. Stu and Didi are often overwhelmed parents, and they get all their advice from the work of child psychology Dr. Lipschitz.

Stu's brother Drew is Angelica's dad, who is married to Charlotte. They are a real power couple, as they both have well-paying jobs. Charlotte is actually the CEO of her company and has a cell phone. In the early '90s! Take that, Zack Morris! Their busy work schedules obviously leave them with limited time to spend with Angelica, which explains why she is always being babysat by Stu and Didi, or occasionally Stu's dad Grandpa Lou, who is also a delightful character. We also, on occasion, see Didi's parents, Boris and Minka. They introduced me to the concept of borscht. They also got the show some stick because they are Jewish characters, and the animation style of Klasky Csupo left them looking a little caricature-y. However, both Klasky and Csupo are of Jewish descent, and this is a show that did both a Chanukah and Passover special, so as a gentile I will cede the floor to the folks who made the show on that front, in terms of everything being acceptable. I almost wrote "kosher" there—pun not intended—before catching myself.

It also makes sense why Chuckie is often dropped off at the Pickles', because his dad Chas is a widower. A young widower at that. Chuckie's mom died soon after he was born, which is strikingly tragic for a show for young kids, but also probably considered more palatable than divorce in some twisted way to the folks making the big decisions. Chuckie looks a lot like his father and also seems to have the same personality, which I guess makes some sense as he is still so young. Phil and Lil have parents too, but they make less of an impact, but I do remember Mrs. DeVille being a brassy woman.

The crux of *Rugrats* is based on the kids not understanding the world. However, the things they misunderstood had to be things that the kids watching the show did comprehend. That was the where the humor was supposed to lie, at least for the child viewers. An eight year old isn't going to understand a nuanced conversation about relationships or jokes about getting hangovers. They do understand that you don't need to be afraid of a toilet eating you. The kids live in their own little world. So many things are fresh and new to them, and they can't really understand what's going on. That makes simple things like getting a ball from the neighbor's yard into an adventure of epic proportions. We knew the reality as older kids—it was just a ball over a fence—and that made the story feel clever and inventive. It also plays into my wondering about if this was a show for little kids who were happy they weren't even younger kids. I mean, you're sort of laughing at Tommy and his friends for not knowing what's really going on.

There also exists within the *Rugrats* world two levels of everything. The little kids talk to each other, but we're to understand this is "baby talk." Tommy can talk on the show, but the adults don't understand him. To them, he's just babbling. All the kids can understand each other, though, and Angelica can understand them because she is still young enough to remember the language of baby talk. That's a bit of a stretch for the sake of convenience, but it's a cartoon about babies. You have to accept some leaps in logic. Even though we hear the kids talking in a more coherent way than they are in "real" life, they still mispronounce a lot of words, mostly because they don't understand what they are hearing. That's how "Sasquatch" becomes "Satchmo," leading to any adult who hears the older kids mention their fear of Satchmo to ask "The trumpet player?"

Which brings me to another aspect of *Rugrats*, which are the jokes for the adults watching with their kids. That means this show actually operates on three levels. It exists on the level the kids on the show operate. Then, there are the kids watching at home who are more advanced and realize how much they don't understand. However, these are still children. They are still super ignorant of the world at large and have a small scope of references. This leads to the level the show operates at for adults. The adults can still get the jokes about the toddler not understanding the world around them and thinking that magicians can, in fact, actually make people disappear. The older viewer can also get a lot of references clearly geared toward them, not to mention many of the jokes that come from the adult characters. Watching the show now, even as a childless man, I see so many jokes about adulthood and parenthood I did not recognize as a kid.

Needless to say, jokes about Louis Armstrong aren't for seven year olds. There is an episode where Chuckie gets swept up in the hora dance and afterwards he proclaims, "The hora … the hora" just like Colonel Kurtz at the end of *Apocalypse Now*. He's even lying on the ground in the same way as Kurtz. Although, I swear somehow I got this reference. Maybe not when it originally aired, but perhaps during a rerun later in the '90s. Obviously, I had not seen *Apocalypse Now*, but I was a kid who watched a ton of TV and had absorbed a lot of pop culture. It's entirely plausible when I was 10 or 11 I had gleaned that "the horror … the horror" was a line from a movie. I did start watching *Mystery Science Theater 3000* in the '90s, after all.

Then, there's the existential streak that runs through *Rugrats*. There is a beloved meme of Stu making pudding at four in the morning. When Didi asks him why he is making pudding at such an hour, he responds, the despair clear in his voice, "Because I've lost control of my life." I'm of two minds about this. On the one hand, that's a great joke. It would work in any sitcom and in any show for adults. And yet, does it make sense in a show that is clearly for kids? I do not believe that something is strictly for kids just because it is a cartoon, or because it airs on a channel like Nickelodeon. Take *Phineas and Ferb*, for example. That show, a Disney original, operates under the premise that they are making a show that doesn't exclude kids from the audience, not that they are making a show for kids. Maybe *Rugrats* felt that way, but most of the show doesn't operate like that. It can be a little "neither fish nor fowl" in that sense. As an adult, I appreciate the jokes for me. As a cultural critic, I think it may be a fault. This show is not good enough to watch as an adult and enjoy it, so what purpose do those jokes serve other than to give an adult a little chuckle here and there while stuck watching it with their kids?

The initial run of *Rugrats* lasted until 1994, giving us 65 episodes. However, most episodes consisted of two stories, as this was one of those cartoons that did two 11-minute stories per episode, by and large. The show went on hiatus at this point, and a lot of people left the show, or straight up left Klasky Csupo. For two years, the only new *Rugrats* we saw were the two aforementioned Jewish holiday movies. So why did this show end up having such a long run and getting so engrained in our lives? Because of the magic of reruns. Nickelodeon loved reruns, and they specifically loved *Rugrats* reruns. While they weren't producing new episodes, they ran reruns constantly. Like, every day. In fact, Nickelodeon aired episodes of *Rugrats* 655 times in the year 1996. The popularity of those reruns led to the show returning in 1997, and to *The Rugrats Movie* in 1998. That movie is when Dil was born, which means everything after that is something I didn't pay attention to at the time. It also starts to leave the realm of the time '90s kids were watching it. Chuckie's dad getting married and Chuckie getting a stepsister and all that stuff is for the author of the book on 2000s Nickelodeon to tackle, and I wish them the best.

Rugrats was a tent pole of Nickelodeon in the '90s. That's in part because of the fact it was one of the three original Nicktoons. It's in part because they ran reruns of it incessantly. And, of course, it's in part because it ran from 1991 through the end of the decade and beyond. Was it the best show of Nickelodeon in the '90s? No, I don't think so. I don't even think it was the best cartoon. Was it the most-important cartoon? I would make the argument that, for the '90s, it was. There are definitely funny moments and strong bits in every episode. The voiceover cast is strong and goes well beyond Jack Riley. I should probably shout out the likes of E.G. Daily, Christine Cavanaugh, Kath Soucie, and of course legendary voiceover actor Tress MacNeille. The theme song, from Devo member Mark Mothersbaugh, is catchy and perfect for a show about toddlers. It was certainly better than the "Rugrats Rap" I remember from ads on Nick back in the day.

I still can't wrap my head around this show as an adult. I still wonder what it was that made it appeal to kids. It could be nostalgia or anti-nostalgia or neither. I feel like I just thought it was funny, though some of what I found was funny was the characters' version of reality versus what I knew reality to be. That's not a bad thing, but it is a weird thing when you are only like six or seven. The idea of a seven year old turning up their nose at a toddler is funny to me now. It's not as funny as Stu Pickles making pudding at four in the morning, but it's funny. I don't feel as fondly for *Rugrats* as the kids on the show felt about Reptar, a dinosaur character that I wish I could have had more time to delve into. The words, "Halt I am Reptar!" are never far from the front of my mind. I feel like there was a version of *Rugrats* I liked as a kid and a version I like now. That could be seen as a strength or a weakness. As *Rugrats* taught us, our reality can be shaped by how we perceive it.

Salute Your Shorts

Nothing lasts forever, even our dear
friendships ... or poorly-crafted fishing poles

For a child of the '90s, the concept of camp had a hefty grasp on our minds. Either you were the kind of kid that went away to camp for the summer, or you were the kind of kid that didn't but was intrigued by the idea. Surely there were some children that only thought of camp as a nightmarish outcome. Like, in their imagination they envision some impractical horror story wherein they are accidentally shipped off to camp and have to be there all summer. You know, those who are colloquially referred to as "indoor kids."

I was, funnily enough, in the camp of kids that didn't get to go to camp. Sure, I wanted to. However, my parents would not allow it. They never explained why. Perhaps they feared I would be unsupervised because the teenaged counselors were off having sex and then being murdered by a machete-wielding maniac with an increasing number of supernatural powers. At the time, it bothered me. Now, I am totally happy with the decision. The strange thing is that I ever wanted to go to camp at all, given that I grew up watching *Salute Your Shorts*. It seems like a show engineered to make the impressionable youth turn against the concept of going to camp.

In a way, *Salute Your Shorts* was a de facto trip to summer camp for kids who did not actually get to go to a camp. Hey, my generation was largely raised by television, so why should TV not also be our camp counselor? There was less sunburn and bug bites this way. *Salute Your Shorts* aired two seasons of 13 episodes, which seems insane to me in hindsight. I feel like I was watching that show all summer, and probably even in the fall, for years. Surely that's probably because of reruns. There is inconsistent information of when episodes aired. What I can tell for sure is that the first season aired in 1991 and the second aired in 1992. If IMDb is to be believed, multiple episodes were aired each week and the entire seasons would be burnt through in about a month's time. Episodes definitely aired in summer, which was fitting for a show about a summer camp. Reruns continued through the bulk of the rest of the '90s, which may be why I intuitively felt like there must have been at least double the episodes they were. *Salute Your Shorts* has had an outsized impact given how few episodes there are. Probably because it was the summer camp experience for many of us.

The show was created by Steve Slavkin, who based it off a book called *Salute Your Shorts: Life at Summer Camp* that he co-wrote with a man named Thomas Hill. Slavkin had another role on the show beyond being the creator, as he also voiced Dr. Kahn, the camp director. He was never seen on screen, but his voice would boom over the speakers running through the camp. Slavkin had something of a poor man's Ben Stein vibes, but if his personal politics happen to be more palatable I am willing to flip the script and start calling Stein the poor man's Steve Slavkin. Kahn's missives occasionally served as jokes, but often were used for exposition and transitions. This was actually a clever way of doing that, and much less clumsy than making characters recite exposition in conversation, especially given the bulk of the cast were kids.

Salute Your Shorts tells the tale of the adventures of a group of kids at Camp Anawanna. The camp feels sort of like a prison compound in some ways. The mail comes by boat. It feels like the kids at Camp Anawanna are isolated from the world, only being watched by one camp counselor, Kevin Lee, known as "Ug." His nickname both points out that he doesn't have much authority over the kids and how not clever children are. While there are many kids running around the camp, much as how there are many kids at Bayside High School in *Saved by the Bell*, we only spend time with about six of them per season.

The first episode of the show, "Michael Comes to Camp," is about, well, a kid named Michael coming to Camp Anawanna for the first time. He is our point-of-view character, which becomes a problem as the season goes on and he has literally no personality. To call him an everyman, or an everyboy as it were, would be to presuppose that the average person is a big zero without anything noteworthy about them. Everybody else is an archetype, which is not exactly rich storytelling in its own right, but Michael just exists to not know things and to be pushed around.

When he gets to camp he is immediately told that he made a mistake. The character who tells him this is Sponge—not his given name—who earned that moniker because he is brainy. He's also smaller than most of the other kids and has glasses, which in a '90s TV show for kids meant he was a nerd. Eddie C. Gelfen, who is known as Donkeylips, is a big lummox. You need to have a dumb character in an ensemble comedy, after all. On the girl's side of things, Z.Z. Ziff is an environmentalist, Dina is shallow and materialistic, and Telly is a tomboy who loves sports. Then, there is the final boy of our septet. Bobby Budnick, a dead-eyed sociopath with a red mullet.

So much of the conflict of *Salute Your Shorts* is driven by Budnick. He's a bully. He's vicious. He cheats and swindles. Budnick is awful to everybody basically all the time. If he's nice to somebody, it's because he wants things. Granted, most of the time the stories end with Budnick getting his comeuppance. For an example, let's take a look at the episode "Toilet Seat Basketball," which is one of the episodes that stick out in my memory. The kids play on a basketball team called the Tigers, led by Telly, but they aren't as good as the Hurricanes. Budnick takes over the team, promising they can win without working. Also, he renames them Budnick's Bombers and gets them pretty dope tie-dyed shirts for uniforms. The team does start winning, but because Budnick stole the Hurricanes' playbook. Let us ignore the absurdity of a bunch of preteens having a playbook for their playground basketball games. At first, the kids other than Telly are OK with it, because they are winning without having to practice. Then, they feel bad and learn their lesson. Budnick is banished to the bench, and only let in during the final seconds. Because his candy stash is on the line, he refused to pass, and his desperation shot doesn't go in. The Bombers lose, and Budnick loses his candy stash. The lessons we learned as kids are clear. Practice is important. You can't get what you want without working. Don't trust promises that seem too good to be true. Also if you have issues with gambling there's a number you can call.

The second season brought change, as Michael was out and in his place came Ronnie Pinsky, played by Blake Soper, now known as Blake Sennett. He's the only actor whose name I mention because he is the only one who has had a notable career as an adult. Not as an actor, mind you. Sennett has become a musician, and a successful one at that. He was a member of the excellent indie rock band Rilo Kiley, fronted by Jenny Lewis, who was also a child actor. If you take away anything from this chapter, it should be the suggestion to listen to Rilo Kiley. Unlike Michael, Pinsky did have a personality. He was suave and clever and people at camp liked him. Pinsky oozed confidence, unlike Michael. Basically, he was a rip-off of a Ferris Bueller or a Zack Morris, but with less sociopathic tendencies. Hey, at least Pinsky was interesting, and he changed the dynamic of the camp and the show. Budnick couldn't really get anything over on Pinsky. They had something akin to a Wile E. Coyote and Roadrunner vibe. Since Budnick was so unlikable, especially when you are a kid and just see characters as people who are cool or not as opposed to characters who have a role to play in a story, it was nice to see him get his comeuppance.

Of course, there were only 13 episodes of that. There was also no closure, as the show was cancelled before a planned third season. Apparently there were budget issues, and they wanted to move production from Los Angeles to Nickelodeon Studios in Orlando, Florida. Producer Courtney Conte said in the book *Slimed* that each episode had a budget of $180,000, which is nothing for TV. With a lower budget, it may have looked like the third season of *Batman '66* when the villains would have their lairs in a black void. As such, the final episode is about the kids starting a birdhouse company, another '90s staple. Kids starting a business, that is. Not birdhouse companies. This feels weirdly grim, because in terms of the story we were privy to, all the kids are still at camp. It feels like they are stuck there forever. It's like how the final episode if *ALF* ends with ALF being surrounded and captured by the United States government. When it aired, it said "To be continued…" but the show was cancelled so that was it. As far as I'm concerned, Sponge, Dina, and the crew are trapped at Camp Anawanna forever.

Make no mistake; Camp Anawanna is a camp you are stuck at. This is the overarching theme of many episodes of the show. The title comes from the practice of stealing boxer shorts and raising them up the flagpole. Within the show, there are murmurs of a punishment called the "Awful Waffle" that is delivered, frontier justice style, by the children. We never see it. We only heard it talked about in hushed and horrified tones. All we know for sure is that it involved syrup and a tennis racket. Naturally, Budnick is a frequent administrator. In one episode Michael tries to convince his grandparents to get him out of camp so the bully Thud Mackie doesn't beat him up. He actually almost gets free, but only with the promise of a summer spent at his grandparents' house, which is even worse apparently. Truly, life is hell for these children. Ug honestly seems to get it the worst. His face is stained blue once. His girlfriend breaks up with him via mail. To be fair, he does start dating the mail carrier, Mona, but she only shows up in a couple episodes. Like *Salute Your Shorts* as a whole, Mona occupies a relatively large area of my brain given how little I actually saw of her.

And yet, it wasn't all bad. Sure, there was the nightmarish Zeke the Plumber episode, which was *Salute Your Shorts*' riff on horror movies. The mask they used for Zeke the Plumber was cheap, but that made it more effectively creepy. This is an episode I would not watch in reruns as a kid, and I am not the only child of the '90s that felt this way. On the other hand, they played capture the flag with water balloons! I think this is what I imagined when I imagine going to camp as a kid. I envisioned the good stuff and not all the bad things. *Salute Your Shorts* may have skewed things further negatively than reality. Or maybe I'm naïve. Maybe if I had gone to camp I would have been as miserable as the crew at Camp Anawanna.

Salute Your Shorts is a middling show in terms of quality. There were worse '90s Nick shows, but *Salute Your Shorts* was definitely not good. It's not one I like to revisit now. If I had not had to check back in with it for the purposes of this book, I would have been content with never seeing it again. The show looked like it was made on a shoestring budget. While none of the kids were bad actors, nobody was really a standout either. It was just a lot of mediocrity baked under the oppressive sun that plagued Camp Anawanna. That being said, because I watched reruns of these 26 episodes (or rather 25 of them while I skipped Zeke the Plumber over and over), *Salute Your Shorts* is indelible in my mind. It is the camp experience of my childhood, and of many kids who either couldn't, or wouldn't, go to camp themselves. In honor of the famous theme song that began the show, all I have say is that when I think about *Salute Your Shorts* I hope we never part. Hey, I made sure to get it right. I didn't want to pay the price.

The Secret World of Alex Mack

If you want to be special, a good
shortcut is to get doused in chemicals

It's a tale as old as time. An ordinary kid becomes extraordinary. Sometimes they find out they were special all along. It turns out they weren't ordinary at all, but in fact had some sort of power within them. Maybe they are the chosen one. They could turn out to be a wizard. Perhaps Zelda Rubenstein tells you that you are about to become a teen witch. Then there are the stories about kids who have something happen to them that suddenly makes them special, particularly giving them powers. This is the case for young Alexandra Mack, known as Alex to most. The idea of suddenly finding out you're special, or becoming special, is a bit of wish fulfillment for kids. When you feel unremarkable you dream of being remarkable. Ideally, though, you don't dream of being drenched in a top secret chemical and getting chased by an evil CEO.

The Secret World of Alex Mack is about what happens when a kid finds themselves in a strange new situation that involves all sorts of fantastical powers but also a lot of fear and dread. The opening credits lays it out explicitly that Alex felt all-too-average but no longer feels that way. Ah, but is that a good thing or bad thing? What does one do when they are suddenly superpowered but also still want to be a relatively normal teenager? This is the heart of *The Secret World of Alex Mack*, with a fair amount of low-stakes thriller built in as well. There's also more serialized storytelling in *Alex Mack* than almost any other Nick show from the '90s.

Alex and her family live in a fictional Arizona town called Paradise Valley. It's home to a chemical plant that just so happens to employ her dad. They seem to do all sorts of insane stuff as a company. For example, they are working on a top-secret drug they call GC-161. The CEO, Danielle Atron, wants to turn it into a weight-loss drug. Now, I don't know if this is how chemical plants tend to do business. I also don't know if that is how weight-loss drugs work. On top of that, most potential weight-loss drugs don't have the side effects that GC-161 has. We find out about this when, on Alex's first day of junior high, she is almost hit by a truck and then has GC-161 spilled all over her.

Alex quickly realizes that she has the capability to do many things she

Alex Mack (Larisa Oleynik) shows off some of her secret powers (Nickelodeon).

couldn't before. The most memorable of these is her ability to turn herself into a puddle that makes her look like liquid metal but is not actually liquid metal, *Terminator 2* style. When she uses the power the first time she is not able to bring her clothes along with her, but then she manages to figure that out immediately. Why this was a necessary step in the process I do not know. Alex also has telekinetic powers and shoots something akin to electricity out of her fingers. I mean, it's supposed to be electricity, but it doesn't look as good as, say, Emperor Palpatine's electricity finger powers. Say, is Alex maybe related to Palpatine? Is she a descendent of Rey!? Only time will tell. There are surely more *Star Wars* movies to come. Also, Alex doesn't have full control of her new powers, such as the fact she glows bright yellow when she's nervous. As a teenager, that happens plenty. I mean, she has crushes! It's so relatable!

Alex only confides in two people, her best friend Ray and her sister Annie. Annie is a scientific super genius. Honestly, she's a more interesting character than Alex in many ways. Alex has remarkability foisted upon her. Annie made herself remarkable. This lets Alex have people to interact with regarding her power, but also Annie is able to do scientific tests. That allows Alex, and the viewer, to find out more about her powers as the show goes on. Alex does not tell her parents, even though her dad works at the very plant that made the chemical that doused her. To be fair, Alex is right to be worried about being found out. Atron wants to find her to keep her under wraps and also to experiment on her. She is quite evil. If Atron had a mustache she would twirl it, and I bet one of the chemicals at her plant could give her a hirsute upper lip. Her right-hand man is her head of security, and he's obsessed with finding the so-called "GC-161 child." Also, his name is Vince Carter, which is very amusing. Vince Carter is also the name of a Hall of Fame basketball player who rose to fame a few years after the show debuted. The march of time can be delightful sometimes. On a more intentional note, Carter is eventually replaced as Atron's lead henchman by a character named Lars Fredrickson, who is purposefully named after the member of the punk band Rancid.

There are other kid characters in the show, though none of them are as important as Ray or Annie. Louis is basically Alex's "other" friend, so she can have a friend who is a little less kindhearted and a little more scheming than Ray. Scott is Alex's crush, but he's usually too busy seeing another girl. One of those girls, by the way, was played by a young Jessica Alba. This is, in fact, Alba's first TV role. She's definitely the one true star to come out of *The Secret World of Alex Mack*, but the actor Will Estes—who is one of the leads on *Blue Bloods*—had a role in the fourth season as well. Meanwhile, lead of the show Larisa Oleynik seemed destined for stardom, or at least a successful career. After starring in her own TV show for four seasons, Oleynik had a recurring role as Tommy Solomon's girlfriend Alissa on *3rd Rock from the Sun*. She also had a big role in the hit romantic comedy *10 Things I Hate About You*. However, after the turn of the millennium Oleynik didn't really transition into adult stardom, or even adult success. She hasn't really been in any movies, and I was sad to see that she was in one of those awful *Atlas Shrugged* films. On TV, she did have a role in a few episodes of *Mad Men*, and I remember seeing her in one episode of *Psych*. I must admit then when I saw her on *Psych* I kind of understood why her acting career didn't take off, as her acting skills hadn't really progressed since I last saw her on *3rd Rock*. Hey, at least she's done a lot of voiceover work for something called *Winx Club*.

Like I said, *The Secret World of Alex Mack* balanced telling a story in every episode with the overarching story going on. In an episode Alex may be dealing with some regular kid problem, like learning to drive or being jealous of her sister, but she's also dealing with the whole GC-161 issue. She's always on the run from Atron and Paradise Valley Chemical Plant. Sometimes they get close to finding her. In fact, the truck driver who almost hit her even realizes who she is once, but decides to keep her secret. This is a pretty cool element of this show, and something you never really saw on Nickelodeon. The network was obsessed with reruns. If they had their druthers, their shows would have been nothing but standalone episodes with no series finales. That way they could show them as reruns in any order and just cycle through them. You couldn't do that with *Alex Mack*. Not only did it have some degree of serialized storytelling, but it has a definitive series finale.

In what was effectively a two-part series finale, called "Paradise Lost" and "Paradise Regained," the events of the show finally come to a head. Louis finds out about Alex's powers, and while he tries to hide them he fails, and Atron finally finds Alex. She has Alex kidnapped and taken to the plant, where her parents are also taken. Then, the Macks finally find out about her daughter's powers. Her plan, in true villain fashion, is to blow up the plant with Alex and her parents inside to keep the secret of GC-161 to get out. That seems a little extreme, but I'm not as business minded. Fortunately, Ray and Will Estes' character Hunter are able to save the day. Atron gets arrested. The truck driver who almost hit Alex alerts the FDA to the truth of GC-161 and those two have a nice moment together. At the very end, Alex's dad gives Alex an antidote for GC-161, but when the episode ends she has not made her decision on whether or not to take it. It's an open ending, just like *Inception*, but better. Seriously though, a show about a girl with superpowers from a chemical spill is less silly to me than dream heists and possibly being trapped in the dream world forever. This series finale was a momentous event, akin to appointment viewing for teens. Never before had there been an overt series finale event like this on Nickelodeon. History was truly made.

The Secret World of Alex Mack aired for four seasons and 78 episodes starting in October of 1994 and just tipping into January 1998, when the two final episodes aired on the same day. The shows aired on SNICK, taking over for *Clarissa Explains It All*. It was a perfect show for SNICK. It was about junior high students, who became high school students, and was a little more mature than other Nick shows. Not necessarily in terms of content, but in terms of storytelling. You had to follow along a bit and keep track of things on *Alex Mack*. For an adult, that's easy. For a 10 year old it's an introduction to serialized storytelling. They had decent enough actors on the show, even the kids, and the show looked better than a lot of Nick's live-action shows. Yeah, the special effects were maybe a little iffy, but by 1994 standards Alex's morphing is fine. It doesn't look realistic, but it passes muster. Also, at the beginning of the fourth season they did a couple episodes with 3-D capabilities. I realized this in my rewatch when Louis was suddenly shooting foam balls right at the screen. Oh, and in that episode Jack Riley, aka the voice of Stu Pickles and Mr. Carlin on *The Bob Newhart Show*, plays Alex's driving instructor. That was awesome.

For a child, the stakes of *Alex Mack* felt substantive to me. I mean, that's still true as an adult, especially knowing that in the end the villain was willing to kill a girl and her parents. It's relatively charming, and I can watch *The Secret World of Alex Mack* as an adult and be totally fine with it. I wouldn't call it good, but I would say that it's decent. As a kid, though, I definitely thought it was good. I thought it was exciting and the premise was cool, and it could even be funny occasionally. There was no show like *The Secret World of Alex Mack* on Nickelodeon, just like there was no kid like Alex Mack. She was special, and maybe you wished you were special. Although not in the way Alex Mack was. It's one thing if a kid wanted to be good at sports or be skilled with an instrument. It's quite another to want to be involved in a severe chemical spill and then be able to melt down into a liquid puddle and move around. *The Secret World of Alex Mack* could serve as a source of excitement and intrigue. It shouldn't have been wish fulfillment. The lesson, as always, is to be yourself. It's true for *Moby Dick*, and it's true for my book as well.

SK8-TV

Rise and grind

I was, for a brief period of my life, a sk8r boi. This was in my early teenage years, when I had stopped watching Nickelodeon and started doing stuff like listening to punk and disliking artists like Avril Lavigne for doing stuff like saying "sk8r boi." By then, skateboarding had gone mainstream. The X Games started in 1994. It was the first chance for many people, especially kids, to see extreme sports. Skateboarding was always the focal point. It was *way* more popular than that weird street luge thing. By the time Tony Hawk was hitting a 900 in 1999, skateboarding was totally integrated into the world at large. Skaters weren't "edgy" anymore. They did not exist on the periphery. There were celebrity skateboarders. Well, there was Tony Hawk. If parents were ever worried about their kids getting into skateboarding, by the end of the '90s they weren't.

Given all that, the fact that Nickelodeon had a skateboarding show in 1990 is kind of a surprise. The way it was executed is even more surprising. I know 1990 was still relatively early for Nickelodeon, in terms of original programming. Even so, going back and watching *SK8-TV* for the first time I feel like without knowing it was a Nick show I never would have guessed it. Obviously, I didn't watch it when it aired. *SK8-TV* only lasted one season of 13 episodes airing between July and September of 1990. I wasn't even tying my own shoes yet, let alone getting hyped to see Tony Alvas skate pools. That also means *SK8-TV* never really factored into my life, even amongst friends of mine who were into skateboarding. For kids who were verging on teenagerdom—or had just passed that threshold—in 1990, though, I bet *SK8-TV* was hugely important.

This is not to say that Nickelodeon has shied away from skating since 1990. I already wrote about *Rocket Power* in this book, and I could have talked about the episode of *Doug* where he desperately wants a Smash-O skateboard. Dogs love it too, don't you know? That doesn't really encompass "skateboarding" in a real sense, though. Those are cartoons that have a very kid friendly sense of skating. The characters are children, after all. *SK8-TV* was not that. It was pure skateboarding. If you weren't super into skating as a pastime, there was nothing in this show for you. If you liked skating, I bet this was one of your favorite shows on TV.

SK8-TV captures '90s skateboarding pretty perfectly. That's not surprising, given the people behind it. The show was created by Nathan Pratt and Mark Ashton Hunt, two members of the legendary Z-Boys. Since I imagine many of you reading this aren't necessarily skateboarding enthusiasts, I will dive in further. The Z-Boys were a skate crew who sort of reinvented skating. That made skateboards not merely a way to travel around. The idea of skating a half-pipe and doing aerial tricks effectively began with the Z-Boys. They were some of the original skating celebrities. This was back in the '70s, mind you. There were even two movies about the Z-Boys, the fictionalized movie *Lords of Dogtown* and the acclaimed documentary *Dogtown and the Z-Boys*. The latter was directed by Stacy Peralta, who was a Z-Boy. He also directed SK8-TV. Yes, this is partially where Peralta made his bones as a director.

The show was done in the style of a magazine-style show. There would be different segments, all of them about skating. Nickelodeon built SK8-TV a set at a hotel in California where they turned the pool into an elaborately-painted skate spot representing the show. It should be noted that skaters used to be obsessed with pools. Empty pools were some of the first big skate spots, and it is wild how much footage of dudes skating pools or talking about skating pools makes up SK8-TV. I watched a segment on Tony Alvas, another Z-Boy, where he says that half-pipes are fine, but to him skating is all about pools. The X Games this was not. These were the old-school skate types who probably considered the X Game for sellouts. Not that only skaters of this vein were showcased on SK8-TV. You could also see segments on youngsters like Tony Hawk, who was just becoming a big name in skating, and guys who weren't even names yet like Bucky Lasek.

While the target audience was kids, obviously, they didn't dumb things down. All it really meant was a lack of swearing or anything graphic or adult. There was a lack of guys wiping out and getting nasty injuries. However, they talked about skating seriously. They had segments about board maintenance and would talk board specs with a lot of detail. To go back to the Alvas segment I watched, they dedicate a few seconds to him talking about how he likes hard wheels and he uses technical specs I don't even understand. This was on a show for kids. They didn't care. Skateboarding was serious business to them, even if they show tried to be fun.

All of these segments were stitched together by the two hosts. This is where SK8-TV somewhat falls apart, at least to me. One of the hosts was a man who went by Skatemaster Tate, whose real name was Gerry Hurtado. Hurtado started skating in the '70s but then got into DJing and making music. He made a song with the clunky name of "Skaterock Rap" in the early '80s and he quickly became a guy you just saw around the skating scene. Basically, he's the exact guy who would end up hosting a show like this in

1990. Skatemaster Tate was an emcee in the skating world with credentials. Unfortunately, Tate's personality is quite grating. He's too much of a performer. His comedy is cheesy. There's something sweaty about him as a host and he rubs me the wrong way, also known as the reverse Christina Aguilera.

The other host was a young man named Matt Lynn who was enthusiastic and doing his best. There was something about his personality that showed potential. Young Matt Lynn grew up, and you now know him as Matthew Lillard. Yes, one of the hosts of *SK8-TV* was Matthew Lillard, the actor who would go on to be in *Scream* and play Shaggy in *Scooby-Doo!* He was only 20 at the time, and this was his first gig. A year later he would get his first acting gig as Stork in *Ghoulies III: Ghoulies Go to College*. He's definitely raw, and sometimes he seems like he's trying too hard to be cool. Still, of the two hosts he's definitely the one I prefer. Lillard also wore some amazing outfits on *SK8-TV*, including a blue turtleneck that makes him look like the rich villain in an '80s campus comedy.

The show really screams skateboarding in the '90s, which is totally fair. That includes the fashions, the editing, the music, everything. Even after writing this chapter, I'm still surprised this was a Nickelodeon show. It just feels like an entirely different beast. It's also quite good for what it is. Due to the nature of my work, I find myself watching a lot of modern skating videos. They are all over YouTube. If you are a kid into skating now, or a kid who wants to get into skating, you have a ton of options. Back in 1990, though, *SK8-TV* surely introduced some kids to skateboarding as a concept. I can see it getting them excited. The segments are pretty good. I mean, the skaters are all legit. They were big names in the scene. Peralta knows how to shoot skating. I wonder if Nickelodeon quickly realized that *SK8-TV* didn't fit into what they wanted the brand to be, or what the brand had become. Maybe kids weren't watching it casually. You were probably either super into *SK8-TV* or you didn't watch a second of it, and the audience of Nickelodeon, even in 1990, was probably not inclined to hang out with Skatemaster Tate and Matt Lynn's turtlenecks.

Now, though, if you're into skating the segments of *SK8-TV* aren't any different than the new skate videos you find on YouTube. There are a bunch of old segments on there with the big names of early skateboarding. That way, you see a little less of the hosts as well, which to me is a positive. While *SK8-TV* failed, at least Lillard went on to bigger and better things. For him, this is an artifact of him starting his career. Sadly, Hurtado passed away in 2015 when he was only 56. Had *SK8-TV* come out a decade later, I definitely would have watched it. The show really succeeded at being what it wanted to be. The problem is that what it wanted to be had nothing to do with what Nickelodeon has ever been. This ain't *Rocket Power*, kids. Everybody into the pool!

Space Cases

Sometimes through getting lost you can find yourself

You know, I really need to give a shout out to Canada for its role in the evolution of Nickelodeon. I've mentioned it before, and I will be mentioning it again, but so many shows from Nick in the '80s and '90s were either Canadian co-productions or were simply shows created in Canada that aired in the United States on Nick. Yeah, Nickelodeon's production wing would get involved, but these shows weren't being shot down in Orlando or out in Los Angeles. Canada actually plays a massive role in American television production in general. You've seen dozens of shows that are set in America but were shot in Canada. If you only knew how many times you've been seeing Vancouver on your screen in recent years. *Space Cases* is one of those Canadian creations, and like many of the Canada-based shows on Nick, you could probably tell that just by the budget.

Have you ever watched the original episodes of *Star Trek*? If you are a sci-fi lover I'm sure you have. They clearly were not splashing cash on that show. Despite being a show about space travel, aliens, and visiting new planets, it feels like *Star Trek* was made on a shoestring budget. Most of those planets were just sets from other shows sitting around at Desilu Studios. That's why they ran into so many gangsters, Ancient Greeks, and what have you. The aliens were often just people painted a different color. And yet, to many that was surely part of the charm. That, or sci-fi diehards have set the lowest bar possible for quality. Me, I prefer at least a little production value in my shows. It keeps me from watching some British sitcoms, like *The IT Crowd*, and it certainly doesn't help with some of the shows that Nick aired in the '90s. Especially a science fiction show that is about space travel featuring aliens.

Space Cases was created by the duo of Peter David and Bill Mumy. They both have bona fides for creating a show like this. David is a prolific and successful comic book writer, and in 1992 he won an Eisner Award for his work on *The Incredible Hulk*. Mumy, meanwhile, wished a bunch of people into the cornfield. That is to say, he plays the evil kid with psychic powers in the iconic *Twilight Zone* episode "It's a Good Life." More importantly, he was Will Robinson in the original series of *Lost in Space*. Hmm, I wonder how he got the idea for *Space Cases*.

The premise of the show is as follows. There are a group of misfit kids at a space academy. They are a variety of aliens by and large, and I will get into that a bit more. After being kept from a school event for not being ready to participate, they all end up sneaking aboard a mysterious alien ship, with the very alien name of the Christa. Two of the school's authority figures follow them to try and find them, but while they are all on board the ship one of the kids accidentally makes the ship take off. To make matters worse, only the kids can control the ship because they've bonded with it or some nonsense. Oh, and then *also* they get shot through a spatial rift, which means when all is said and done they are light years away from the Star Academy and it will take them over seven years to make it back at maximum speed. So now these misfit kids and two adults are on a journey through space, trying to make it back home. Ah, but there are still lessons to be taught, so the kids aren't off the hook educationally. Basically, that makes *Space Cases* effectively *Lost in Space* meets *Welcome Back, Kotter*. Which, honestly, probably oversells the quality of the show. Now I can only think of Dr. Smith saying "Up your nose with a rubber hose." Or Horseshack saying, "The pain, the pain of it all!"

As this is a sci-fi show there is a ton of lore and character detail and I don't want to go into all of it. Reading over all the info makes my eyes glaze over, but then again I'm not a huge sci-fi fan. The adult characters are Theresa Davenport and Commander Seth Goddard. Davenport is not a space traveler type and her role is to freak out and faint when there's danger. She's the serious, stuffy vice principal who becomes the teacher to the kids on the ship. Goddard was a "Stardog," which seems to be the show's slang for a space soldier, but he got demoted from captain and was made to teach at the Star Academy. In space, though, his role is to, you know, actually command the ship. He's also quite serious, but he's sterner and action oriented. The only other "adult" character on the ship is Thelma, who is an android who doesn't understand these humans. Does Goddard ask for a hand with the dishes only for Thelma to give him her actual hand? Yes indeed. Hey, it was good enough for *Get Smart* in the '60s. Why mess with a classic?

Among the kids, Harlan Band is the ostensible main character and the de facto leader. It may be because he was being played by an actor in his mid-twenties. By the way, that actor is Walter Emanuel Jones, who also played Zack the Black Power Ranger. So even if you didn't watch *Space Cases*, Jones was probably a part of your childhood. He's cocky and wants to be a Stardog like his dad. Somebody needs to whip him into shape and get him to be more humble and take more help from others.

Catalina is from Titan, Saturn's moon, and has rainbow hair. It's not exactly the most convincing wig. She can unleash sonic screams and has a friend named Suzee who she can only see because she's in another dimension. Within the show, the other people on the ship assume she is Catalina's imaginary friend, but for anybody watching it's obvious that's not the case. In the second season Catalina and Suzee swap spots, and Suzee becomes an actual character on the show. The actress who played Catalina, Jewel Staite, would go on to have a role in another sci-fi show, in this case *Firefly*.

Radu is from Andromeda and was born from an egg. He's sort of the Spock of the show, as he has emotions that are uncommon for his people. Radu is super strong and has long hair. The makeup and hair for Radu look goofy as hell. It was impossible for me to take the character seriously. And yet, he probably looks better than Bova and Rosie. Bova is from Uranus and is deadpan and pessimistic. Unfortunately for the poor kid stuck trying to convey that as an actor that mostly just made him seem like he was struggling to remember his lines. To be fair, he may have also just been a bad actor. Bova has these super fake looking antennae on his forehead that shoot out electric blasts. Rosie is from Mercury and is the optimistic one. She can control heat. She's also pink, and in the *Star Trek* way they just covered the actress in pink makeup so she looks ridiculous.

You can see the lack of budget on *Space Cases*. Apparently they repurposed a lot of props from other Nick shows, and they would use toys in control panels and stuff. In a way, I appreciate the ingenuity. I mean, I'm a huge fan of *Mystery Science Theater 3000*, and those sets were so cheap looking. Why do I find it charming there and roll my eyes at in on *Space Cases*? I think it's in part because *MST3K* is a comedy and it's mostly about showing a bad movie and making fun of it. *Space Cases* took itself seriously as a sci-fi show. There is no winking or embracing of their situation. They just sort of ignored it, but I can't ignore it in the same way. Plus, the animation used for the ship whenever we see it looks bad even for 1996.

I did not watch *Space Cases* as a kid, and in fact before starting this book I did not remember it existing at all. Which is weird, because it's the only show from '90s Nickelodeon that aired later than, say, 1993 that I did not remember. That's strange. It aired on SNICK, and I definitely watch SNICK. Granted, it only aired for two seasons and 26 episodes between March of 1996 and January of 1997. *Space Cases* was barely a blip on the radar for Nick. I imagine on the show they would have made a radar out of one of those handheld video games where you're fishing. While I almost certainly saw ads for the show given how much I watched Nickelodeon at the time, the show must have not appealed to me. It's possible I saw the ads and thought it looked bad. This is a mystery I will never solve.

That means my first experience watching *Space Cases* was for this book. The show is really lacking in quality. A lot of that is the production design and the costuming, of course. It's a cheap-looking show but in a way that lacks charm. The kids aren't really very good actors, and neither is the woman who plays Ms. Davenport. I felt like Staite was fine as Catalina, but that's about it. Even Jones, who again was already a twentysomething when he took on the role of Harlan, isn't very good. The writing is decent enough, I guess. There are definitely worse written shows, even from '90s Nickelodeon. Admittedly, the storytelling was decent enough to give me a twinge of intrigue. It wasn't totally boring, but this is definitely not a hidden gem from Nickelodeon's past. Maybe if I was into sci-fi lore things would be different. Or maybe if I had watched the episode that had guest appearances from Danny Tamberelli and Michelle Trachtenberg. Any connection to my beloved *Pete & Pete* can go a long way.

There is one absolutely positive thing I can say about *Space Cases*, though. The opening credits are amazing. They have this goofy, infectious theme song, the kind of old-school theme song where they explain the premise and who the characters are. Oh man did I have fun with that. You should absolutely watch the opening credits for *Space Cases* on You-Tube. Otherwise, I don't recommend returning to the show. The kids on the Christa never got back home. Hey, when you say you have a seven-year journey in front of you but your show barely lasts more than a year that will happen. They are lost in space, and even Bill Mumy can't save them. It's not a good life. It's not a good show.

Let's Briefly Talk About *Nick at Nite*

The past is full of joys and wonders

As a child, there were many things I wanted to do. I wanted to be a professional hockey player. I wanted to thwart bumbling burglars with booby traps a la *Home Alone*, although I did not have the sadistic streak of Kevin McAllister. Mostly, though, I wanted to stay up all night watching television. There were so many nights where I tried to secretly stay up literally all night, or at least late into the evening, watching TV. Of course, my parents weren't OK with this, because they weren't negligent. On Saturdays during hockey season, I would watch *Hockey Night in Canada*, since I grew up in the Detroit area and thus was able to watch CBC, Canada's answer to the BBC. My clever ploy was to close my eyes like I was sleeping when I would hear one of my parents come down the stairs to get me to go to bed under the theory they would just say, "Oh, he's sleeping" and just leave me on the couch. Shockingly, this plan didn't work. During the week during the summer, though, there was only one channel my TV would be parked on when I tried to stay up all night watching television. That would be Nickelodeon, where I could watch Nick at Nite.

Nickelodeon is a channel, but it really exists as three separate channels. This was true in the '90s as well. Early in the day, it was Nick Jr., which was programming for preschool kids who were home during that time. Then, it would become Nickelodeon, which was for kids to watch after school until it was time to go to bed (or for the family to watch primetime programming). The SNICK block, which I did not give a full chapter to, folds into this. When Nick would sign off, it would become Nick at Nite, which had a target audience of adults, but was still family friendly. Nick at Nite was both a throwback and innovative in equal measures. It also absolutely ruled, at least in the '90s.

The early days of cable were weird. I went into this a bit in the introduction. In the early '80s, Nickelodeon only existed during the day, when kids were watching TV. At night, it would become A&E. That's right, it was basically two channels in one. However, as cable grew, so did the channel opportunities. In 1984, A&E decided to become its own channel. It was time for them to spread their wings. MTV Networks President Bob Pittman turned to Geraldine Laybourne, who was running Nick at the time, to figure out what to do with all that time they now had to fill. As Laybourne had done previously, she turned to Alan Goodman and Fred Seibert. You may remember them from their role in rebranding Nickelodeon after being the guys who basically built the MTV brand. They invented the orange splat logo (with the help of graphic designers, of course) and the all the iconography we remember from '90s Nick. The tricky thing was that the bigwigs did not want programming targeted toward kids. They would be in bed, after all, and it would be a bad look for Nick to seem to be enticing kids to stay up late on a school night. Plans for original programming weren't working. What would Goodman and Seibert do? Would they just combine their greatest hits and create an orange astronaut character and have him dance about on the screen all night?

Alas, no. They did not go with the terrible idea I just made up. Goodman and Seibert didn't have much to work with, but they did, for reasons I do not know, have 275 episodes of *The Donna Reed Show* at their disposal. *The Donna Reed Show* was a decent enough sitcom that aired from 1958 through 1966 as a vehicle for Reed, who was transitioning from movie stardom. You likely know her best as Mary from *It's a Wonderful Life*, though she did win an Oscar for Best Supporting Actress for *From Here to Eternity*. Kids of the '90s remember it best for Ernest Borgnine's role a Sergeant "Fatso" Judson, of course. Having all these episodes of *The Donna Reed Show* sitting around gave the dynamic duo of MTV Networks an idea. Well, they really just took a well-established idea and tweaked it for television. Inspired by oldies radio networks, Goodman and Seibert came up with the idea of an oldies TV network. The idea was a hit, they branded it at Nick at Nite, and on July 1, 1985, the programming block made its debut.

Nick at Nite would run from 8:00 p.m. until 6:00 a.m. seven days a week at first. Its schedule would be tweaked over the years. Some nights it would start at 9:00 instead of 8:00, and eventually it would run until 7:00 in the morning. Saturdays eventually had to make room for SNICK, so it started later. The channel grabbed more old-school shows to fill up the programming. It was not an all *Donna Reed Show* all the time network. In the early days, they would often show classic movies as well. The *Nick at Nite Movie* would air at 9:00 every night, but they stopped with that at the end of the decade. That means it isn't relevant to this book about '90s Nickelodeon. This is about the shows that we grew up watching at night, the classic sitcoms—and the occasional drama—that showed us a world of television from before we were born.

I was introduced to so many classic shows by Nick at Nite. Well, classic shows and also shows that were at least notable. They weren't all classics, with all due respect to *Mr. Ed*, the show about a man who can talk to his horse. The horse's real name was Bamboo Harvester, which is a great name for a horse. I definitely watched *Mr. Ed* on Nick at Nite, but it was not necessarily a favorite. The shows that aired early on Nick were usually more family friendly. That doesn't mean they were showing "adult" stuff later in the night. The shows they put on first just tended to be sillier or broader. This was when I would see shows like *Bewitched* and *I Dream of Jeannie*. *Get Smart*, a silly spoof of spy stories, often opened the evening, at least in the early '90s. They also showed *F Troop*, which was a weird choice that would never be made now, as it featured a lot of Jewish comedians playing Native Americans.

A longtime staple of *Nick at Nite* was *I Love Lucy*, one of the first iconic sitcoms. It was also a vitally important show. After all, it was built around a woman's comedy persona and Lucille Ball managed to convince the network to let her cast her real-life husband, Desi Arnaz, as her husband in the show. This was in spite the fact he was a Cuban immigrant with a thick accent. When Ball got pregnant, they worked it into the show, even they pregnancy was a taboo subject at the time. *I Love Lucy* also popularized the three-camera sitcom format, using live-audience laughter as opposed to canned laughter, and showing reruns. Basically, Ball and company were geniuses. *I Love Lucy* sticks out in my childhood because it was the last show me and my siblings got to watch before bedtime. It came on at 9:00 where we lived, which started as my bedtime then. Eventually, it became "after the first commercial break of *I Love Lucy*," which feels insane. On my part, not my parents' part. Why was I jonesing just to stay up a few more minutes to see the start of a story I wouldn't see finished? Because I love TV. Eventually, the bedtime became 9:15, and eventually it became 9:30, after *I Love Lucy*.

Ball's physical style of comedy and the shows scenery-chewing performances were right up my alley as a kid. As an adult, *I Love Lucy* is not a favorite show of mine. I don't consider it a classic, even if it was a favorite then. I have another favorite from the early days of Nick at Nite that no longer has as much appeal to me. This time, though, it is truly insane that I enjoyed this show so much. For some reason—I kid you not—there was a brief period of time where I considered my favorite show *in the world* to be *Dragnet*. Jack Webb created and starred in *Dragnet*, which began life as a radio show in the '40s. He then turned it into a TV show in the '50s, before reviving it in 1967. This revival, which was in color, was the one that aired on Nick at Nite.

The show was a half-hour police procedural set in Los Angeles. Webb starred as Sergeant Joe Friday. In the revival he was joined by Harry Morgan (no relation that I know of) as Officer Bill Gannon. Gannon taught me about the concept of isometric exercise as a kid. The theme song of *Drag-net* is iconic, and rightfully so. Episodes would begin with a voiceover by Webb, usually beginning with "This is the city." You may also think of the show for giving us the phrase "Just the facts ma'am," although at this point any TV aficionado knows he didn't really say that. There is a lot of good stuff in this show, except for the fact Webb was kind of a nut. The dude was a straight-laced middle-aged man from a different generation, and he was really against hippies and marijuana and all that stuff he presumably considered "un–American." Sometimes, it feels like he only revived *Dragnet* to rail against a younger generation he feared and didn't understand. By far the most famous episode of *Dragnet* features a character known as "Blue Boy." It's actually the first episode of the new revival, which means it sort of set the template and established the ethos. The episode is called "The LSD Story."

Friday and Gannon are sent to the park to investigate a person acting strangely. They find a teenager with his head literally buried in the ground, and when they pull his head out his face is painted half blue and half yellow. He calls himself "Blue Boy," and they find LSD on him. There is a bunch of talk about the dangers of LSD. Blue Boy is placed on probation. He starts selling LSD. He has an acid party that Friday and Gannon break up. Does the party involve a painter eating paint? You bet! In the end, when they go to arrest Blue Boy they find he is dead, having "overdosed on LSD." The episode is insane. Webb wrote it himself, presumably having heard one secondhand story about acid. *Dragnet* is kind of laughable now, even if it has the trappings of a solid procedural.

It is odd to be that I loved *Dragnet* when I was, like, six, and it is also a little odd that I wanted to stay up late to watch shows like *The Bob Newhart Show* and *The Mary Tyler Moore Show*. Granted, those are really good sitcoms. I have them on DVD and I watch them now and really enjoy them. They just aren't aimed at kids at all. Sure, I probably laughed at Ted Baxter being dumb, but could the subtle comedy of Bob Newhart really land with me? Did I enjoy the complex and realistic depiction of a marriage as told through Bob and Emily Hartley? Honestly, I just didn't care. I loved watching TV and all these shows fascinated me. They were a look into a world I never lived in. I'm sure that was true of many '90s kids. We weren't there for the '90s, but the shows from the '70s were there for us. I was being educated by Nick at Nite. If that meant staying up until two in the morning and watching *Phyllis*, that worked for me. Back in the '90s, Nick at Nite was basically the only way to watch classic sitcoms. They had what was effectively a monopoly, and Nick had a near monopoly on my television watching.

Not that I enjoyed every Nick at Nite show as a kid. While I liked *The*

Munsters, Addams Family didn't do much for me. Now the script has been flipped on those two shows. The Lucille Ball shows other than *I Love Lucy* didn't wow me, and I feel like *The Brady Bunch* didn't work for me, which is obvious, because it's a bad show. I kept watching Nick at Nite a little longer than I watched Nick, but I gave up on it eventually too. They started showing more recent shows and that appealed to me less. TV Land, owned by Nick, became the place for classic sitcoms. Now, that's not true either. Nick and Nite is so foreign to me now. They currently show *Friends* and *Mom* and shows like that. Fortunately, it's never been easier to watch classic TV shows. I'm not talking about DVDs either. There are many over-the-air networks dedicated to old-school TV. We have MeTV, Cozi, Antenna TV, and so many more. Some of these shows are available to stream as well. I've watched episode of *My Favorite Martian* and *Green Acres* on demand. *Rockford Files* is always just a couple clicks away. Nick at Nite used to be vital for people looking to watch shows from the past, and often from their childhoods. Now, it's outlived its usefulness in some ways.

Once upon a time, though, Nick at Nite was an innovator. Before the concept of "binge watching" was the norm, it was all about binge watching. During summers in the '90s, they would have "Block Party Summer," where each day of the week was dedicated to a single show. You'd have *Munsters* Mondays, *Bewitched* Be-Wednesdays, and *Welcome, Back Kotter* Fridays, to give a few examples from throughout the years. Speaking of shows I used to enjoy but now realize were bad, *I* give you *Welcome Back, Kotter*. Catchy theme song, though. Also, it's kind of amazing that there was a beef between Gabe Kaplan, who played Mr. Kotter, and Marcia Strassman, who played his wife Julie and Strassman won that battle. Kaplan became barely featured in his own sitcom vehicle. The network would also do countdowns of the 25 best episodes from the shows that were airing on Nick at Nite at the time. Casey Kasem hosted, naturally. "Lucy Does a TV Commercial," an episode of *I Love Lucy* where Lucy accidentally gets drunk while filming a commercial for Vitameatavegamin, seemed to win most years. The episode "Death Be My Destiny" of *The Bob Newhart Show* won in 1993, which I think fueled my fascination with that show. Although, the best episode of that show is clearly "Over the River and Through the Woods," which also features plenty of drunk acting.

I have many fond memories of watching Nick at Nite in the '90s. I remember so many late nights awash in sitcoms. I remember "Block Party Summer" and the New Year's Eve countdowns with Casey Kasem. I guess what I'm saying is, Nick at Nite, this is my god damn death dedication.

SpongeBob SquarePants

Try to be positive. Do not try to live in a pineapple

Within every generation there are microgenerations. This doesn't really matter as an adult, but it is significant as a kid. There is a sizable difference between a 10 year old and a 7 year old from a developmental standpoint. These microgenerations have things in common from a life experience standpoint, but there is not total overlap. Even among those of us in the Gak Generation there are different groupings separating us. Take, for example, the *Harry Potter* series. I was just barely "too old" for it. I did know some kids who read the books, and ended up seeing the movies, but they were rare in my grade. I was aware of the books, but felt they were too childish for me, and that was a fair assessment at my age. For people even two years younger than me, *Harry Potter* was a massive part of their childhood. It was unavoidable. To not indulge in *Harry Potter* was to be contrarian. I have never read a *Harry Potter* book or seen a *Harry Potter* movie, and I'm comfortable with that, especially since it turned out J.K. Rowling is a creep. I am starting this chapter with talk of microgenerations amongst '90s kids for a reason. That reason? *SpongeBob SquarePants* was not part of my childhood.

For some of you, this is going to be a deal breaker. If you slam this book shut and throw it across the room I get it. I have to admit, *SpongeBob SquarePants* is the biggest show in Nickelodeon history. No Nick show, animated or otherwise, has been more popular, and no show has had a greater cultural impact. I would love to sit here and say that *Adventures of Pete & Pete* is the most-beloved Nick show and that "Endless" Mike Hellstrom and bus driver Stu Benedict are icons. That would be a lie. Even though I did not grow up watching the show, I have been around for its entire run. It is profoundly obvious just how huge of a cultural landmark *SpongeBob* is. Many '90s kids consider it their favorite Nick show ever, or even their favorite cartoon full stop. They are all younger than I am.

To be fair, *SpongeBob SquarePants* barely eked into this book. The show debuted on May 1, 1999, with a sneak preview and then had its official premier on July 17 of the same year. By then, I was almost 13. I was in junior high school. Nickelodeon was a channel for kids, by reputation and by marketing. This was just some random cartoon on a network I had grown out

204

of, as far as I was concerned. I did not expect it to become a legitimate phenomenon. To be fair, how could I have? Not because I wasn't clairvoyant, but because there is nothing on the surface of this bizarre show that indicated it would become the jewel of Nickelodeon's crown.

SpongeBob SquarePants' life began with creator Stephen Hillenburg's love of the sea. As a kid, his two passions were marine life and art. Those passions stuck with him throughout his life. In college, Hillenburg majored in marine science and minored in art at Humboldt State University in California. Eventually, he got a job teaching people about marine biology for the Orange County Marine Institute, now known as the Ocean Institute. While he was teaching, one of the educational directors at the Institute suggested he could create a comic to teach kids about life in tide pools. He did just that, creating a comic he called *The Intertidal Zone*. With a name like that, you might think its main character would be a chain-smoking fish named Cod Serling. Instead, the "host" of the comic was a little guy named Bob the Sponge. This Bob was designed to look like an actual sea sponge. They do not look like kitchen sponges. They look weird. You would not want a sea sponge chilling on your sink. This was in the mid–'80s, so it may not be surprising to know that *The Intertidal Zone* did not take off. Instead, in 1987 Hillenburg quit his job to become an animator.

He graduated with an MFA in experimental animation from CalArts and student loan debt in 1992 with a couple of student films in tow. Hillenburg wasn't out looking for work long, as he was fairly quickly hired as a director for a new Nickelodeon cartoon called *Rocko's Modern Life*. That was a pretty nice first gig, as *Rocko's Modern Life* is my personal pick for the best Nickelodeon animated program. While he was there, a writer for *Rocko* named Martin Olson read *The Intertidal Zone* and suggested to Hillenburg that he could turn it into a TV show. Apparently Hillenburg hadn't thought of this, but he jumped at the chance to combine his two passions. In the process of creating the show, he realized that an actual sea sponge might not be the best choice for a main character. Thus, Bob the Sponge became a kitchen sponge, a much more recognizable "sponge" design. I mean, how many of you could describe what a sea sponge looks like without Googling it right now? That square, yellow, porous image is what we think of when we think "sponge." Bob the Sponge had a new look, and he would soon have a new name. I don't need to tell you the new name, right?

SpongeBob SquarePants is about a group of animals living in an underwater city called Bikini Bottom. Obviously, one of those is SpongeBob. He wears brown shorts and an extremely small white dress shirt with a red tie. When I was a kid, I assumed SpongeBob was a child, because a lot of Nick's shows were about kids. Also, because the way he sounds and acts seems fairly childish. Then I realized he had a job and lived alone and realized he had to be an adult. He's just an adult sponge brimming with enthusiasm and wonder. SpongeBob loves life. Even though he works as a fry cook as the Krusty Krab, a fast food restaurant, he seems happy with it. Needless to say, if you've ever heard the theme song, he lives in a pineapple under the sea. He also has a snail for a pet named Gary who meows. Normally I don't like human names for pets, but Gary is a pretty solid name for a snail.

His best friend is Patrick, a starfish who lives under a rock. He's not terribly bright, a staple of secondary characters in comedies. Fittingly enough, he's voiced by Bill Fagerbakke, who played the dim-witted Dauber on *Coach*. The man has been typecast, but he's also gotten to be rich. It all works out in the end. I should also note that SpongeBob is voiced by Tom Kenny, a well-respected voiceover actor who was the voice of Heffer on *Rocko's Modern Life*, where he met Hillenburg. He was also a cast member on *Mr. Show*, a raunchy sketch comedy show on HBO, right before he started voicing SpongeBob. That's a fun little bit of whiplash.

Other notable characters include Squidward, an unhappy and misanthropic octopus who hates his job at the Krusty Krab and hates living between SpongeBob and Patrick. For kids, he's probably the character you root against. For adults, he's the most relatable character by far. Mr. Krabs is, well, a crab who owns the Krusty Krab and is always trying to save a buck. He also talks like a pirate for some reason. His daughter is a sperm whale. Don't ask me how that works. Plankton is a villainous fellow who owns a restaurant called The Chum Bucket. His wife is a computer named Karen. Then, there's Sandy, a squirrel who lives underwater anyway. Don't worry, she has a diving suit, and also an oak tree under an airtight dome.

When you read all this, your first thought might be that *SpongeBob SquarePants* is built around what is often called "random" humor. There are many who are derisive of this. I get that. While I enjoy a bit of oddball comedy, weird for the sake of weird just doesn't cut it. I want inventive and unexpected comedy, but throwing together a de facto "game of Madlibs" world certainly warrants skepticism. There is no depth to it. You might chuckle at, say, a pineapple house, but that's not a joke. It's a slightly clever and outside-the-box concept. In truth, it's very easy to be "random." Literally anybody the least bit creative can do it. If *SpongeBob* was just a collection of quirks and "weird" tics, that would make for a lackluster program. Does the show have more going to it than a crazy world full of left-of-center choices?

While I did not watch a single episode of *SpongeBob* until 2019, I have to say it has a little more substance to it. Not a lot, but some. *SpongeBob* is a genuinely unusual show with a flair for the avant-garde. Do you remember the "Wacky Delly" episode of *Rocko's Modern Life*? I feel like one out of every 20 *SpongeBob* episodes is up to that level of oddness. That I do admire. There is ambition to the randomness of *SpongeBob*. However, at the same time it does still float on the surface of storytelling a lot of the time. They go deeper narratively than just doing the whole Madlibs thing, but that definitely seems like where the creativity is focused. There aren't a lot of strong, hard jokes in *SpongeBob*. A lot of the entertainment seems to want to come from "Isn't this wacky?" or "Isn't this fun?" It's frothy, and it seems more dedicated to creating a bright, colorful world than telling stories and writing jokes. That isn't too surprising. *SpongeBob* comes from the branch of animation where they don't really write scripts, but instead write outlines and then do storyboards. These shows are driven by animation and direction. As a writer, and as a joke fan, that isn't as much up my alley.

Given all this, I'm not surprised that *SpongeBob* has a reputation as being a favorite of stoners. Although, that may be in part because people I know didn't grow up watching *SpongeBob* as kids, unless they were a little younger than me. If they were watching it, it would have almost certainly been while under the influence of marijuana. As such, there may be some confirmation bias there. Even so, it does have a lot in common with other stoner favorites. The random humor, the absurd lack of logic, the eclectic character designs and lush animation. If *SpongeBob* was a little more adult and threw some swearing in, it would fit right in on Cartoon Network's Adult Swim.

I feel like I've seen the "greatest hits" of *SpongeBob*, given that I've either been shown episodes by people pitching the show to me or—for the sake of this book—looked up the most popular episodes. That's the way to do it, because there are a ton of *SpongeBob* episodes, and even more story segments. Like many Nick cartoons, *SpongeBob* episodes consist of two 11-minute stories except on special occasions. On top of that, there have been over 250 episodes since the show debuted in 1999, and that is not the end of it. Yes, over 20 years later, *SpongeBob SquarePants* is still on the air. In fact, current Nickelodeon President Brian Robbins—of *All That* fame—has declared that the show will be on as long as Nick is an extant network. That's a bold claim, especially for a guy who will not be president forever, but *SpongeBob* isn't going anywhere. I can see why, because, again, this should is just so incredibly popular, and has been for decades at this point.

Evidently it didn't even take a month for *SpongeBob SquarePants* to become the most-popular Saturday morning cartoon. Its popularity led to it being added to the Monday-Through Nick lineup that aired in the evening, right before Nick at Nite. This was when many older viewers started watching it. Apparently at its peak of popularity one-third of its audience was in the coveted 18–49 demographic. The demographic that can make "Nuts 'n' Gum" happen if they really want. It wasn't just college stoners, either. A lot of adults apparently really just dug the comedy and oddball nature of *SpongeBob*. Critics have loved it. It's won a ton of awards, and not just Kids'

Choice Awards. In 2007, Barack Obama called SpongeBob his favorite TV character. Hey, when you're running for President, it's probably safer to say that than talk about your love of *The Wire*. There have been two *Sponge-Bob* movies with a third on the way, this one a prequel. Why they are doing a prequel I do not know. There is no origin story here. Hell, they even had a Broadway musical with a Flaming Lips song and 12 Tony nominations. The popularity of this show, and its main character, can't be overstated.

Not that the popularity is what it used to be. *SpongeBob SquarePants* is a bit of a legacy show at this point. It happens. *The Simpsons* is the greatest show of all-time, but mostly on the strength of its first 10 seasons. They have had over 30 now. Hillenburg actually wanted to end the show after the first movie, afraid it would jump the shark. He resigned as showrunner after the third season, but the network didn't let the show go with him. Instead, the reins were passed to Paul Tibbitt, but even he has since relinquished that role. That's what happens when a show last the long time. Sadly, the show has outlasted Hillenburg as well. He was diagnosed with ALS, also known as Lou Gehrig's Disease, in 2017 and then died of heart failure in 2018. Hillenburg was only 57. *SpongeBob SquarePants* has not ended, as Hillenburg hoped, and he will have no say in how it ends. It's hard not to feel queasy about that.

Most of the hit Nick shows covered in this book I know like the back of my hand. I can tell you the plot of every single *Pete & Pete* episode off the top of my head. This was the chapter that I felt a little unprepared for. *SpongeBob* was a cornerstone of the childhood of so many kids, but I was not one of them. It wasn't in my childhood at all, except on the periphery. I did not see a single episode until my thirties, and I have only seen a handful of episodes. I consider myself an impartial observer on all of these shows, not bringing any childhood feelings to the table. With *SpongeBob*, though, I didn't have to do that.

If you love this show, that's great. I think it's a totally solid cartoon. The characters are a little one-dimensional and SpongeBob's voice can be a bit grating. I would appreciate a little more substance and a little less absurdity for the sake of absurdity. As an adult, or at least an adult who isn't stoned, that kind of comedy doesn't really hit me as it may have as a kid. Even so, when you talk the history of Nickelodeon, *SpongeBob SquarePants* is one the vital points to hit. It's the biggest show the network has ever had. It's the biggest hit it will ever have. Stephen Hillenburg loved the ocean and he loved to draw. Combining those loves ended up giving people so much joy. He's given me a little bit of amusement. Maybe I just wasn't the right age. All I know is that a talking kitchen sponge who lives in a pineapple is an iconic TV character. He will be remembered well after any other '90s Nickelodeon character. No wonder he's so happy all the time.

Think Fast

*There is always something new to discover, and
it may be in a fake locker room*

Do you remember the chapter on *Make the Grade*? It was a game show
on Nickelodeon that began in 1989 and ended in 1990. After the first season production moved down to the newly opened Nickelodeon Studios in
Orlando, which meant having to get a new host. All of that is also true of
the game show *Think Fast*. However, while *Make the Grade* was kind of drab
and uneventful, *Think Fast* is overstuffed with action and kinetic energy.
It's a game show that never stops moving. It's like a bucket of confetti being
thrown in your face. And I am not saying any of that to knock the show.
I've found out that I don't have much negative to say about *Think Fast*. I
can only hope to explain it properly, since it throws so much at you in each
episode.

There are two teams on the show, each consisting of one boy and one
girl. There's the blue team and the gold team. Each episode consisted of
five games, three in round one and two in round two. Some of the games
involve both team members, while others involved the boys squaring off
with each other or the girls taking on each other. There are so many games
to this show, and since *Think Fast* was new to me I can't explain them all.
Some of them are puzzle based. I watched an episode where the kids had to
put together an approximation of the Mona Lisa (in a *Think Fast* shirt) that
had been cut up into puzzle pieces. They also had different version of what
you would call "Simon-style" games, in reference to the handheld game
Simon. They are about remembered a pattern that gets increasingly lengthy.
It could be about punching in numbers on a giant telephone or about putting ingredients on a banana split, but rarely if ever putting ingredients on
a giant telephone.

There's a game called "The Feelies" where one contestant is blindfolded
and wearing gloves and their partner hands them an object and gives
them a one word clue. If they guess the object they get a point. I mention
it because the episode where I saw it both teams were really good at it. The
one team used one of their friend's names as the clue for the skateboard—
evidently he was an early adopter of skateboarding—and they got it right.
That was delightful. Kids would throw giant spitballs at a blackboard or pull

letters out of alphabet soup. While games have a lot of business going on and can be messy they are rarely sloppy, to borrow a phrase from the *Double Dare* vernacular. People aren't getting slimed or making any crew members pull out a big mop after every round.

Winning a first-round game got you $50, while winning a second-round game got you $100. When you won a round you also got to take a crack at the Brain Bender. This was a puzzle that was unveiled one piece at a time. There might be a rebus under the puzzle pieces, a la *Concentration*. There might be a photo of a celebrity you had to guess, a la Kirk Cameron. I'm not saying that Kirk Cameron is known for making people guess what celebrity is being obscured by puzzle pieces. I'm saying he was the answer in one of the episodes I watched. When you got the Brain Bender right you won 200 bucks, and technically there could be two Brain Benders in a game, though I did not see that in any of the episodes I watched. In fact, it seems more often than not the puzzle isn't solved until the very end, when the teams take turns guessing the solution. If you lost, you got some parting gifts, the kind of random stuff I miss from old-school game shows. The winners went to the Locker Room round.

In the Locker Room, there were 15 large lockers, 14 of which contained one half of a pair of characters or other objects, such as balloons or a bunch of rubber balls. Although, to be honest I only care about the characters. You might see a pair of cowboys or bank robbers or, in one instance, Julia Child. I got to watch some local actress ham it up as a fake Julia Child and it brought me unbridled joy. It must have been fun to mug as these characters, but I personally have an affinity for people in small roles or doing what is sometimes glorified background work. I find it fascinating and when I see somebody who stands out it's always cool. I'm much rather, say, spend my time thinking about the career of an actor who had a recurring role as a student in *Strangers with Candy* than pontificate on, like, whatever Paul Newman got up to. It's way more interesting. Anyway, each locker had a button in front of it. When you opened the locker that matched with the open locker, you then had to run to the starting point to hit another button to close all the lockers. The cosmic dance would continue.

During the first season, one player had 30 seconds to start. One locker contained the time bomb, and if you didn't open that locker within the first 20 seconds it would "go off," and that meant the second player on the team only got 20 seconds as opposed to 30 seconds. However, having watched the show I can't imagine that ever happening unless the first contestant totally messed up. Each match would win you a prize, with the prizes getting increasingly nice. You'd better believe I saw Space Camp as a grand prize. In the second season, the two team members alternated for 60 seconds. Additionally, you won $200 for four matches and then the final three matches each had a prize attached as well. On top of that, the time bomb disappeared and was replaced by the Red Herring, which is some real *A Pup Named Scooby-Doo* type stuff. The Red Herring had no match, and when their door was opened the contestant had to go to the center of the room to pull the "Herring handle," which dumped a bunch of little plastic fish on the unmatchable character.

Like I said, *Think Fast* had two homes and two hosts. The first season was shot at the same studio in Philadelphia where *Double Dare* was shot. Then, they moved down to Orlando because Nick's studio down there had opened. The second season was hosted by a guy named Skip Lackey, which seems like a fake name. It too could be the name of a character on *A Pup Named Scooby-Doo*. Lackey is a pretty good host. He has good energy and he explains the game well. In fact, I might even say Lackey is a good host. I may just be grading him against his competition, the man who hosted the first season of *Think Fast*. His name is Michael Carrington, and he rules. I knew Carrington's name, because he co-wrote one *Simpsons* episode, "Homer's Triple Bypass," which is a good episode. He also did some voiceover work on the show (shout out to Sideshow Raheem) and has had a successful career as a TV writer with a little bit of acting on shows like *The Critic* and *Martin*.

Carrington absolutely crushes it as the host of *Think Fast*. From the second the first episode I saw with him began I bought into him as a game show host. He's naturally funny and brings great energy. Carrington never goes over the top but he's always engaged. He knows when to mug but doesn't steal the spotlight. His skills as a host are strong. Carrington introduces the games well, and he can even make the little interviews with the kids bearable. I'm not being hyperbolic when I say that Carrington is now my favorite game show host in Nickelodeon history. In fact, he's maybe one of the best game show hosts I can recall. I don't know why Carrington didn't get to do more of this. I wish he had been able to host the second season as well. Seeing Carrington in action was a pleasant surprise in all this.

In fact, *Think Fast* was the most-pleasant surprise in writing this book. Since the show's 160-episode run ended in the middle of 1990, I had no personal memories of this show when I started this book. *Make the Grade* and *Think Fast* were the two game shows that were totally new to me. *Make the Grade* made me snooze, but I can genuinely say that *Think Fast* is a good game show, especially the first season hosted by Carrington. The games within the show are inventive and fun. It's dedicated to being silly but takes its games seriously. Everybody seems like they are having a grand old time. The challenges may not be anything you can play along with, but they are engaging enough to watch that it doesn't matter. *Think Fast* clearly made an effort to keep the show entertaining to watch, not just to be a part of. Throw in Carrington's hosting acumen, and I am here to tell you that, as an adult, *Think Fast* is now my favorite Nickelodeon game show. I can actually enjoy watching aspects of it as an adult. If they rebooted it as a show for adults, I would watch it. Especially if they brought Carrington back as a host. Seriously, had I been a TV executive in the '90s I would have cast him as the goofy but good-natured jokester in a workplace sitcom. Also, I would have paid him what he wanted to move down to Orlando to host the second season of *Think Fast*. Again, I'm not slagging off Lackey. In a world where Carrington didn't exist he would be getting praise for his hosting work. And in a world without the Great Wall of China we might spend more time talking about Hadrian's Wall. That's just how life goes sometimes.

U to U

They have the internet on computers now

When did your family get on the internet? It was probably in the '90s. I recall when my family got America Online, allowing me to hear that "You've got mail" sound whilst I surfed the web to submit captions for images from episodes of *Mystery Science Theater 3000* on the Sci-Fi Channel website and read wrestling rumors, as 12 year olds did at the time. Or, at least this 12 year old did. Of course, the internet existed before I got on it. Sandra Bullock used it to order pizza in *The Net*, a movie that came out in 1995. Also coming out that year was *Hackers*, where Johnny Lee Miller and Angelina Jolie use the power of their hacking skills and inline skates to hack the planet and take down Fisher Stevens and Lorraine Bracco. Before I would ever get on the internet, Nickelodeon would dip their toe into that world in an interactive show that was connecting viewers with the world around them. It was called *U to U*, and it is a stark example of what interconnectivity meant in the mid–'90s. Hint: It involved more fax machines than it does now.

The show, also sometimes stylized as *U-2-U*, aired episodes from 1994 through 1996, but seemed to air intermittently. It would appear that only 20 episodes were ever produced. I understand that, given the amount that must have gone into making each episode, even with how much of the content was viewer submitted. There is no overarching premise or anything beyond "Here's a bunch of ways we are interacting with our fans, and also have you heard about this internet service called Prodigy?" The show was hosted by Ali Rivera and Sertrone Sparks, and the *U to U* set is large and ambitious. After all, they had to have a section of it dedicated to being able to play virtual reality video games.

Fan submissions drove the content of *U to U*. While they provided an address and a phone number, they also of course provided an email. It feels like, in retrospect, this show was Nick's attempt to showcase the fact they were now getting involved in the online realm. You could write a song and then somebody at Nick would turn it into a music video. Other times a story or script would be submitted and then they would turn it into a cartoon. Both of those things must have been awesome for those kids. Games would be played, sometimes in person and sometimes over the phone. The latter makes *U to U* a forerunner to *Throut and Neck*. I'm not dropping that name as if though it is a commonly-referenced show. I just happened to watch it as a kid in 1999, when I was newly on the internet. *Throut and Neck* was a Game Show Network show that didn't last too long but contestants would call in and use their phones to control Throut and Neck in competition. They were these monsters who were sassy and would trash talk you and each other. There was also a human host named Rebecca Grant to handle everything. Anyway, I feel like it was as close to "late night programming" that Game Show Network got.

On *U to U* kids could also submit questions to celebrities, call in and leave voicemails, and also kids would send videos in for their pen pals. I got to see a kid from Estonia explain what life in Estonia is like to his pen pal. This also seems like it must have been incredibly cool to a kid in the mid-'90s when connecting to each other was much more difficult. Now you can just slide into DMs willy nilly, even when nobody wants to hear from you. All that said, here's my favorite part of *U to U*, and inexplicably it just involves reading emails. Rivera and Sparks would enter this computer lab area of the set where they would sit in front of '90s-era chunky computers and face each other. Then, they would log onto Prodigy and read emails from kids and talk to each other. One, the graphics are just so much fun. It's a pile of retro beauty. If I saw something like this on TV now it would be tedious. Seeing a clip of that from the '90s, though, is just so glorious. The idea of it being cutting edge to read emails online scratches an itch for me here decades later. These sections are a little clunky in a way that is fun to watch as well. Rivera and Sparks aren't the most natural TV hosts, though I wouldn't say they are bad. It's just very clear when they are reciting lines that were written for them.

That, in a nutshell, is what *U to U* is. I can't really break down much else about the show, because there is nothing else to it. It was an act of fan service in TV form, and also a way for the network to farm out content creation to fans. Not that they were complaining. If you would have told me as a kid that I could write a song and then it would be turned into a music video I could see on TV I would have been hyped. It is definitely a show that sought to connect people and to show how the world was changing. *U to U* brought the internet to Nickelodeon, but also insured that the show couldn't help to be incredibly dated. There is no mistaking *U to U* as anything but a relic of the '90s. One look at Ali and Sertrone at their computers reading emails makes that clear. *U to U* is fascinating as a time capsule, but not necessarily good as a show. Maybe that's because it is barely a show. It's more a collection of unrelated segments thrown together by a couple of hosts who don't have a ton of chemistry with each other. The show is from a world of dial-up modems and phones that still had cords. Even if having an internet-heavy show in 1994 was ahead of the curve then, it's hopelessly dated now.

Still, I admire the ambition of *U to U*. We all know technology always gets dated in time. You can't let that stop you from embracing it in the moment. We may laugh at Zack Morris' giant cell phone or Ali Rivera chilling on a computer promoting Prodigy, but someday in the future our cell phones and computers will be laughed at as well. Time isn't going to let you off the hook. Make your peace with that. And then fax in a question for Ben Savage.

Weinerville

Some places are nice to visit but you wouldn't want to live there.
This is an original sentiment I just made up.

Evidently I can't get away from writing about puppets. After writing an entire book about *Mystery Science Theater 3000* (available from McFarland Books now!) I now find myself writing about a Nickelodeon sketch show that was heavy on the puppets. It's not the first show involving puppets I have written about here. *Cousin Skeeter* involved a puppet, and in the Nick Jr., chapter I discussed *Eureeka's Castle*—and my nightmarish experience with said show—which was also puppet based. Outside of Nick Jr., though, no show involved puppets more than *Weinerville*. Also, like *Mystery Science Theater 3000* it was created by a former standup who had made a handful of appearances on *Saturday Night Live* before getting swept up in the burgeoning world of cable programming.

In this case, the man in question is Marc Weiner. His show took place within a world of his own devising, hence *Weinerville*. I do recall as a child both adults and kids hearing the name of the show and giggling to themselves. Some of them even asserted that the name was a double entendre. To which, as a preteen child, I had to inform them that, no, Weiner was just the star's name. I feel like some were skeptical about this, but it's true. His last name was Weiner. Lots of people have the last name Weiner. Don't blame your preoccupation with penises on him. Go back in time to talk to Sigmund Freud about that between cocaine binges.

Much like Paul Reubens, Weiner created a world for himself to inhabit. The difference is that his little town of Weinerville was much more puppet centric. This was very much an old-school variety show for kids. I don't think they make shows like this anymore, for kids or for adults. Weiner would do sketches, show old cartoons, have audience members play games, you name it. Episodes would have overarching themes and storylines, at least most of the time, but this was not a show driven by story. It was driven by Weiner's desire to basically do a one-man show on TV. I don't know if it was hubris or ego or it just happened to be the idea he had, but Weiner appeared as himself and as dozens of other characters in a show that named after him set in a town named after him. Must be nice to have that much self-possession. I can only assume he enjoyed his particular style of comedy more than I did both then and now.

You see, as with many variety shows the comedy on *Weinerville* is corny as hell, even by the standards of kids' shows in the '90s. One of the most-famous puppets from the show, probably the most famous in all honesty, is Boney the dinosaur. See, he's like Barney, but he's a skeleton and he hates kids! That's facile, but it's not bad. It's also not good. Maybe you can get the slightest of chuckles from that. It has just enough cleverness to register as a joke, but a barely passable one. There's a character named Eric Von Firstensecond and a game show host named Soup Tureen, presumably a pun on Soupy Sales, a name kids in the '90s definitely knew. What was the runner up name, Art Phlegmy? Soup was, of course, performed by Weiner, as was almost every character, be they human, puppet, or human-puppet hybrid.

If there is anything that makes *Weinerville* stand out all these years later it's the fact that Weiner had "puppets" on his show that were puppet bodies with his head poking through a curtain as if though his head was the puppet's head. Technically, these were puppets, because the bodies were puppeted. These tiny bodies were overshadowed by the big human heads on top of them, though. Every single one of the regular puppet characters of this variety were portrayed by Weiner. The primary one was Dottie, who appeared in every episode, would welcome us to Weinerville, and who served as the mayor of the town. You could almost credit Weiner for not making himself mayor if not for the fact that Dottie was just him in drag doing a falsetto lady voice. There was also Baby Jeffrey, Big Pops (who picked his nose quite a bit, which is always gross and barely a joke), and Commander Ozone, a space captain who is a parody of sci-fi heroes.

Weiner would tape these segments where he was a puppet earlier so that he could interact with them as his normal self. Because if one Marc Weiner is good, two is better. Or something. Each episode would features sketches interspersed with cartoons and some other bits. There was a fake game show called "That's Not Fair," the one hosted by Soup Tureen, which would features kids and adults squaring off. Needless to say, the kids usually won, on account of a lack of fairness to the questions. Every episode would also feature a trip to Playland, where two members of the audience would compete against each other in a game of some sort. However, before they could compete they had to be "Weinerized." The premise here was that they were being turned into puppets a la Weiner's own performance as Dottie. They would enter a contraption in order to be Weinerized, at which point the episode would throw to a cartoon. This was ostensibly to give the contestants time to be shrunk down into puppet form. I regret to inform a trusting nation that these people were not in fact turned into puppets. They just went behind a curtain and stuck their heads through.

After being turned into puppets like in a cheap '80s horror film—with slightly less nudity than most cheap '80s horror films—the contestants would play a game in Playland. The purpose of the game would be seeing how the players could control their little puppet bodies. It was an exercise in sight gags and puppetry. Some contestants would get a handle on it, while others just couldn't figure it out at all. The loser would receive the silver hot dog, while the winner won the golden hot dog, which came with a special topping. This being Nickelodeon in the '90s, that topping would be slime, which was dropped on their heads. Yes, *Weinerville* was the rare Nick show that decided to slime the winners. Although, given that I bet a lot of kids wanted to have the experience of being slimed, it kind of makes sense to do it that way.

Weinerville began airing in July of 1993, and at first would air episodes in marathon blocks on Sundays. Eventually, it would prove popular enough to end up as part of the Nick in the Afternoon lineup hosted by Stick Stickly. The second season began airing in 1994, but that would also be the year it was cancelled. According to Weiner, Nickelodeon wanted to move in a slightly "edgier" direction. Looking at the lineup of new Nick shows that came out in the immediate aftermath, I don't really see that. After all, a couple years after *Weinerville* got cancelled the President of Nickelodeon bleeped *The Angry Beavers* saying "shut up" because it was a bad example for children. We are all the heroes of our own story, though.

It's perhaps a little surprising that *Weinerville* got cancelled, given that Weiner and his puppets were the hosts of Nickelodeon's New Year's Eve coverage in both 1993 and 1994. The man had to talk to puppet versions of himself for four hours to entertain kids who were probably getting to stay up until midnight for the one time in the year. That's a lot of pressure. Weiner also made a Chanukah special and an election special during his time. Joe Lieberman, Pat O'Brien, and Bill Maher were all on his election special. What a murderer's row of creeps. At least John Tesh and Mary Hart were also there. Thanks for taking a break from going to Dodgers games, Mary!

Speaking of going places, as a kid I went to see *Weinerville Live* at a theater near me. I don't remember much about it other than the fact I was not chosen to be Weinerized. This was the primary thing I was excited about, along with seeing a person from TV in real life. Who would have thought many years later I would be living in Los Angeles and meet Marc Cherry the creator of *Desperate Housewives* and feel nothing? Seeing Lori Beth Denberg at *Simpsons* trivia was cool, though! To get back on track, I was not necessarily enthused specifically to see Marc Weiner and *Weinerville*, because while I liked the show it was far from my favorite. It was good enough to keep me entertained, but I was never particularly looking forward to it.

As an adult, the heavy cheese factor is obvious. It's cheesier than a Chicago deep dish pizza. It's cornier than the entire state of Iowa, especially since they cut down all that corn to make a baseball diamond for ghosts. As a kid, I may not have noticed, which leads to me cutting some slack for Weiner. I'm sure a lot of kids thought a parody of Barney was just brilliant. See, he was mean, not nice! Broad comedy tends to work on kids, whereas nuance can be lost on them. Weiner wasn't necessarily talking down to kids, but he figured he could get away with some sweatier, more well-worn material since it wouldn't register that way for his young audience. He was in the grand tradition of variety shows in that his comedy played it safe. The goal was to entertain, to be family friendly. Don't swing for the fences, when you might strike out. Just try and hit a single every time. Don't even try and stretch it out for a double. Better not to risk anything. Look, I have to express at least a little contempt with a show that has an episode called "Tooth Hurty" and included a Donald Trump parody named "Donald Rump." I don't care if you're writing for kids, that's just lazy. Which is weird, because Weiner's ambitions make him seem anything but lazy. Maybe if he was spending less time playing 10 different characters and more time on writing the show would have been better.

Weinerville fell out of the Nickelodeon rotation long after a relatively short shelf life for reruns. To be fair, variety shows rarely get shown much in reruns. They tend to be disposable. Plus, if they wanted to keep showing episodes, they'd have to keep paying for the rights to the old cartoons that were included. Why do that when you can just show *Rugrats* a dozen more times in a week? Weiner would be just fine, and even stay in the Nickelodeon family. He voiced Swiper the Fox and the Map in *Dora the Explorer*. For a man that didn't seem interested in edge, that's the kind of work he seems perfect for. Also, it's kind of funny in a way that a man who wanted to make a corny, family-friendly variety show for kids had a last name that made people assume the name of his show was a penis joke. Funny, but also kind of sad. Marc Weiner created an entire world, but so did the people of Atlantis. Both worlds were eventually lost to the sands of time. Only one featured a restaurant owner who was always picking his nose. That I know of. I actually don't know what restaurant owners in Atlantis got up to.

Welcome Freshman

Childhood is a time for learning.

When you think of sketch shows on Nickelodeon, your first thought is probably *All That*. That was the first truly successful sketch comedy show to air on Nick, but it wasn't the first. Far from it, in fact. Years before *All That* showed up to introduce us to Kenan, Kel, and some people whose names didn't start with a "K," *Welcome Freshman* was airing on Nick, bringing something close to a '90s slacker edge to the usually bright and bubbly world of Nickelodeon.

Welcome Freshman debuted in February 1991, the same year that the first Nicktoons hit the airwaves, meaning that Nick was still in the very early stages of figuring out what they wanted the network to be. It feels like early Nick skewed a little older, and *Welcome Freshman* is an example of that. After all, it's a sketch show set in a high school about high school life. Granted, they were freshman, but teenagers are not necessarily thought of as the primary makeup of the Nick audience. It's kids and their parents, but *Welcome Freshman* has the vibe of a show aiming to grab onto the last vestiges of Generation X. After all, while there are different definitions, the general thought is that Gen X gave way to the Millennials sometime between 1977 and 1985. Somebody born in 1977 would be turning 14, the same age many freshman are, in 1991. Now, I'm not saying that a 10 year old in 1991 had Gen X vibes, but it all lines up for *Welcome Freshman* to be a Gen X starter kit for tweens and teens.

With its rocking theme song and black-and-white credits full of quick cuts and handheld camera work, I was immediately put into mind of another sketch show from the era. That would be MTV's *The State,* which would debut in 1993 and air until 1995. This means *Welcome Freshman* actually conceived those aesthetics first, and given that *Welcome Freshman* ended in 1994, I can imagine a lot of kids graduating from watching *Welcome Freshman* to watching *The State*. It all lines up so conveniently. *The State* was not a huge success at the time for MTV—like Nick owned by Viacom—but it did feature many future stars in its cast. Several future members of the *Reno 911* crew, including Tom Lennon, were in The State. So were Michael Ian Black, Michael Showalter, and David Wain. The crew of *The State* is largely responsible for the cult hit movie *Wet Hot American*

Summer. They were young, rising comedians when MTV gave them a sketch show. Eventually, they would grow into successful fixtures in comedy, especially "alt" comedy.

You can't quite say the same thing about the case of *Welcome Freshman*. While this was a sketch show, it operated under different rules than many sketch shows. Namely, it wasn't actors playing different characters in a series of sketches. Instead, in the first two seasons we followed five students from Hawthorne High School. Obviously, they are all freshman, which is to say ninth graders. Merv is a scheming brainiac with some stereotypical nerd vibes. Walter is the dumb one. Kevin is the smooth one, in that he fashions himself a bit of a ladies' man and considers himself relatively worldly. Alex, who is a girl, is popular and materialistic. Lastly, Tara is an activist and eco warrior, but unlike Jessie Spano she's quite nice and laidback. Why these five all hang out I do not know. It's classic TV show for kids logic. They want a diverse mix of personalities so they eschew the fact that popular vain girls and scheming arrogant "nerds" rarely hang out. Lastly, there is Mr. Lippman, the Vice Principal. He's your classic antagonistic authority figure, in that he's mean but dumb. He also hates freshman.

I do not know why he hates freshman. It seems weird. What, exactly, about somebody being in ninth grade makes these kids so loathsome to Lippman? I feel like there was lingering stuff in culture about freshman that seeped into *Welcome Freshman*. In older works of media, freshman are often bullied and the butt of jokes. There's a running gag in *Rock N' Roll High School* of a freshman being pranked repeatedly. A big plot point in *Dazed and Confused* is the next group of freshman being hazed by the next group of seniors. That I can understand a bit culturally. Dead-eyed sociopaths continuing a cycle of abuse. Why would this grown man hate freshman so much, though? What is Mr. Lippman's deal? Hey, this show already had more established story and character than most sketch shows, let alone a sketch show for kids. I guess I shouldn't dig too deep into that.

Anyway, most episodes in the first two seasons would be about a theme, like money or friendship. We would see the cast joined together hanging out and talking, and that would set forth the theme of the episode. There would be little blackout scenes here and there happening in the action, but then there would also be sketches thrown to in one way or another. All of the sketches took place within the world of the show and these characters, though they found ways to stretch the possibilities a bit. Take, for example, the recurring sketch premise "Mr. History." In those, the titular Mr. History's voice would boom and the kids would talk to him, then it would throw to a sketch where the kids from the show would be in a different historical period. Suddenly, they would be in pirate times learning pirate lessons or what have you, while keeping the same personality traits.

Welcome Freshman wasn't mere sketch after sketch after sketch. Instead, it would be sketches woven together by character and setting based on a theme, usually one that kids could relate to.

In a way, that's admirable. It certainly makes doing a sketch show much more difficult than having an open sandbox to play in. Granted, they did rely on a few recurring sketches in most episodes. Mr. Lippman would be doing the morning announcements, and then suddenly he imagines himself as a standup comedian roasting freshman, replete with a drummer doing rim shots. There is no really story or premise to these sketches. It's just joke writing, and all the jokes are insults. They aren't even necessarily freshman specific. Generally speaking, they are just jokes about dumb people or gross people. You could replace freshmen with, say, the ethnicity of your choice and tell jokes in the Catskills in the 1950s. It's not exactly imaginative or terribly fun. On the other hand, Merv's documentary series, where he tries to break news and find scoops within the school, are much more ambitious and pretty funny.

None of these five kids is particularly talented, and it is probably worth noting that none of them were successful enough to even end up with their own Wikipedia pages. I wouldn't say they were bad actors, or didn't have any comedic timing, but the main crew definitely wasn't on the level of the cast *All That* put together. Still, the performance issues are enough to be apparent when watching, and it does hurt the comedy. As much as I enjoyed Merv's "Merv-U-Mentary" sketches, David Rhoden is probably the least capable of the main quintet from the first two seasons. Not to be all negative, I will say that Chris Lobban, who played Kevin, was the best of the bunch.

I keep noting the first two seasons, because *Welcome Freshman* veered severely in the third season. For starters, it was no longer a sketch show. Yes, suddenly *Welcome Freshman* was just another sitcom, and it lasted for 23 episodes like this. Given that the first two seasons were both only 13 episodes long, that means it was an episodic comedy show for almost as long as it was a sketch show. That surprises me, since I did not remember it becoming a sitcom at all. The cast also changed. Merv and Tara were written off the show, for starters. Meanwhile, Walter flunks ninth grade, so he remains a freshman. On the other hand, Kevin and Alex do become sophomores. The trio was joined by three new characters. Replacing Merv in like-for-like fashion was Manny, who even had a name that starts with an "M." He is also a "nerd," but again he somehow gets to hang with Kevin and Alex, though they do tend to just pick on him. Erin and Grant. Erin is defined by being into grunge in 1994. Grant is defined by being Erin's brother. This is normally where I would make a bold proclamation and declare the final season of *Welcome Freshman* heretical or non-canonical. However, I will not be doing that. For starters, like I said it was a sitcom for almost as long as it was a sketch show. Secondly, I don't care enough about *Welcome Freshman* to do that.

That being said, this is one of the shows that I enjoyed more as an adult than as a kid. Given that I was only seven when it got cancelled, and given that it only aired in reruns until 1996, many of the times I watched it I was probably a little young for it. I'm not saying *Welcome Freshman* is super edgy or incredibly cerebral. However, it was probably over my head when I was six. Now that I've been to high school and seen a lot of sketch comedy, I can appreciate it more. The writing isn't all that bad, and if they had put together a stronger cast it could have even been a good show I imagine. That is, in the sketch version. The sitcom version is just a generic sitcom for teenagers. It's forgettable and far from Nickelodeon's best. On the other hand, as a sketch show *Welcome Freshman* is honestly on par with *All That*. The cast can't compete, but the show gets points for having more ambition than just doing sketches—which feels fresh—and for having slightly better writing.

I should also note I cannot relate to any freshman experiences. My high school only went 10th through 12th grade so when I was a freshman in ninth grade it was at a school that went from seventh to ninth grade. Ben Affleck never chased me down to hit me with a paddle. Not that you need to have a "freshman experience" to watch, understand, or enjoy *Welcome Freshman*. It would help to enjoy hearing street jokes about dumb people recontextualized to be about freshman, though.

What Would You Do?

Whipped cream is surprisingly versatile

Whipped cream is sometimes called Chantilly cream. It has apparently been around since the 1500s, and used to be known as "snow cream" back then. You want a high butterfat content in your cream in order to make sure your whipped cream is stable once it is in its colloid form. However, you also don't want to overmix your cream, because then it will become butter. The same is true with overchurning ice cream, but that's a story for another time. Canned whip cream, the kind that sprays out due to nitrous oxide, has been around since the 1930s. There are also imitation whipped creams you may think of as actually being whipped cream, but in actuality they are merely "whipped topping." They tend to be made from oil as opposed to dairy, which is cheaper but also better for the lactose intolerant. There are several different ways one can use whipped cream. Oftentimes it is used to top a dessert, such as shortcake or an ice cream sundae. You can also put it on top of pie, or even occasionally make a pie just straight up out of whipped cream. This is called a "cream pie," and it isn't typically served as food. Instead, it tends to be used as a comedic prop. That brings us to the show *What Would You Do?*, which worshipped at the altar of whipped cream.

What Would You Do? aired on Nickelodeon for two seasons and 90 episodes running from August 1991 until November 1993. It was hosted by Marc Summers, already a staple on Nickelodeon due to his stint hosting *Double Dare*. In fact, he was still hosting *Double Dare* when *What Would You Do?* debuted, meaning he was pulling double duty. Oddly enough, both shows also ended in 1993, making that kind of a down year for Summers, one imagines. Robin Marrella, who also served as a stagehand and foil on *Double Dare*, was part of the *What Would You Do?* crew as well, though she left the show before it ended. She stuck with *Double Dare*, so it was not about being tired of cleaning up messes. The title of the program was a question, and personally I have a question myself. What kind of show, exactly, was *What Would You Do?* Answering that question has proven a little trickier for me than I had expected.

It definitely wasn't a sitcom or some sort of scripted show. That much is certain. It also wasn't a talk show or a medical drama or a cop procedural or an alien autopsy. My initial instinct is to call it a game show, but that doesn't feel quite right. There's not much in the way of a "game" to *What Would You Do?* They play some games, sure, but so much of the show's time is not dedicated to them. Plus, there aren't always prizes and we don't get to know the contestants. *What Would You Do?* was a revolving door of kids—and occasional adults—joining Summers to do one thing or another. Mostly they were low-stakes stunts or challenges. If it is a game show, *What Would You Do?* is a game show in the vein of something like *Let's Make a Deal* or the outré, ironic shows that spawned from the mind of Chuck Barris, such as *The Gong Show*. I could imagine the executives that greenlit the show being asked "What kind of show is this?" And their answer being "A show that kids will watch." Based on my own personal experience, they were right.

The question of the title did come into play on occasion. Evidently, during episodes Summers would show footage of some unusual situation playing out. Then, he would ask the audience members to vote on what they thought would happen, or what they would do in a similar situation. Basically, they were asked "What would you do?" I said "evidently" because I need to be honest and say I literally did not remember this being part of the show when I was a kid before I started researching. This was not what *What Would You Do?* was about. It was entirely a show dedicated to the worship of cream pie, and the cream pie was the kind of god that demanded sacrifices.

I feel like roughly 75 percent of any given episode of this show is dedicated to somebody either being hit with a pie, or being doused in whipped cream, or prepping to be hit with a pie. There were many different ways the folks on *What Would You Do?* concocted to make sure people got covered in whipped cream. The primary creation was the Pie Pod. This was where a person would sit in a chair, which could be adjusted to make sure their head was in the target, and then four cream pies would be whipped at their faces. Don't worry, they were wearing goggles ... well, eventually. The very first episodes of *What Would You Do?* were a little looser on the safety regulations. If this show was about anything, it was putting people in the Pie Pod. However, that is just the tip of the whipped cream iceberg.

The Pie Slide is exactly what it sounds like. Participants would go down a big slide and land in a vat of whipped cream. Sometimes they would go feet first, but other times they would go head first and get themselves drenched in creamy goodness. There was the somewhat lackluster Pie Wash, where you got squirted with whipped cream and then brushed off like in a car wash. This was more about novelty than mess. The Pie Coaster had both of those going for it. It was a miniature roller coaster that ended with you getting hit with a giant pie! What kid wouldn't want to have that experience? There was also the Pie Pendulum and Pie Roulette. These are just the contraptions. Games of Musical Chairs or Rock, Paper, Scissors would end up with somebody being pied. In the first season, they had "Pie-A-Thon" episodes. I assume whipped cream was cheap, because it was the crux of everything *What Would You Do?* was about.

There would be different reasons why people would end up getting pied. Sometimes two audience members would be brought down to the staging area for a competition. It would be something simple and almost always involving a race to complete a task, even if that task was drinking a glass of milk. Did the loser get pied? Of course. The only real question was how they would be pied. All roads on *What Would You Do?* led to a pie. Sometimes that would even be true for Summers himself. After all, it's the height of comedy for a kid to see the authority figure in question—the reasonable adult in the room—to be taken down a peg. Summers was always a sport about that kind of stuff, especially given his well-known preoccupation with tidiness.

The first season fueled the pie lust with something they called the "What Would You Do? Medley." Here, audience members, and Summers, would have index cards stuck to their foreheads. There would be a stunt, really more akin to a dare, on the card, and they had to either do the dare or go to the Pie Pod (or sometimes a different pie device). Usually the stunts would be gross, and more often than not they involved food. Man, did *What Would You Do?* love using food not for its intended purpose. If you looked at your card and then decided that, say, you didn't want to eat a Twinkie covered in gravy you could resign yourself to the Pie Pod. I say that fully knowing many of the people in the audience were probably stoked to get pied. They got to be on TV and partake in a wacky gag! What else do you want when you are a kid in the audience of a show like this?

In the second season, the index cards went by the wayside for a new concept called the Wall O' Stuff. The wall contained 20 doors, and audience members would win tokens—either through stunts or a lottery—they could use to open one of those doors. The wall had a real *Pee-wee's Playhouse* vibe in terms of its aesthetics, but it still was definitely more dynamic and cinematic than a bunch of index cards stuck to heads. Behind some doors you would find a prize, usually Nickelodeon merchandise. Other times you would be hit with a pie (or shot with whipped cream). Some of the doors contained a card, which usually featured a poem that would invariably send you to a pie contraption. Now that I think of it, the addition of the Wall O' Stuff really aligns *What Would You Do?* with *Let's Make a Deal* even further. Not that the shows are exactly the same. For example, Marc Summers is a good game show host, while Monty Hall is the most-overrated game show host of all time.

There would also sometimes be special guests that would bring audience members down for stunts and occasional hidden camera prank bits. Again, though, none of that mattered. I'm not saying that simply because I don't remember any of that from my childhood. I'm saying that the fact I only remember the pies is indicative of what the show was all about. I remember the Medley and I remember the Wall O' Stuff, and I vividly remember all the pies. When I tuned into *What Would You Do?* it was to see people getting hit by pies. I wanted to see the Pie Pod and the Pie Coaster in action. It was funny to me. It also wasn't that sustainable of an idea. I'm not surprised that *What Would You Do?* only lasted two seasons, even if it was 90 episodes. Even by the standards of kids' television it was bound to get repetitive. Hell, they completely revamped the show between the first and second season, and that was probably necessary. Eventually, people would tire of the Pie Pod. How many different pie contraptions could they manage to create? Go down that road long enough and you find yourself tying pies to bats and letting them loose like some sort of misguided World War II weapon.

No show has ever made more use of whipped cream than *What Would You Do?*, both in terms of quantity and quality. They got clever about the ways in which they reached the end goal of "person covered in whipped cream." And yet, there was still bound to be diminishing returns and pie fatigue. *What Would You Do?* was flimsy, and not as good as *Double Dare*. It was barely a show, if I'm being honest. Despite that, if you wanted to see people getting hit by pies, it gave you everything you could have ever wanted. I would probably still even ride that Pie Coaster. I'll skip on the Pie Pod, though.

Wild & Crazy Kids

Sometimes the journey is the destination,
especially on a game show without prizes

Chuck Barris created *The $1.98 Beauty Show* in 1978. It was part of his particularly bizarre career in the world of game shows. Also, he claimed to be a CIA assassin. *The $1.98 Beauty Show* was hosted by Rip Taylor, which should give you a sense of what the show was like. It was basically a parody of beauty pageants featuring six contestants. While the outcome was previously arranged, they still went through the motions, and in the end a winner was declared. They received a cheap plastic crown, a bouquet of rotten vegetables, and, yes, $1.98. As far as game shows go, this was a paltry prize. It was more than anybody got on *Wild & Crazy Kids*.

Due to its rocking theme song and collection of much-desired brightly-colored shirts, *Wild & Crazy Kids* has a pretty big piece of our collective memories for a show that was arguably about less than *Seinfeld*. There was not much point to it other than chaos and mess. The show ran for three seasons and 65 episodes from 1990 through 1992. There was a 2002 reboot, but it only lasted 10 episodes. Maybe kids of the 2000s wanted more from their "game shows." I put that in quotes, because I feel like *Wild & Crazy Kids* is barely a game show. It's more just an excuse for ridiculous games and the misuse of cream pies. As the opening credits would say, the show was out there trying to "find kids having fun," which was a weird way of phrasing it. That makes it sound like the hosts stumbled upon kids in matching shirts dumping food on each other and just documented it anthropologically.

For the first season those hosts were Donnie Jeffcoat, Omar Gooding, and Annette Chavez. Chavez was replaced by Jessica Gaynes for the final two seasons. If you were wondering, yes, Gooding is related to Cuba Gooding, Jr. They are brothers. Omar Gooding actually had an acting career himself, probably highlighted by ESPN's short-lived football drama *Playmakers*. The hosts were all teenagers at the time, which made them authority figures to the younger kids left in their stead.

Each episode featured three games, and each one emceed by one of the hosts, though multiple hosts would sometimes be involved in a game. The games would feature massive teams of kids competing against each other, though sometimes parents or adults would be involved as well. Oftentimes, the hosts would be at the helm of one of the teams. There was little to no rhyme or reason, near as I can tell, for the team sizes. It just seemed like they would have kids show up and then they got thrown onto teams and given shirts. Like I said, the *Wild & Crazy Kids* shirts came in a variety of colors. Those shirts were definitely a desired article of clothing when I was a kid, first when the show was on, and then later as a piece of nostalgia.

It should be noted the teams didn't really carry over from game to game. Usually, you got to be in one event and that was it. Maybe you won, and maybe you lost. And when you won, you got … nothing. There were no prizes on *Wild & Crazy Kids*. The prize was the feeling of accomplishment, I suppose. I assume both teams got to keep their shirts. Is this where I make a joke that if they rebooted *Wild & Crazy Kids* they'd have to give both teams a trophy? In truth, the idea of a game show without a prize or reward airing on TV feels odd. That being said, I imagine these kids not really caring. They were there to have fun. You did things on *Wild & Crazy Kids* you could never do in your day-to-day life. It was like a school's field day on steroids, or playground games run amok. Hey, it was fun to watch the show, despite the fact there weren't winners and nothing to really root for. It's not like I knew anything about any of these kids. Really, if you wanted to root for a team, there was one of two reasons to do it. Either you rooted for the host you liked the best if hosts were involved in the game, or you rooted for your favorite color. Is that any less inane that rooting for the chef you find most attractive to win on *Chopped*? I rest my case.

A lot of the games on the show would take something familiar to kids and make it, dare I say, wild and crazy. On multiple occasions they played a game called "Dizzy Bat Home Run Derby." A bunch of kids would try and hit home runs, and then a team of adults would try and best them. The difference was that the adults had to put their head on the bat and then spin around three times before trying to hit off a tee. Thus, the adults would often have trouble maintaining their balance or hitting the ball, presumed hilarity ensuing. Similar games in this vein would feature kids playing three-legged soccer or playing basketball on donkeys like in that one episode of *Saved by the Bell*. There were massive games of Twister and Simon Says. This was not the crux of the show, though.

Mostly, *Wild & Crazy Kids* was in the vein of many a Nick show in that it was all about mess, especially food mess and slime. I have a distinct memory of kids solving a massive word search with different foods hid in it, and when you found a food you could dump a bucket of it on your opponent, like chocolate sauce and raw eggs. Many a pie was put to use by being thrown into faces. There was a game of Red Light/Green Light where kids who failed had to put their pie in their face but kids who succeeded got to pie their parents. Also, if not for Nickelodeon, would "pie" ever be used as a verb? I don't need to go into every game and tell you all the different ways kids, parents, and the hosts got slimed or gunked.

Celebrities would stop by sometimes. Arnold Schwarzenegger made his way into the opening credits of the show after his appearance. There was one episode where three of the cast members from *Salute Your Shorts* helmed a team while the *Wild & Crazy Kids* hosts led another. I swear some kid from *Hook* was on an episode but I cannot find that information now. It would be a weird false memory, but also it was almost 20 years ago. I don't have the cast of *Hook* memorized, because unlike many of my fellow '90s kids I think it's a bad movie and I don't get the nostalgia for it. There was also an episode I vaguely remember involving pro wrestlers having a tug of war with a bunch of kids, but I do not recall the wrestlers and their identities can't be found online. I'm going to assume one of them was Duke "The Dumpster" Droese, the wrestling garbage man.

When I was a child, I certainly wanted to be on *Wild & Crazy Kids*. As an adult, I don't really get why. Maybe just to be on TV? I also probably didn't really think it out. It didn't occur to me that I would barely be involved, might get a bunch of food dumped on me, and wouldn't win anything of note for maybe 10 seconds of screen time. Watching, though, allowed you to enjoy all the fun with none of the mess. I do admire *Wild & Crazy Kids* dedicating itself to coming up with creative ways to have messy, sloppy contests. They really knew how to work within the framework of "dumping food on the heads of children." Watching it as an adult is pretty dull. The hosts are teenagers doing their best, but they aren't getting any help from their writers. The games aren't really all that interesting to see in action. It's not like you're watching skills on display. You're just watching random kids shooting ketchup and mustard at each other. There wasn't even a need to watch a full episode for this book to get the gist of it. The contestants on *Wild & Crazy Kids* got nothing for being on the show, and I got nothing from revisiting it. Hell, I don't even really want one of the shirts anymore … not that I'd turn one down.

The Wild Thornberrys

Travel can broaden your mind,
especially if you can talk to animals

Nickelodeon's cartoons, by and large, consist of two 11-minute segments per episode. That has been the tradition since 1991 when the very first Nicktoons debuted. What would it take for Nickelodeon to break that pattern? Apparently a family of world travelers and a feral boy voiced by the bassist of the Red Hot Chili Peppers. *The Wild Thornberrys* stands out from other Nick cartoons in a few ways, even though it is yet another show from Klasky Csupo. It may not be as massive a hit as *Rugrats*, but it has aspects of it that are more impressive.

To be fair, this show was a collaborative effort beyond the duo of Arlene Klasky and Gabor Csupo. While they did co-create it, and it's animated in that classic Klasky Csupo fashion, Steve Pepoon, David Silverman, and Stephen Sustarsic are all considered creators as well. Silverman is a big name in animation, mostly due to his work on *The Simpsons*. He directed all the shorts, dozens of episodes of the show, and *The Simpsons Movie*. Having listened to many a *Simpsons* audio commentary, I am well-versed in Silverman. You can see an animated version of him in my favorite episode, "The Itchy & Scratchy & Poochie Show." Pepoon wrote one episode of *The Simpsons* as well, but also 14 episodes of *ALF*. He did not, unfortunately, write the episode where ALF calls up Ronald Reagan and they think he's a terrorist.

The Wild Thornberrys basically imagines the Irwin family before they became a thing, and also if Steve Irwin hadn't died so young. While the show takes its name from the Thornberry family, the point-of-view character of the show is Eliza, an 11-year-old girl with Pippi Longstocking vibes voiced by Lacey Chabert. Every episode we get a narration over the opening titles that explains the situation. Eliza's dad, Nigel, is the star of a nature show, so the family travels around shooting nature documentaries. They live in an RV, which would suck as a kid. The matriarch of the family, Marianne, is the director of the show, filming everything for her husband. Eliza has an older sister, Debbie, who is more sardonic and glum, Daria for kids. The family has also taken in a child, Donnie, who is effectively feral. Apparently he was raised by apes a la Tarzan. They also have a chimp named Darwin.

You know who I feel terrible for? Debbie. Imagine being a 16 year old and spending all your time with your family. You're stuck in an RV with your mom, dad, little sister, a feral boy, and a chimp. You don't get to go to school with friends. You don't get to date. Debbie has a terrible life. She comes across as "emo" or "grunge" in the writing of the show, but I have to imagine she'd be profoundly depressed all the time. Eliza I understand enjoying it more. She's young and naïve. Oh, also she can talk to animals.

Yeah, you read that right. As the opening narration says, "And between you and me, something amazing happened ... and now I can talk to animals. It's really cool, but totally secret. And you know what? Life's never been the same." Really, Eliza? Life hasn't been the same since you got the ability to *talk to animals*? What a shocking revelation! That's an understatement if I ever heard one. Anyway, Eliza was given the power to talk to animals magically, because she saved a shaman pretending to be a trapped warthog. Apparently this shaman, who had the ability to turn into animals, would just chill and try and see if a human was worthy of this incredible gift. Ah, but Eliza can't tell anybody she can talk to animals (for no good reason) or she'll lose the power. That's an inane bit of logic within the world of the show done just for storytelling purposes. Also, the philosopher Ludwig Wittgenstein said that if a lion could talk, we could understand them, because our perceptions of the world are so different. *The Wild Thornberrys* disagrees, clearly.

The Thornberrys are going on adventures for Nigel's show, but within that Eliza goes on other adventures. Sometimes she's joined by her sister Debbie, but oftentimes she's joined by Darwin the chimp, who she can talk with obviously. So basically the show becomes a girl and a talking chimp going on adventures. That's not too shabby an idea for a kids show. The premise of *The Wild Thornberrys* is a smart one to me, because it inherently creates drama and spectacle. They have an excuse for why the Thornberrys are doing crazy things like climbing mountains or traversing the jungle. It's all part of their lifestyle, and Nigel's show. Eliza gets to meet all sorts of animals and talk to them. Given all this, it makes sense that *The Wild Thornberrys* was the first Nickelodeon cartoon that did one story per episode. There weren't two segments, but one sole story. That's a lot trickier to do, but *The Wild Thornberrys* gave themselves plenty to work with to fill those 22 minutes up.

What I've also realized while working on this book is that *The Wild Thornberrys* is not a comedy. Yes, it's a cartoon and it's on Nickelodeon. Most of those shows are comedies by nature. Maybe they aren't laugh-a-second romps, but they are by their nature defined as comedic. I would not say that's the case with *The Wild Thornberrys*. It has some moments, sure. You don't have a feral child voiced by Flea on your show if you don't want to have some laughs. The show has better comedic tim-ing, from the directors and actors, them some of the shows that are actually comedies as well. I was going down the Klasky Csupo vortex while doing my research, so I watched *The Wild Thornberrys* after *Rocker Power*. The comedy and directing is stronger in *The Wild Thornberrys*, even though it isn't first and foremost a comedy show.

It's, fittingly, an adventure drama. There are pretty heavy stakes a lot of the time. The Thornberrys will face landslides, monsoons, and other nat-ural disasters. They often face off with Neil Biederman, a poacher who is their sworn enemy. Which, you know, makes sense. Eliza's ability to talk to animals establishes a level of intelligence in animals pretty much equivalent to humans. That makes killing them, for sports or otherwise, much more disconcerting. While the show is animated, and thus inherently feels less dramatic than if it were live action, the show does feels adventurous. The stakes feel real. Again, this show is well directed. I was legitimately engaged in the action moments and they feel earned. This is the best directed of the Klasky Csupo shows. It looks the best as well.

Not only does the adventure pay off, I will say that they manage to handle emotional moments better than a lot of other Nick shows. Granted, a lot of them didn't try it. *Ren & Stimpy* did not care for human emotion. I watched an episode where Eliza befriends an elephant named Rebecca that Nigel had saved years prior. An elephant never forgets, after all. Alas, Rebecca is dying, and Eliza is with her when she dies. I will say that they earned the pathos. It was genuinely well-written and emotional. That kind of stuff can feel cheap and manipulative, but that was not the case at all when Rebecca the elephant kicked the elephant bucket.

I'm also going to shout out the voice cast of the show! Flea just does his goofy Flea thing, but you know who plays Nigel Thornberry? The one and only Tim Curry! He's a delight and is right at home in doing animated voiceover work. Chabert is pretty good as Eliza, but she was still a little young and unpracticed when the show began in 1998. I also particularly liked Danielle Harris as Debbie the older sister. She's a scream queen with horror movie bona fides. She's even in the Fangoria Hall of Fame!

As I just noted, *The Wild Thornberrys* aired its first episode in 1998, specifically September 1. They did three seasons with a ton of episodes, 77 total. There were then two more seasons, but they were very brief. The fourth season is only six episodes, and then they released *The Wild Thorn-berrys Movie* in 2002. This was a straight-up theatrical release that even got an Oscar nomination for Best Original Song. The movie has a rating of 80 percent of Rotten Tomatoes. I have not seen it, but that sounds impressive. There was then a five-episode fifth season, which aired from February 2003 through June 2004. Obviously, there were some gaps between episodes.

There was also *Rugrats Go Wild*, which hit theaters in June of 2003. Yes, this was a full-length theatrical crossover film between two Klasky Csupo animated shows. I also did not see that film, as I was in high school at the time. It has bad reviews, so I'm not necessarily interested in it.

In truth, I'm also not interested in *The Wild Thornberrys Movie*, which is not to say I don't like the show. I would call it perfectly pleasant. It's neither good nor bad. It's just fine. The animation is solid, the voice work is good, and each episode keeps my interest. I may not just be the target market for an animated adventure drama for kids. If it were live action, and well made, it might be a bit more gripping. Then, though, you'd have to eschew the whole talking to animals thing. If I've learned anything in my life, it's that live-action movies with talking animals suck. Even in *The Wild Thornberrys*, the whole aspect of Eliza talking to animals is the least interesting thing to me. I'd prefer a little more big adventure moments and globetrotting personally. Still, I liked *The Wild Thornberrys*. It stands out among Nickelodeon's cartoons with its 22-minute stories and dramatic elements. I appreciate the fact they took a big swing, and I feel like they connected. In fact, I might go as far as to say this is Klasky Csupo's best effort. Is it the power of Tim Curry? I wouldn't argue against that.

You Can't Do That
on Television

I don't know

By sheer dint of the alphabet, the last show being covered in this book is *You Can't Do That on Television*. In a way, though, it feels fitting. Sure, the bulk of the show aired in the '80s, with only the final 15 episodes airing in 1990. By May of that year, it was done. However, it still aired in the '90s, which counts. Also, reruns continued to air on Nickelodeon until 1994, so kids of the '90s got plenty of chances to check out *You Can't Do That on Television* well into the decade. Mostly, though, this was the show that changed Nickelodeon. I would argue it pointed the network into the direction it ended up going. And it all began in, of all places, Ottawa.

This is where Nickelodeon and Canada began their fruitful relationship. The show began way back in 1979. Yes, the legacy of *You Can't Do That on Television* goes back that far. At the time, it was a locally airing one-hour variety show for kids that aired on Saturday morning. It would be a mix of sketches and music videos. There were also disco dancers. Needless to say, those didn't last long into the show's history. You know who was also there at the beginning? Canadian comedian Les Lye. Lye would go on to be a cast member for the show until it ended in 1990. Almost every adult man and authority figure in the show was played by Lye.

Local success in Canada's capital led to a national show, which they called *Whatever Turns You On*. Which, to me, is a weird name for a sketch show for children. They made the show a half-hour long and replaced the music videos with actual live performances from Canadian bands. If you wanted to see Trooper in action, and who didn't in 1979, this was the place to do it. They even got Ruth Buzzi to join the cast. She had been a cast member on *Rowan and Martin's Laugh-In*, which made her casting make total sense, as if this sketch show had any predecessor it's *Laugh-In*. For '90s kids, you might remember Buzzi best as Screech's mom on *Saved by the Bell*. The woman who loved Elvis. This version of the show was a failure and was cancelled after 13 episodes. No matter. It allowed *You Can't Do That on Television* to be reborn in 1981.

This revamped version did away with the disco dancers and started to theme the sketches around a specific topic. Around this time, creator Roger Price and director Geoffrey Darby decided to try and make a syndicated version of the program. The 1981 episodes were an hour long again, so they edited them down to a half hour. Mostly, they removed the Canadian content and got rid of anything that wasn't sketch comedy. That caught the attention of Nickelodeon, which was desperate for content at the time. They showed a few of those edited-down episodes as trial run in 1981, and they were successful enough that Nick got into the *You Can't Do That on Television* game. In 1982, they were simply making the show in a half-hour format full of sketch comedy, and by 1983 *You Can't Do That on Television* was the highest-rated show on Nickelodeon. Granted, competition was slim then, but it was clearly connecting with their audience. They began to air the show five days a week, and then seven days a week. Interestingly, the show was way more popular in the United States than Canada. A lot of the time Canadian pop culture doesn't cross over into America. I would argue that most Americans have likely never heard of The Tragically Hip, but they are legends in Canada. *You Can't Do That on Television* was the inverse of that, in part because Canada didn't have the wherewithal to showcase children's programming like we had down in the United States. Eventually, in 1988, the channel YTV debuted in Canada, and *You Can't Do That on Television* finally got love north of the border.

Between 1983 and 1990 there were ups and down and changes, of course. Cast members came and went. Ratings fluctuated. Once Nickelodeon had opened its own studio, it became time for them to move away from airing *You Can't Do That on Television*, and without Nick's backing the show didn't have enough support solely in Canada. The run came to an end after 10 seasons and 144 episodes, though that final season was a mere five episodes.

This is the arc of *You Can't Do That on Television*, but what did the show consist of? Well, sketch comedy obviously, usually of the broad variety. Most of the cast was children, some of them teens, some of them younger. The two primary adult cast members were the aforementioned Lye and also Abby Hagyard, who played a lot of the female adult characters. Over the course of the show's run, over 100 kids appeared in the cast. The numbers of kids per season would fluctuate, and some were there mostly as filler. Others were regulars who became familiar faces. You have probably heard that Alanis Morissette was a cast member on *You Can't Do That on Television*. That's one of the show's primary claims to fame. It is true. However, she was only on five episodes, all during 1986. She has a short haircut and is far from the woman who would someday write a song that is partially—but not entirely!—about Dave Coulier. By the way, Coulier is not Canadian, despite what many people think. He's actually from

Metro Detroit. If you have been telling people he's from Canada, well, cut it out.

Of the kids on the show, three primarily stood out as cast members. Certainly the most-iconic of the bunch is Christine "Moose" McGlade. Now, that may seem like an awkward, even insulting, nickname. The nickname came from her early childhood, when she was kind of a smaller kid. Her classmates started calling her "Moose" after Moose from the *Archie* comics, who got his nickname because he was gigantic. So it was an ironic nickname, and she is the one who brought it up to the producers of *You Can't Do That on Television*, so it seemingly didn't bother her. Thus, a generation of kids grew up with a girl called "Moose" on their TV. McGlade was a cast member from the very first episode way back in 1979 through 1986. When she started she was 15, but by the end of her run she was 23 and an adult. Fortunately, she looked a little young, so she could still plausibly play a kid. By the end, she would step into adult roles in sketches as well.

McGlade was also the first person to serve as the host of the show. That meant introducing the show, introducing sketches, leading interstitial segments, and generally just leading the viewers through the hectic world of *You Can't Do That on Television*. She also played the straight woman in many interactions and sketches. McGlade was a natural in this role. For a young performer, McGlade knew how to host. She had a natural knack for it. Not every sketch performer can do that. It makes sense they made her a host. Yes, she was a veteran on the show, which probably in part gave her the role, but she earned it with her skill. Moose is definitely a standout, and it's only partially because of how much screen time she got, and how often she was called by her own name (or nickname).

A common foil for McGlade was Lisa Ruddy, known as "Motormouth" for her tendency to talk fast and ceaselessly. Not the best trait to have in an ensemble show, especially in unscripted moments, but it became part of her persona so it worked. She paired swimmingly with McGlade, who again was served well in the straight role. They had a Carl Reiner and Mel Brooks dynamic, if I may flatter them with that comparison. Also, I would totally watch a show called "Moose and Motormouth." Ruddy was an original cast member as well, leaving the show in 1985. The other name I have to mention is Alasdair Gillis, who was on the show from 1982 through 1986 and served as the second-ever official host. You may have noticed none of these three were on for the final few seasons. Indeed, some of the charm of the show was gone by then. The cast was missing some key pieces. Some fans of the show complain it got too lowbrow by the end, including in the '90s episodes. The "glory days," such as they are, seem to run adjacent to Gillis' run on the show, though that's only in part about him at most. Once Gillis, Moose, and Motormouth were gone, a little of the luster was lost.

The show would always begin with a fake preemption. It might be something along the lines of "Rudolph the Red Nose Reindeer Joins the A-Team will not be airing." *The A-Team* seems to have been riffed on multiple times as a popular show of the era. Then, they would cut to the opening credits, which are something of a *Monty Python* rip-off. They are clearly heavily influenced by Terry Gilliam's animation style. One of the key features of the show was the locker jokes. We'd see closed lockers, and then two cast members would open lockers and emerge from them so one could tell the other a (usually cheesy) joke. They'd do a few of these per segment. There were also a ton of sketches about a firing squad. Here, Lye would play El Capitano, a military dictator type who would be preparing one of the kids on the cast to be executed by his firing squad. Usually the kid would trick El Capitano and he would be shot instead. Sometimes, though, the kid would actually be executed. Most of the time they'd cut before the shot was fired, but on multiple occasions they didn't. Now, imagine a sketch show for children today that would include a kid being shot by a firing squad. It's more likely we'd see "Rudolph the Red Nose Reindeer Joins the A-Team" become a reality, and George Peppard is long dead.

Another common sketch featured the kids at Barth's Burgery, a (very) greasy spoon burger joint owned by Barth. Barth, played by Lye naturally, has real Zeke the Plumber vibes to his look. He's a crass, gross, chain-smoking chef who will use just about anything to make burger meat. You'd think the kids would stop going to Barth's restaurant, but they never seem to learn their lesson. Personally, I only need to be served one rat-meat burger before I move on. Other than these recurring sketches, most of the sketches are around whatever the theme of the episode is, be it Christmas, divorce, or the mall.

Of course, it's not the sketches *You Can't Do That on Television* is remembered for. They are remembered for "stage pollution," specifically the thing that became an iconic totem of Nickelodeon: slime. Not that it was all about slime. There were pies in the face. There was also a ton of water being thrown on cast members. If a cast member said water, or anything even tangentially related to water, they faced the potential of having a bucket of water dumped on them. In the early days, it would be thrown at them from off stage, but eventually the water started to rain down from above. Moose even got hit once for saying "Oh," on the presumption that it sounded too much like "eau," the French word for water. Hey, it was Canada after all. She also got drenched for saying "what're," which happened a couple times in the show's run.

Now, though, I just need to get to the slime. While it became the trademark of the show, and the American network it aired on, the slime was not born from intent. In fact, it was born from something truly disgusting.

Way back in 1979, Darby had planned to dump a bucket of food leftovers, softened with water, on cast member Tim Douglas. By the time they were ready, though, the food had gotten moldy. This was low-budget local Canadian TV, so Darby dumped it on him anyway, which is truly messed up. Price agreed. It was also quite popular with viewers, so they figured they had stumbled onto something. Mercifully, they did not stick with the rotten food. The slime was made of gelatin powder, oatmeal, and water, with baby shampoo added to the mix to make it wash out of hair better (tear free, of course). They decided to make it green, to truly give it a slime vibe and to match that originally moldy food. The green slime was debuted on the St. Patrick's Day episode in 1979. Ruddy was slimed a whopping six times in that one episode. Eventually, they learned restraint. They also eventually, if the stories are true, changed the recipe to simply a bucket of cottage cheese with green food coloring, which apparently smelled terrible.

The premise was that any time a cast member said "I don't know" they would be slimed. This happened quite often, much to the chagrin of the cast. You might think the kids would enjoy being slimed. It's wacky and messy and they didn't have to clean it up. And yet, they apparently largely didn't enjoy it. McGlade in particular despised it. Naturally, she got slimed as much as anybody. As the straight woman, the show took great glee in sliming her. McGlade would on occasion try and use other phrases to avoid saying "I don't know," but she would get slimed anyway. Basically, if the show wanted to slime you and could get away with it, you were being slimed. Viewers apparently loved it, which meant Nick loved it. They were behind an increase in slimings as the show went on. Nickelodeon would even host a "Slime-In" contest where the winner would be sent to the *You Can't Do That on Television* studios to be slimed. See, apparently some kids liked it. Take that, Moose!

The kids may not have liked it, but the slime became the show's signature, and became Nick's signature in turn. Slime became part of *Double Dare*. Eventually we got Gak, which is one variation of the iconic green slime, one you could buy for your very own home. They made green slime shampoo. Slime was everywhere. Although, not all the slime was the same. Indeed, the slime of *You Can't Do That on Television* definitely has a more lo-fi feel to it. In my memory, slime was pretty watery and smooth. The slime I saw dumped in the episodes I watched was often quite thick and viscous. You can see the oatmeal. It just sort of gloops down on people's heads with a sloshy sound. When Nickelodeon does it themselves, there definitely seems to be a higher quality to the consistency of the slime. Slime's come a long way, baby.

You can't argue with the indelible mark *You Can't Do that on Television* made on Nickelodeon. It was one of their first successes. They aired it on the network, including reruns, for over a decade. Years before *All That*, or even *Welcome Freshman*, it was the sketch show of record for the channel. It's definitely a low-budget show. They never lost the local Ottawa show origins in its DNA. I don't mind that, though. Now, it reads as charm. As a kid, I wouldn't have appreciated that. I probably just wondered why the show looked so cheap. While it eked into the '90s, *You Can't Do That on Television* definitely feels like an '80s show. I think it had run its course when it ended. This wasn't *Saturday Night Live*. It couldn't go on forever. Les Lye needed a chance to do other things. The sketches aren't always great. Well, they are never great. I should say they aren't always good. If not for the introduction of slime into our world, it would have probably been entirely forgotten. Instead, it's remembered forever. It has a lasting legacy that goes beyond the trivia of the future artist behind *Jagged Little Pill* being on it for a minute. She got slimed a couple times, by the way. They had talented people in the cast, especially for kids. I can imagine being a young child and enjoying spending time with Moose and Motormouth and seeing what Barth was serving up this week. Nickelodeon may not have found its voice or its vision if not for being introduced to this Canadian export. For that alone, I have to thank *You Can't Do That on Television*. I don't know if I can forgive them for dumping soggy, moldy food on a kid, though. Oops, I just said "I don't know." Maybe somewhere Moose is getting slimed on my behalf. I'm sure she still hates it.

You're On!

Don't trust anybody, because they might be
on a terrible hidden camera show

Oh man, do I dislike hidden camera shows. I also can't stand prank shows. Even when I watched *Jackass* as a teenager it was only for the stunts. The pranks and hidden camera stuff didn't appeal to me. For starters, the obvious issue is that they are filming people secretly for the sake of making television, using them as unwitting props for their production. That sucks. I know everybody that ends up showing their face on a show signed a release, and a lot of times people seem amused, but I think it's garbage. Don't secretly film people. Also, don't mess with people. Let people live their lives. I can't stand pranks, filmed or otherwise. What, exactly, is the appeal with inconveniencing people or making them uncomfortable? What's funny about pranks? How does Jimmy Kimmel do a bit every single year where he has parents film their kids while they tell them that they ate all the kid's Halloween candy? I can't think of anything more profoundly stupid and obnoxious.

In addition to the ethical problems with secretly filming people while you mess with them, hidden camera shows aren't funny. The bits are never good or clever. For whatever reason, the people who like hidden camera shows just don't have good senses of humor. Well, I get why that's the case. They think this bad idea is good, so why would they have other good ideas? I know those *Impractical Jokers* guys are truly inexplicably popular, but any time I have seen them for even a split second—in any context—they seem like the most boring people alive. They are paint drying in human form. This is a lot of frontloading for the topic at hand, and so now there are going to be no surprises. This chapter is about Nickelodeon's hidden camera game for show for children, *You're On!*

There is one thing that *You're On!* definitely had going for it, and that was the fact Phil Moore was the host. As I mentioned in the *Nick Arcade* chapter, Moore is a strong game show host. He is actually talented. He was thrust into a terrible idea built on a foundation of trash. The man deserved a paycheck, though. I hold nothing against Phil Moore. Unfortunately for him, but luckily for fans of good television, *You're On!* had a short lifespan. It only lasted for 26 episodes, and those episodes were burnt through swiftly. The first episode of *You're On!* aired on August 3, 1998, and the final one aired on October 4 of the same year. That's basically two months. Clearly, they were burning through episodes. Whether or not that was the intent I do not know.

As I noted, this wasn't merely a hidden camera show. It was a hidden camera *game* show. Teams of two kids would be sent out into a naïve, unsuspecting world along with one of the remote hosts, Vivianne Collins and Travis White. They would be given three tasks around a theme. The kids had to get people on the street to perform these tasks, without being able to just say, "Hey if you do this for me I might win a Nintendo 64!" So, you know, they were just kids asking adults to waddle like a penguin or play hopscotch. Now that I think about it, a lot of those adults had to know something was up, right? No kid is clever or convincing enough to make it seem like their ask isn't part of something larger. How many of the adults figured out they were on a hidden camera show? Or how many at least knew that, for one reason or another, they were being messed with?

While you could ask a kid to complete the first task, the second and third tasks were usually trickier and thus required an adult. You had 10 minutes to get all three prompts checked off, and if that happened you got a prize that was fine, but not on the level of Space Camp. You might get a snowboard, but you weren't getting a trip to, like, Vail. If they failed, they still got a small prize so that they didn't go home unhappy. The people who were inconvenienced by these kids and had their days interrupted to be strong armed into being part of a TV show? They won nothing. Needless to say, you didn't have to see through the full 10 minutes. They did three of these contests in every episode, and they only had 22 minutes without commercials.

Plus, they had to do the Runarounds! What was a "Runaround"? Before the second and third game, after the premise had been established, six people would be called down from the audience. In the first round it was all kids, in the second it was three kids and three adults related to said kids. They got to see the three tasks and then had to guess how many tasks the kids could get done in time. If you were right you won a prize. If you were wrong, there was a chance you would get called back over for the end of the episode to be slimed or something along those lines. After all, could you have a game show on Nickelodeon without slime? Yes, yes you could, but when you had a sweaty premise like *You're On!*, anything that could earn you a bit of entertainment value was called upon.

I don't need to tell you I don't like this show at all, right? As much as I like Moore, this show is bad. Hidden camera shows are garbage, and this is a bad premise for a game show. There is something vaguely interesting, anthropologically speaking, about seeing how kids would try and convince a person to, say, kiss a fish. There was an episode where the kids had to get somebody to eat out of the trash. Why the hell was this on television? Also, were these kids being taught how to lie and manipulate to get what you want? Saying that is closer to pearl clutching than I'm comfortable with, but it's not an entirely invalid concern. Not that kids need to be taught to lie. If anything, this show was probably more about showcasing which kids had already learned to lie and manipulate. Although, again, a lot of the adults had to know what was up. Watching it now, that just feels clear. If I were walking down the street and two kids were trying to convince me to kiss a fish I would immediately think, "Something is going on here." Also, I would just keep walking and wouldn't make it on TV.

You're On! genuinely annoys me. I am against the very premise of it, and the execution isn't good either. It's probably still better than *Impractical Jokers*. Phil Moore is as talented as those four guys combined. At least with kids doing it the process feels less gross. There is little to no fun to be had watching *You're On!* as an adult. I could see a kid enjoying it, mostly because adults do wacky things. This was one of the final game shows Nickelodeon did. It's the last one in this vein, maybe because it fell flat. This was also one of the last gigs for Moore, who has mostly disappeared since *You're On!* Apparently he hosted some educational show called *Aqua Kids* and played himself on a couple of *Robot Chicken* episodes. The fact this was the end of Moore's legacy is a shame. He was better than this show, and he deserved a chance to get another hosting gig. *You're On!* was a failure as a concept, and a failure in execution. To paraphrase the tombstone Patty and Selma bought for Homer, we are richer for having lost it.

Conclusion

We all grow and change. So do TV networks

And so, we reach the end of this journey. I have covered all the original Nickelodeon shows from the '90s. This trip down memory lane has come to a close. The '90s came to a close decades ago. My childhood ended over a decade as well. As a member of the Gak Generation, your childhood is long since over as well. We are living in the past with this book, but that's just fine. Part of why I wanted to write this book was to treat '90s Nickelodeon as a legitimate topic for critical discussion. Also, to make a bunch of jokes and to tell people I wrote a book about Nickelodeon to seem cool. Mostly though for the noble thing I said. This culture is as valid as any other culture. Yes, some of it involves a cartoon about a dog and a cat that are conjoined twins. It all has its merits as a topic for discussion. Some of us just want a flicker of a fond memory of sitting on the floor of our childhood living room even though there were perfectly good couches to sit on as we watched the Blue Barracudas try and avoid the temple guards. We want to remember the simplicity of a Saturday night spent with Clarissa Darling while we either babysat or were babysat. I hope maybe this book triggered some of those memories, Proust style. *The Adventures of Pete & Pete* is more enjoyable than any Madeleine dipped in tea.

When Nickelodeon began life in the early days of cable, they surely had no idea what might become of them. Many channels flamed out. Nickelodeon found their footing. They became the preeminent network for kids by the late '80s, and they were a juggernaut in the '90s. I'm not a child, and I do not have children, but I do believe that are still the pinnacle of children's programming by reputation. Or maybe I can't believe anything else could be true. The pieces started to fall into pace. *You Can't Do That on Television* introduced slime, which became a staple of the network in the '90s. Even into the new millennium they were dumping Gak on celebrities at the Kids' Choice Awards. I feel like they just call it slime now, though. I don't remember the last time I heard the word "Gak" being used contemporaneously. Maybe they got wise to the drug lingo that spawned it. Maybe we've lost something else.

Double Dare was the first game show that knocked it out of the park. Marc Summers became a staple of the network and a legend to an entire generation of kids. *Hey Dude* brought original live-action programming that wasn't strictly aimed at the preschool set. It didn't totally land, but it was a noble effort. In 1991, *Rugrats*, *Doug*, and *The Ren & Stimpy Show* all debuted one after another. They all became favorites of '90s kids. They stuck with us. They shaped our senses of humor. Maybe we grew out of them. I know I largely have, especially when it comes to *Ren & Stimpy*. That's fine. We're allowed to change. It'd be weird if we loved all the same stuff as adults than we did when we were 11. We're smarter now, and we can have a critical view of Nickelodeon of the '90s. Maybe you have trouble with that. It may hurt you to admit *The Angry Beavers* isn't as funny as you remember, or that *Figure It Out* was kind of dumb. This book might have been rough at times. Many of the shows I rewatched, or watched for the first time, for *The Nickelodeon '90s* fell below the standards of good. Some of them were ones I enjoyed back in the '90s. They don't hold up.

On the other hand, not everything falls apart under the weight of time and age. Some of the shows are still good. I watched *Think Fast* for the first time and found it to be a delightful game show. *Roundhouse* surprised me. Luckily for me, my favorites held up as well. *Rocko's Modern Life* is still the best cartoon from the network. *Clarissa Explains It All* is still a strong sitcom, and way better than *Sabrina, the Teenage Witch*. Then, of course, there's *The Adventures of Pete & Pete*. That show remains so good. "Hey Sandy" is still a jam. I have been listening to that song for decades, and I will listen to it for decades more.

All these shows are trapped in time. Well, except *SpongeBob SquarePants*. It's our relationship to the shows that change, or sometimes don't change. Someday *SpongeBob* will stop airing as well. Two *Double Dare* reboots have already come and gone. *All That* has gotten a reboot as well. Kenan Thompson is still doing sketch comedy. Mike Maronna and Danny Tamberelli may not be brothers, but they are friends who have done a podcast together. Child actors have come to reconcile their careers. Reunions have happened. They've made movies for *Legends of the Hidden Temple*, *Rocko's Modern Life*, *Hey Arnold!*, and more in recent years. There's money in nostalgia. As long as the Gak Generation exists, we will be catered to. Eventually we'll just be catering to ourselves. Let's try not to be as obnoxious as Boomers though, everybody.

I have seen very little of Nickelodeon since I stopped watching in after the '90s. It seemed to become mostly about live-action shows. I've heard of *iCarly*, *Victorious*, and *Drake & Josh*. I think Ariana Grande was on at least one of those shows. Most of them came from Dan Schneider, who has since been disgraced. He was vital to '90s Nickelodeon as well. So was the loathsome John Kricfalusi. Does any of this change our memories of our youths spending TV? Maybe. It's really how you unpack your pop culture.

Was Nickelodeon in the '90s the pinnacle of children's programming? Or do I just feel that way because it's when I was a child? It's hard to figure out which one of those is leading the charge. I'd definitely take a *Rocko* or a *Doug* over, say, *Scooby-Doo* or *The Flintstones*. I haven't watched much in the way of new shows since I, you know, became a teenager and then an adult. It definitely doesn't seem as good as Nickelodeon's programming from my youth. Not that all of the shows were good. Some of them are bad. Programs like *My Brother & Me* and *Animorphs* are abject failures. Others are good. It's a television network. It has its hits and misses. For kids' programming over the course of a decade and some change, though, I am impressed with Nickelodeon's output. The network became behemoths in the '90s, and they earned it. How much credit goes to Stick Stickly? Who can say?

I've lived to see Stu Pickles losing control of his life become a popular meme. I've lived to see *SpongeBob* get a musical. I didn't get to see Eddie McDowd turned back into a boy. He will remain a dog forever, and I don't care. When I was 10, I liked *Pete & Pete* because I thought it was funny a kid had a tattoo of a dancing girl. When I was 20 I thought it was clever to note that *Pete & Pete* was actually funny, and not just funny for a kids' show. When I was 30, I admired *Pete & Pete* for being more openly emotional about the fact life is hard than any other children's show I can think of. Like I said, we change, the world changes, but these shows don't. Us '90s kids have grown into adults and we've carried these shows with us. We have our favorites, the ones we think are overrated, and the ones we have basically forgotten. They are all here in this book. Our experience as a generation now been cataloged, to the extent it can be. It's not as simple as all that. It never is. As I bring this book to a close and try and think of some interesting way to end it, I'm annoyed Nickelodeon was so opposed to traditional series finales. Wouldn't it be nice to take some show's final words and recontextualize them here? I have to turn to my personal favorite show of '90s Nickelodeon, because this can't help but be an inherently personal experience. Remember the motto of the bus driver: Trust, Loyalty, Niceness. Farewell, my little Vikings.

Index